BIRDWATCHER'S
BRITAIN

Mam + Dad —
Thought you might
enjoy these!

D1025224

BIRDWATCHER'S
BRITAIN

The unique pocket guide to birdwatching walks

Pan Books/Ordnance Survey

First published 1983 by Pan Books Ltd.
Cavaye Place, London SW10 9PG and
Ordnance Survey, Romsey Road, Maybush,
Southampton SO9 4DH

Conceived, edited and designed by Duncan
Associates, 64, Fullerton Road, London,
SW18 1BX with Mel Petersen &
Associates, 5 Botts Mews, Chepstow Road,
London W2 5AG.
9 8 7 6 5 4 3 2

Designer	**Linda Abraham**
Deputy Editor	**Lionel Bender**
Editorial assistance	**Fred and Kathie Gill**
Picture Research	**Jackum Brown**
Editor/Art editor	**Andrew Duncan/ Mel Petersen**

Pan ISBN 0 330 28028 7 (Paperback)
ISBN 0 330 28109 7 (Hardback)
OS ISBN 0 319 00020 6

Printed and bound in Great Britain
by Collins, Glasgow

Note on 1:25 000 mapping

The old 1:25 000 First Series maps are gradually being replaced by a new Second Series, called *Pathfinders*. Whereas the First Series appeared in 10 km × 10 km format, the Second Series is generally published in 20 km × 10 km format, except in those areas where it is economically and cartographically more desirable to change the format, e.g. in coastal areas.

For this reason the sheet containing the Hayle Estuary, formerly *SW 53* in the First Series, now appears on *SW 63* & parts of *SW 53* in the Second Series. There is, in effect, no longer a sheet *SW 53*.

All *Pathfinder* numbers are listed on an index published by Ordnance Survey but several of these will be incorporated into the 1:25 000 *Outdoor Leisure Map* series before being published as *Pathfinders*, towards the end of the series. Hence the sheet which features Whitestone Cliff, which was sheet *SE 58* in the First Series, is now incorporated into *OLM North York Moors, West,* and is not yet a Second Series *Pathfinder*.

Outdoor Leisure Maps are produced to Second Series specifications, but, because they are regularly updated and revised, often contain more current information than either the First or Second Series sheets.

Single 1:25 000 sheet numbers appearing in the text of this book indicate that the First Series is still the only available sheet at that scale, in the 10 km × 10 km format, at the time of going to press. The areas covered by these sheets may, however, also be covered by the more up-to-date *Outdoor Leisure* Series.

Double sheet numbers indicate that a Second Series *Pathfinder* is available.

GENERAL EDITOR
John Parslow

**Principal contributors
(walks featured on
1 : 25,000 mapping)**

THE SOUTH-WEST:
Stanley Davies

SOUTH-EAST ENGLAND:
Tony Prater

WALES:
Roger Lovegrove, Stephanie Tyler (Llanthony Valley) and **Graham Williams** (Holyhead Mountain)

MIDDLE ENGLAND:
Philip Burton (Grand Union), **Linda Williams** (Malvern Hills), **P. W. Richardson** (Salcey Forest, Pitsford Reservoir), **Michael F. Wallace** (Long Mynd), **Frank Gribble** (Cannock Chase), **Barrie Robertson** (Mid-Churnet Valley) and **David Cohen** (Charnwood Forest)

EAST ANGLIA AND REGION:
John O'Sullivan and **Peter Rumsey** (Epping Forest)

NORTHERN ENGLAND:
John S. Armitage (Ribble Estuary, Langsett Moors, Worsborough) and **Ian Armstrong** (Bempton Cliffs, Whitestone Cliff, Ullswater, Tyne Valley and Budle Bay)

SCOTLAND:
Ray Hawley (Balcary), **Peter Bowyer** (Lunderston Bay), **Stephen Warman** (St Abb's), **Alister Clunas** (Tyne Estuary), **Stewart Taylor** (Loch Garten, Glen More)

**Introductory features
Philip Burton, John Parslow, Ken Smith
and John Hunt**

Other walks researched and compiled by
Claire Appleby

Illustrator	**Ken Wood**
Other illustrations by	**Peter Hayman** and **Ian Wallace**
Cartographic artist	**Nigel O'Gorman**

Our thanks to John Paddy Browne of the Ordnance Survey Cartographic Library for invaluable help.

John Parslow is Director (Conservation) of the Royal Society for the Protection of Birds. For further selected biographical details of contributors, see page 256.

A full list of picture and illustration credits appears on page 256.

Contents

England, Scotland and Wales are covered county by county, in a sequence corresponding to the Ordnance Survey's grid reference system. This works from west to east, and from south to north. Cornwall, furthest west and furthest south, comes first. Grampian Region, furthest east and furthest north, comes last. For additional ease of reference, the book is divided into seven regional sections.

FOREWORD

Birdwatching as a hobby has grown enormously in popularity in recent years. Membership of the Royal Society for the Protection of Birds, for example, has increased tenfold since 1968 and now numbers 350,000. Its Young Ornithologists' Club has over 100,000 members. If one includes people who put out food in winter for garden birds, there must be millions who have at least a passing interest in the subject.

The aim of this book is to help guide birdwatchers in the direction of the birds. So the walks have been selected to cover not just a wide geographical area but an extremely wide variety of habitats and hence different bird communities and species.

By and large birds are not very adaptable creatures. Most are confined to a particular kind of habitat – woodland, heath, fen, seashore and so on – though the habitat they occupy sometimes varies from one season to another. The greatest variety of species is to be found where several habitats come together, especially when these are on or near coasts, where in spring and autumn there may be the added bonus of concentrations of migrants resting or feeding after a long overseas flight.

The places chosen for *Birdwatcher's Britain* vary from classic birdwatching sites, such as Cley on the north Norfolk coast (where on the famed 'East Bank' just about everyone carries binoculars and is on the look-out for newly arrived migrants), to some known only to a few and where a wide variety of common species can be seen in a particularly pleasant or varied piece of countryside. What they all have in common is that they are good for walks *and* birds.

We have been careful to avoid walks which pass close to the nesting sites of rare or timid species except where these occur on protected reserves managed by a conservation body. Thus one walk takes in the observation hide overlooking the famous osprey eyrie at Loch Garten, but none of Scotland's other 20 or more osprey nests are included – most locations are kept secret to avoid disturbance.

Ospreys, and indeed many other rare or uncommon breeding species (including even the barn owl, kingfisher and little tern), are listed on Schedule 1 of the Wildlife and Countryside Act 1981: these birds must not be disturbed at or near their nests.

A portion of the walks are centred on country parks, nature reserves or other 'managed' places. There is one main reason for this. Especially in England, but increasingly in Wales and Scotland too, areas of natural and semi-natural habitat are being lost at an alarming rate – to developments of various kinds and particularly to agricultural 'improvement'. For example, in the last 40 years between a third and a half of all ancient broad-leaved woodlands in lowland England have been felled, approximately 50 per cent of all lowland heath has been ploughed, planted or built upon, and a similar proportion of coastal grazing marsh has been converted to arable fields.

But thanks to the efforts of the voluntary conservation bodies, notably the county trusts for nature conservation and the RSPB, as well as the official Nature Conservancy Council, a good and growing share of the important sites that are left are being acquired and managed as nature reserves. For this reason alone do consider taking out membership of the RSPB and your county trust.

I hope that you enjoy undertaking the walks from this book. Beginners might do best to start on open country walks, especially where there is open water, and where birds are easier to see. Certainly they should read the advice given under *Using This Book*. In woodland a keen ear as well as eye is needed, particularly in summer when it really is worth noting that song birds tend to be more vocal and active in the early morning than at other times of the day. Also, make good use of the ornithological index. If there is no hint on identifying a species on a particular walk – usually for reasons of space – there may well be one on another page.

At all times please follow the *Birdwatcher's Code* and obey the *Country Code*. Good walking; good birding!

John Parslow

The Birdwatcher's Code of Conduct
Today's birdwatchers are a powerful force for nature conservation. The number of those of us interested in birds rises continually and it is vital that we take seriously our responsibility to avoid any harm to birds.

We must also present a responsible image to non-birdwatchers who may be affected by our activities and particularly those on whose sympathy and support the future of birds may rest.

There are ten points to bear in mind:
1 The welfare of birds must come first.
2 Habitat must be protected.
3 Keep disturbance to birds and their habitat to a minimum.
4 When you find a rare bird think carefully about whom you should tell.
5 Do not harass rare migrants.
6 Abide by the bird protection laws at all times.
7 Respect the rights of landowners.
8 Respect the rights of other people in the countryside.
9 Make your records available to the local bird recorder.
10 Behave abroad as you would when birdwatching at home.

This code has been drafted after consultation between the British Ornithologists' Union, British Trust for Ornithology, the Royal Society for the Protection of Birds, the Scottish Ornithologists' Club, the Wildfowl Trust and the Editors of *British Birds*. The full version is available on request from the RSPB, The Sandy, Bedfordshire, SG19 2DL.

REGIONAL AND COUNTY BOUNDARIES

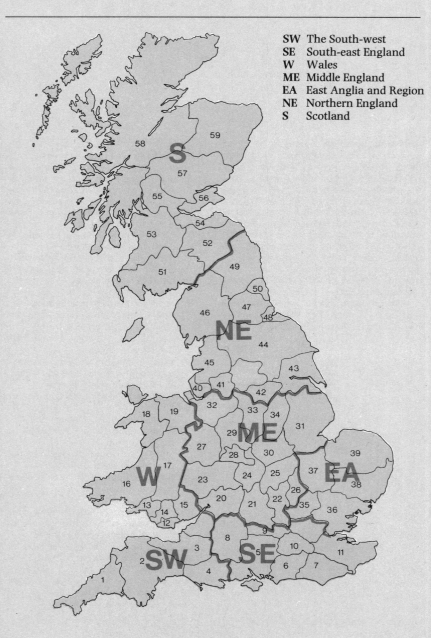

SW The South-west
SE South-east England
W   Wales
ME Middle England
EA East Anglia and Region
NE Northern England
S   Scotland

REGIONAL AND COUNTY BOUNDARIES

THE SOUTH-WEST

1 Cornwall
2 Devon
3 Somerset
4 Dorset

SOUTH-EAST ENGLAND

5 Hampshire
6 West Sussex
7 East Sussex
8 Wiltshire
9 Berkshire
10 Surrey
11 Kent

WALES

12 South Glamorgan
13 West Glamorgan
14 Mid Glamorgan
15 Gwent
16 Dyfed
17 Powys
18 Gwynedd
19 Clwyd

MIDDLE ENGLAND

20 Gloucestershire
21 Oxfordshire
22 Buckinghamshire
23 Hereford and Worcester
24 Warwickshire
25 Northamptonshire
26 Bedfordshire
27 Shropshire
28 West Midlands
29 Staffordshire
30 Leicestershire
31 Lincolnshire
32 Cheshire
33 Derbyshire
34 Nottinghamshire

EAST ANGLIA AND REGION

35 Hertfordshire
36 Essex
37 Cambridgeshire
38 Suffolk
39 Norfolk

NORTHERN ENGLAND

40 Merseyside
41 Greater Manchester
42 South Yorkshire
43 Humberside
44 North Yorkshire
45 Lancashire
46 Cumbria
47 Durham
48 Cleveland
49 Northumberland
50 Tyne and Wear

SCOTLAND

51 Dumfries and Galloway
52 Borders
53 Strathclyde
54 Lothian
55 Central
56 Fife
57 Tayside
58 Highland
59 Grampian

OS CONVENTIONAL SYMBOLS

ROADS AND PATHS

Main road

Minor road in towns, drive or track (unmetalled)

Path

RAILWAYS

Multiple	Standard	
Single	gauge track	

Narrow gauge

Mineral line, siding or tramway

Bridge

Station

Level crossing

Tunnel

Cutting

Embankment

WATER FEATURES

Marsh

Lake or loch

Canal and tow path

Ferry F — Ferry foot

Ferry V — Ferry vehicle

Foot bridge

Cliff

Flat rock

Sand and mud

Sand and shingle

Low water mark

High water mark

GENERAL FEATURES

Electricity transmission line
(with pylons spaced conventionally)

Quarry

Open pit

Wood

Park or ornamental grounds

Bracken, heath and rough grassland

Dunes

Broadcasting station (mast or tower)

Bus or coach station

Church { with tower

or { with spire

Chapel { without tower or spire

Glasshouse

Triangulation pillar

Windmill (in use)

Windmill (disused)

Wind pump

ABBREVIATIONS

PC	Public convenience (in rural areas)	P	Post office	N T	National Trust
.T	Telephone call box	PH	Public house	N T S	National Trust Scotland

RELIEF

Contours are at 10 metres VI or at 50 feet VI with values to the nearest metric equivalent

1:50 000

2 centimetres to 1 kilometre (one grid square)

1 kilometre = 0·6214 mile   1 mile = 1·6093 kilometres

OS CONVENTIONAL SYMBOLS

ROADS AND PATHS

———————— Main road
———————— Other road, drive or track
·················· Path
Unfenced roads and tracks are shown by pecked lines

RAILWAYS

———————— ⎤
⚊⚊⚊⚊⚊⚊ ⎬ Standard gauge
———·———·— ⎦

———·——·—— Narrow gauge

▭▭▭▭▭ Embankment

⊢╌╌╌╌╌⊣ Tunnel

▭▭▭▭ Cutting

⬛ Station

⚊⚊⚋⚊⚊ Level crossing

WATER FEATURES

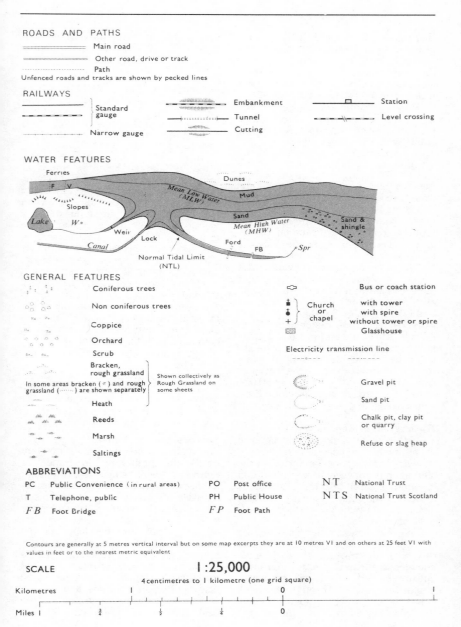

GENERAL FEATURES

Coniferous trees

Non coniferous trees

Coppice

Orchard

Scrub

Bracken, rough grassland ⎤
In some areas bracken (⌀) and rough grassland (·····) are shown separately ⎬ Shown collectively as Rough Grassland on some sheets

Heath ⎦

Reeds

Marsh

Saltings

⇔ Bus or coach station

⚐ ⎤
⚑ ⎬ Church or chapel
+ ⎦

with tower
with spire
without tower or spire

▥ Glasshouse

Electricity transmission line
·──○──·····──○──·

Gravel pit

Sand pit

Chalk pit, clay pit or quarry

Refuse or slag heap

ABBREVIATIONS

PC	Public Convenience (in rural areas)	PO	Post office	NT National Trust
T	Telephone, public	PH	Public House	NTS National Trust Scotland
FB	Foot Bridge	*FP*	Foot Path	

Contours are generally at 5 metres vertical interval but on some map excerpts they are at 10 metres VI and on others at 25 feet VI with values in feet or to the nearest metric equivalent

SCALE

1:25,000

4 centimetres to 1 kilometre (one grid square)

Kilometres |‒‒‒‒‒‒‒‒‒‒‒1‒‒‒‒‒‒‒‒‒‒‒0‒‒‒‒‒‒‒‒‒‒‒1

Miles 1‒‒‒‒‒‒¾‒‒‒‒‒‒½‒‒‒‒‒‒¼‒‒‒‒‒‒0

You can do the major birdwatching expeditions in *Birdwatcher's Britain* just by following the textual directions linked to the numbers on the maps. The same generally applies to the less complex walks shown on the smaller scale maps.

However, some knowledge of maps and map-reading will greatly add to your enjoyment of the book, and enable you to devise your own routes.

The map extracts featured in the book are made by Ordnance Survey, Britain's official surveying and map-making organization, founded in 1791, and usually referred to simply as OS.

OS maps are based on detailed surveys: accurate measurements of the ground combined with aerial photography. Few other maps of Britain are precision instruments in this sense.

The range of OS maps covers a wide variety of scales for differing purposes (all are listed in a free brochure, available from Ordnance Survey, Romsey Road, Maybush, Southampton, S09 4DH). Here, the 50 major expeditions, fully described and annotated with symbols, are featured on extracts from the 1 : 25 000 Pathfinder series. All other mapping is from the monochrome version of the Landranger series, 1 : 50 000 scale. (For further details about these series see pages 4–5 and 230–231.)

The large-scale maps

1 : 25 000 scale mapping is as detailed as birdwatchers normally require. It shows field boundaries and some of the different types of vegetation, the latter in fascinating detail. At the scale of $2\frac{1}{2}$ inches to the mile (4 cm to one km) distances in hundreds, even tens of yards have meaning.

This has enabled the local experts who compiled the major expeditions in this book to translate their intimate knowledge of the birds on the ground, and in the air, into a genuine cartographic record. All through the book you will find specific, often relatively tiny physical features on the ground

pinpointed and highlighted in ornithological terms by means of the symbols.

First walks

If you are a beginner, it is strongly recommended that the first routes to be attempted are those on 1 : 25 000 mapping. Not only do they give a step-by-step approach to map-reading, they show graphically how to approach the countryside in search of birds.

After doing a few of these walks, in a range of habitats, it will become clear that certain types of birds tend to crop up in certain types of country, indeed in certain types of vegetation, in certain types of trees, in particular parts of woods or ponds or coastlines. There are, of course, exceptions; but in general, a pattern will emerge; and once understood, it can be applied to most places you go in search of birds.

With this understanding, try some of the routes marked on 1 : 50 000 maps. These are located in outstanding places for birds and the list of habitats in italics at the end of the introductory paragraph, combined with the seasonal species list, will give a good idea of what to look for, and where.

The species list represents birds recorded at the site with reasonable regularity. You should not expect to see every bird on the list; indeed most of them contain something unusual or rare.

Approaching the symbols

The symbols were devised with certain needs and limitations in mind. To represent every single species with its own silhouette would have overcrowded the maps. Too few symbols to cover the great variety of British birdlife would have required some ornithologically uncomfortable leaps of the imagination on the part of the user. It is hoped that the 20 different symbols adopted will be easy to memorize, and that they are visually self-evident. *Please note that they are not drawn to scale.*

The contributors, working in the field, have taken every care to plot

- The symbols simply alert you to stop and look: always read the 'key'.
- An asterisk * means keep looking for the bird(s) all round the route.
- Symbols and key are in sequence for the route followed as directed.

Aquatic waterfowl, and some offshore sea birds.

The gannet in flight denotes sea birds on passage.

Tern and gull colonies, passage sites and concentrations.

Breeding auk colonies and other cliff-nesting sea birds, including puffinries.

Birds of prey, excluding falcons.

Falcons.

Owls.

Nightjar only.

Game birds.

Waders, except on dry inland sites.

Heronries and all heron species.

Kingfisher only.

Cuckoo only.

Woodpeckers.

Swallows, martins and swift.

Pigeons and doves.

All small passerines (song birds), except hirundines, nuthatches, treecreepers and dipper.

Dipper only.

Nuthatch (and treecreeper).

Crows.

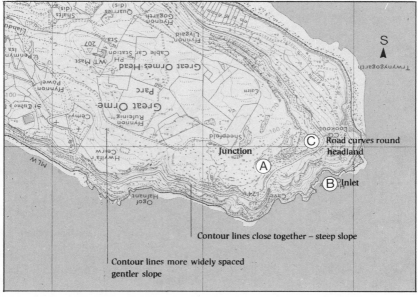

C Road curves round headland

Junction

A

B Inlet

Contour lines close together – steep slope

Contour lines more widely spaced gentler slope

the symbols in accurate positions on the maps, but no claims are made to total reliability. Apart from anything else, the countryside changes constantly, and the activities of man can, and do, cause birds to change their habits and localities. The true purpose of the symbols is to alert walkers when to stop and look, and used in this way, they should be a helpful, revealing 'key' to the countryside.

The position given for a species, or group of species, on the map may not be the only one on the route; it is likely to be where the contributor, trying to give an even spread of interest all round the route, thought it best to concentrate the attention.

Hints on map-reading

As a beginner, first familiarize yourself with the meaning of the map's conventional signs (see pages 12–13). Contour lines are the only ones which are not entirely self-evident. They are surveyed lines showing the height of the land above sea level (see map and photograph opposite).

Before starting to walk, set the map by pointing the top edge of it towards north. In featureless country it is usually necessary to do this by compass, but it is also worth remembering that the sun rises in the east, is south about midday and sets in the west.

Next, get your bearings by singling out two or three features on the ground and identifying them on the map. Check that the direction in which they lie as seen on the ground tallies with the direction as shown on the map. If they do not, rotate the map until they do. (See map and photograph opposite, which have been approximately aligned.)

Beginners often find it is best to set the map in this way whatever the direction of travel. Check progress regularly against landmarks.

It is also important to understand the implications of scale. At an average walking pace of 3 mph (5 km/h) you will cover $7\frac{1}{2}$ inches (19 cm) on the 1 : 25 000 maps or $3\frac{3}{4}$ inches (9.5 cm) on the 1 : 50 000 for every hour walked. Remember, however, that in hilly country walking speed can be reduced by at least half; and to take into account the time spent watching birds rather than covering the ground.

To devise your own routes, use the full colour OS Landranger sheets in conjunction with 1 : 25 000 Pathfinder or Outdoor Leisure maps. Both show public rights of way, though the first is more convenient for planning. Apply knowledge of where you can walk with the larger scale mapping's details of vegetation and habitats and the possibilities for walking and birdwatching are limitless. Indeed, using this book in conjunction with OS colour sheets will suggest extensions and variations on the existing routes, and give a great deal of extra interest and pleasure.

- The OS mapping used in the book does not show all **rights of way**, but the routes as marked are on rights of way or land with open access.
- Both 1 : 50 000 and 1 : 25 000 **sheet numbers** are given below the title of walks shown on 1 : 25 000 mapping. For further information about these maps and their availability in varying degrees of update, see pages 4–5.
- The **six-figure number** below the title of each walk is the grid reference of the starting point.
- **Mud after rain** means the route has a chance of drying out; **mud** means wear suitable footwear at any time.
- Remember **stiles** are of widely varying construction.
- **Path** usually means a narrow way, sometimes just beaten-down grass. **Track** is usually broader and better defined.
- All **distances** are approximate.
- Remember the countryside changes frequently. **Landmarks disappear**, especially stiles, and paths or rights of way across fields may be ploughed out.

WALKING, BIRDWATCHING AND THE LAW

The law's protective net around our wild birds is tightening slowly but surely. The penalties for destroying or disturbing birds, their young, nests and eggs have recently become stiffer, and are likely to grow more so. At the same time, the law is more and more encouraging to those who seriously want to enjoy the country, and birds, on foot.

In England and Wales, the public footpath network – more than 120,000 miles (193,000 km) of it – has always provided much more than a lifetime's access to superb birdwatching. In Scotland, where the law is different, there is, in theory, even greater freedom.

The key to these riches is the Ordnance Survey 1:50000 Landranger map series, on which public rights of way are marked with a dotted, magenta line. The major birding expeditions in this book are shown on map excerpts at the larger, 1:25000 scale in order to give precise locations of species; but planning them, or any other birding expedition, inevitably begins with a close look at the appropriate Landranger sheet, and a knowledge of the walker's rights when following a public footpath.

The right of way

In England and Wales, a right of way is the right of passage across someone's land. The landowner has a right to object if the walker does damage or leaves litter, but has no complaint in law if the walker pauses to watch birds or eat lunch. In Scotland you are generally free to wander the moors and mountains at will, though landowners may, and do, impose restrictions.

If the walker strays from the right of way, he or she is trespassing. The landowner has the right to insist the trespasser returns to the right of way, or leaves the land. If refused, the landowner may use the minimum possible force to achieve this object. In Scotland, the landowner may not intervene unless damage is done.

Trespass is not in itself an offence, and you cannot be taken to court simply for losing the footpath 'deliberately', or accidentally. If the landowner wishes to prosecute, this can only be for damage done by the trespasser. It may not amount to much in terms of cash; but if found guilty, the walker would have to pay the landowner's (and his own) legal fees – not cheap.

Obstruction

If a public footpath is blocked, the walker may stray from the right of way in order to skirt the obstruction, or climb it, causing the least possible damage. In Scotland, the walker may remove as much of the obstruction as is necessary to restore the passage of traffic.

This rule applies to less obvious forms of obstruction, such as shooting; if a shoot has barred a right of way on grounds of safety, you may walk round, with the object of regaining the footpath. However, if a footpath disappears as a result of subsidence – as frequently happens on sandy cliff tops – the law, caught out by its own logicality, does not recognize an obstruction, and the walker must turn back.

Ploughing

The Ramblers' Association, the privately funded lobby group which protects these rights on our behalf, may well improve this state of affairs in the future, as it recently did in the case on the most common form of obstruction, ploughing. Since the 1981 Wildlife and Countryside Act, farmers must return ploughed-out footpaths to usable condition within two weeks, weather permitting (previously there was no time limit). In Scotland, it is more usual for a right of way to be diverted as a result of ploughing.

A major source of confusion for walkers is whether to keep to the line of a right of way when it is ploughed-out, or to avoid damage to crops by walking round the field edge. In legal, and practical, terms the best course is always to keep to the line of the right of way. There is minimal damage to crops if the walkers keep in single file; and it is always better not to trespass if it can be avoided.

Bulls

The other perennial source of irritation – though not so serious as ploughing – is bulls. Do not be unnecessarily frightened, or foolhardy, when you meet bulls or cows. Cows have a disarming habit of rushing up to walkers. They will not do any harm, though it is best to call your dog to heel. Simply continue on your way. They may follow you, but they will not hurt you; and they will eventually lose interest.

If you see a bull alone in a field where there is a public right of way, it is probably there illegally. If it is with cows, it is probably there legally. The law in this area was tightened, and simplified, by the 1981 Act, although it is still not entirely satisfactory to the walker. Those who have actual encounters with aggressive bulls while on a right of way should tell the police and Ramblers' Association about their experience.

The landowner

Remember the landowner's point of view, whatever your feelings about private ownership of land. Farmers, rich or poor, are indispensable. Their chief quarrel with walkers centres on dogs, which all too often upset livestock and disturb game. Other sources of friction are damage to crops and property.

The Country Code
GUARD AGAINST FIRE
FASTEN GATES
KEEP DOGS UNDER CONTROL
KEEP TO PATHS
AVOID DAMAGING FENCES,
   HEDGES AND WALLS
LEAVE NO LITTER
SAFEGUARD WATER SUPPLIES
PROTECT WILDLIFE, PLANTS,
   TREES
GO CAREFULLY ON COUNTRY
   ROADS
RESPECT THE LIFE OF THE
   COUNTRYSIDE

WALKING, BIRDWATCHING AND THE LAW

Bird protection law

All wild birds are protected by the law. It is an offence to kill, injure or take any wild bird; take, damage or destroy the nest of a wild bird while in use; take or destroy the eggs of a wild bird; to disturb certain wild birds while nesting; to possess a wild bird which has not been shown to have been killed or taken legally.

There are exceptions to these blanket rules, but they do not concern normal birdwatchers: the only way to be sure of keeping on the right side of the law is to adhere to this general principle.

The law states these exceptions by dividing birds into categories or 'schedules'. The most important, First Schedule birds, with over 70 species or groups of species, are protected by extra-heavy penalties at all times: birdwatchers should know these birds – see list opposite. The other schedules (four of them, including First Schedule, Part II) list species which may, at certain times and under certain circumstances, be shot (for sport) or culled (for conservation purposes) or killed as pests.

The Wildlife and Countryside Act also prescribes that no one may practise falconry without a licence, or collect birds for keeping in aviaries, or ring birds. You need the authority of the Nature Conservancy Council to examine the nest of or photograph a First Schedule bird while on or near its nest.

Walkers and bird photographers should be particularly aware of this point, and also that the Act allows orders to be made at short notice for the protection of birds from disturbance. Disturbance includes simply being near the bird or its nest: some species really will abandon a nest if they detect humans in the neighbourhood.

Maximum penalties for offences under the Act are a £1,000 fine. The fine can be imposed in respect of *each* bird or nest or egg involved. So three eggs stolen from the nest of a First Schedule bird could cost £3,000. There are lesser fines for offences against common species, but they still make egg collecting not worth the while.

The RSPB publishes a useful leaflet, *Wild Birds & the Law*, which gives the conservation position in some detail. If you think you have discovered someone breaking conservation law, first tell the police, giving an accurate and detailed description, then inform the RSPB.

Lastly, remember that you can do almost as much to protect birds as the law by one simple expediency. If you find or sight a rare species which could be vulnerable to disturbance, *keep it to yourself.*

Safety on the hills

Britain's mountains and hills are not high, but they are dangerous. They are all relatively near the sea, their weather changes fast, and even a thousand feet in height can bring radically deteriorating conditions. If birdwatching takes you into upland or moorland areas, observe the few simple rules that can prevent most accidents and tragedies:

- Wear the right clothes and footwear (see pages 22–3).

- Be equipped with maps of at least 1:50 000 scale, a compass and the ability to use them.
- Say where you are going, or at least leave a note on the car windscreen.
- Allow enough time to be home before nightfall; allow an extra hour for every 1,500 feet (457 m) climbed.
- Ring the local pre-recorded weather forecast, or met. office for a report.
- Do not go alone. Three is the minimum safe number. In an accident, one stays with the injured, the other goes for help.
- If caught in poor visibility and unable to find the way down, stop until the weather clears. Find shelter, put on spare, dry clothing; sit on something dry; eat part of any remaining food; build an emergency bivouac or shelter. Keep the limbs moving and huddle close to companions for warmth.

Avocet	Grebe, Black-necked	Sandpiper, Purple
Bee-eater	Grebe, Slavonian	Sandpiper, Wood
Bittern	Greenshank	Scaup
Bittern, Little	Gull, Little	Scoter, Common
Bluethroat	Gull, Mediterranean	Scoter, Velvet
Brambling	Harriers (all species)	Serin
Bunting, Cirl	Heron, Purple	Shorelark
Bunting, Lapland	Hobby	Shrike, Red-backed
Bunting, Snow	Hoopoe	Spoonbill
Buzzard, Honey	Kingfisher	Stilt, Black-winged
Chough	Kite, Red	Stint, Temminck's
Corncrake	Merlin	Swan, Bewick's
Crake, Spotted	Oriole, Golden	Swan, Whooper
Crossbills (all species)	Osprey	Tern, Black
Curlew, Stone	Owl, Barn and Snowy	Tern, Little
Divers (all species)	Peregrine	Tern, Roseate
Dotterel	Petrel, Leach's	Tit, Bearded
Duck, Long-tailed	Phalarope, Red-necked	Tit, Crested
Eagle, Golden	Plover, Kentish	Treecreeper, Short-toed
Eagle, White-tailed	Plover, Little Ringed	Warbler, Cetti's
Falcon, Gyr	Quail, Common	Warbler, Dartford
Fieldfare	Redstart, Black	Warbler, Marsh
Firecrest	Redwing	Warbler, Savi's
Garganey	Rosefinch, Scarlet	Whimbrel
Godwit, Black-tailed	Ruff	Woodlark
Goshawk	Sandpiper, Green	Wryneck

Birdwatchers do not necessarily cover great distances, but their pursuit does keep them out for long periods; being well clothed and shod is worth the effort.

If you walk regularly in rough, upland country, or heathland, there is no substitute for proper, leather walking boots. Leather is porous, and allows some ventilation of the feet; an airtight casing, such as a rubber gumboot, traps the perspiration inside keeping the feet continually damp and overheated. The rigid construction of a purpose-designed walking boot gives the feet and ankles vital support. And only leather moulds to the shape of the feet, giving the near-perfect fit necessary for maximum comfort.

Genuine walking boots cost more than £30, and it is worth taking advice from an expert, or a reputable walking manual, on buying and fitting.

Birders who walk mainly in easy terrain – country paths and lanes – have a wider choice. The lighter, cheaper version of the stout walking boot – often advertised as a Spanish fell boot – is popular, and so is the lace-up walking shoe. Gym shoes or 'kickers', even with the thicker soles available, are not recommended.

Clothing

Brightly coloured anoraks such as those designed to make walkers visible when the mist comes down, are wholly unsuitable for birdwatching. Brown or olive green blend in with most natural backgrounds, and the camouflage can be assisted by wearing a hat drawn well down over the face.

The inherent problem of waterproofs is that when tightly closed their impermeability causes condensation on the inside. Some modern materials claim to minimize the dampness so caused.

Binoculars and telescopes

Binoculars are the only essential hardware for birdwatching; a telescope is

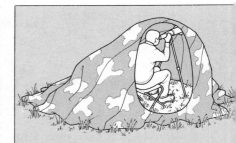

Possibly the simplest and most portable type of hide is cloth with a dull green camouflage pattern, mounted on metal hoops or even wooden stakes.

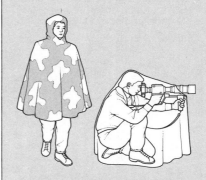

Above, *dual-purpose cape; the hole for the camera lens is covered by a simple patch fastened with 'Velcro' when not in use for picture taking.* **Below right**, *roof prism binoculars, and* **above right**, *the stepped prism type. Buying binoculars requires care, especially if they are second-hand or an inexpensive make. Some firms allow free trial; but one can make some useful tests standing at a shop door. First, ensure the focusing wheel moves freely and that the body, including the piece linking the lens barrels, is rigid and sound. Then look through the binoculars the wrong way round to check for lens flaws or deterioration. Check the coating by looking*

Camera and telephoto lens – increasingly common companions to birdwatching – can often be firmly mounted on a hard support with a bean bag.

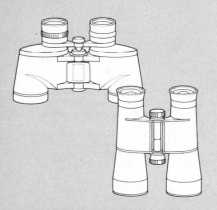

at the lenses (not through them) – they should be tinged uniformly. Next, look at a distant object; there should be no double image. Swing the glasses away from the object: there may be blurring towards the edges of the lens, but the central field should remain sharp. Ensure the image has no blue or yellow borders. Check vertical lines appear straight, at least at the centre of the field of vision. Check how close the binoculars focus: is this adequate for your purposes? Compare sharpness with other makes by focusing on, say, a sheet of newspaper pinned up about 20 yards (18 m) away. Compare brightness of image, and the instrument's weight, with other makes.

invaluable, but it is something to which most birders graduate when experience justifies the cost.

The numbers stamped on binoculars indicate magnification or 'power' and the diameter in millimetres of the large lens furthest from the eye. The first number gives the power, the second the diameter; 6 is a rather low power, 8 is ideal for most purposes but according to a recent survey 10 is most popular with birdwatchers. An average diameter is 40; 50 is for poor lighting conditions. Dividing the diameter by the power gives a factor for the brightness of image. For most conditions, a factor of four is adequate.

Beginners should buy binoculars with an adequate field of view – 'locking on to' a bird is not always easy; minimum recommended field is 7°, equivalent to 120 yards (110 m) at 1,000 yards (914 m), and this is normal for 8 × 30 binoculars. Beware of some cheap models which have 'wide angle' lenses at the expense of image quality.

There are two types of binocular – conventional, with a 'stepped' prism, and 'roof prism', with eye-pieces and front lens in line. The latter are the most compact, lightweight, and expensive. Other factors affecting choice should be the feel of the instrument – if they handle well they will be easy to use; and whether they are suited to spectacle wearers.

Field guides and sound recordings

The choice of field guides is nothing if not wide; possibly the two most telling indicators of quality are whether any of the illustrations are drawn to scale and whether indication is given, preferably by means of illustration, of bird behaviour, an extremely useful factor in identification. Sound recordings are expensive. The most comprehensive album of British bird calls costs more than £80. The RSPB's, covering calls of groups of birds, is excellent, and much more reasonably priced.

BIRDWATCHING TECHNIQUE

Wren   Bullfinch   Jay

The walks in this book have been selected to give birdwatchers the chance of seeing a wide range of species, but there are no guarantees in natural history. Having a sound birdwatching technique is bound to improve your chances of sighting the birds.

Here is how an expert birdwatcher (or 'birder' – the term often used in the United States) would set about a day's birdwatching. Because techniques vary according to habitat, his imaginary walk runs through woods, open heath, marshland and along a coastal estuary – not as fanciful as it seems: in many parts of Britain it is easily possible to cover such varied terrain in just one day.

Preparation

The right time to prepare for an outing is the evening before. The prudent birder would consult the local weather forecast, which, contrary to popular belief, is very often right. Rain and poor visibility keeps birds to the relative comfort of cover, and discourages them from singing. Moreover, they tend to be hard-pressed to find food in these conditions, especially during the breeding season; disturbance by humans only adds to the pressure. So a hardy disregard for the elements, though admirable in itself, is not necessarily an advantage for birdwatching.

It is also worth looking up the time of high tide (local papers often carry tide tables). At high water, waders tend to be concentrated along the high-water mark rather than scattered over areas of mud.

Probably the commonest pitfall in bird identification for beginners is wrong impression of size. The four silhouettes, drawn precisely to scale from dead birds, look different enough on the page – but the inexperienced often report jays as pheasant-sized, and make no distinctions at all between smaller birds. To develop a sense of size, compare birds with their backgrounds (a wren, for instance, is more or less oak leaf-sized). Then, know the typical sizes of the various bird groups, so that species can be noted as 'tit-sized', 'crow-sized' and so on. Beware of the distorting effect on size of binoculars and telescopes.

Weather conditions

In the event, the day starts cloudy but dry – ideal conditions because the glare of bright sun can cause visibility problems. It is worth starting early, for in the breeding season (it is early May), the first two hours of the day see much activity among birds preparing to nest.

Entering the wood, the birdwatcher will almost certainly begin by using his ears as much as his eyes. Even if uncertain of exactly what calls he can hear, they will guide him to an area that *sounds* interesting. He looks for a seat, sits down, and scans the undergrowth for the source of the loudest sound.

In a few seconds, he locates it: a male

Pheasant

blackcap perched high on a spray of rose-bush. As the bird pours out its song, the observer is aware of another movement lower down, amongst the briar. The binoculars are switched to this new target, a female, probably the mate, carrying a piece of dead grass. Obviously, nest building is going on. A few impatient 'chack' calls tells the birdwatcher he has been observed. This is enough and he continues on his way.

Several important points are evident from this interlude. First, it is as important to listen as to watch, especially in woodland, because so many birds are skulkers. A knowledge of the different calls is invaluable; it is also a matter of

experience in the field, although you can develop it to some extent with the help of sound recordings. Actually, bird sound consists of two main kinds – calls and song. The first are generally everyday 'conversation'; the second specialized methods of advertising territory and attracting a mate, heard mainly in the breeding season.

Secondly, it is vital to *stop* and watch, remaining motionless. In five to ten minutes, the birds become less shy of human presence, and the observer, with nothing to do but sit, notices more. Then, never give up after seeing just one bird: many birds go around in pairs, especially during the breeding season.

Finally, always move on as soon as you have alarmed a bird, especially in the breeding season, because the simplest disturbance can cause some species to give up nest building there and then.

It is worth bearing in mind, however, that out of the breeding season, when woodland birds tend to move about in parties, the static observation approach is not so useful, and the birdwatcher depends more on walking further afield and looking for signs of feeding – fallen nuts perhaps, or, on field edges, pecked apples or even cherry stones (indicating tits, fieldfares and hawfinches respectively).

Diagnostic features
Moving slowly, with frequent pauses, the birdwatcher progresses down an open ride fringed with rose and bramble bushes under the shade of oak and birch. A pair of birds, with conspicuously white rumps and black tails, flit ahead. Moments later a much larger bird dashes across the ride into the canopy of an oak, soon emitting ringing screeches.

These birds present the simplest of identification problems. The first are bullfinches, whose black and white rumps are 'diagnostic': no other species has such markings. Recognition is a question of the simplest, fleeting observation combined with knowledge, or the help of a field guide. Likewise the second bird, a jay: no other bird has a similar, ringing, screeching call.

The calling continues, and is joined by the 'clinking' alarms of a pair of blackbirds: a commotion which should arouse any birdwatcher's curiosity. Our birder ventures quietly to the foot of the tree to investigate. Well camouflaged, and perching close to the trunk, is the object of the blackbirds' indignation – a tawny owl. It tolerates the disturbance for a minute or so, then takes off, sweeping silently through the wood.

This illustrates the importance of detective work in birdwatching; this instance, with smaller birds 'mobbing' a predator in order to browbeat it away from their territory, being possibly the commonest method of sleuthing out owls. One does need to know the signs, however, and building up this kind of theoretical knowledge from books, and other birdwatchers, pays dividends.

In fact, the single most valuable piece of experience a beginner can have is going out with an expert.

Jizz
The path passes out of the wood on to open heath studded with gorse and a few low birch trees. Near the woodland edge, a bird is performing a distinctive song flight, rising to a height before parachuting to earth and ending with a flourish of repeated notes.

This presents an identification problem of a different order to the bullfinches

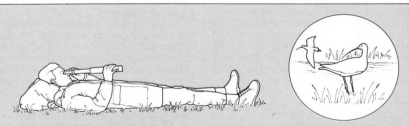

One way of using a telescope in the absence of a tripod or other support: the rucksack steadies the head while the field of forward vision is clear for horizontal sweeping movements. Lying flat also makes the observer less conspicuous – especially important when viewing shy waders.

This is a draw tube telescope, and its suitability for being used in this way gives it a measure of popularity over the 'spotting scope', which may have an impressive power of magnification and a wider field of view, but must be used on a tripod.

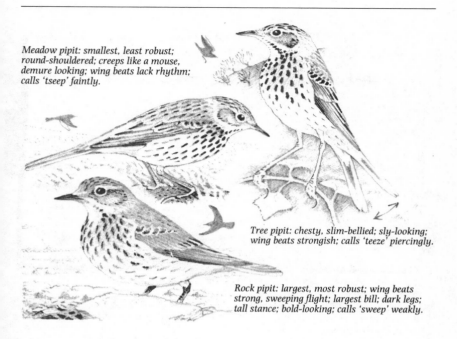

Meadow pipit: smallest, least robust; round-shouldered; creeps like a mouse, demure looking; wing beats lack rhythm; calls 'tseep' faintly.

Tree pipit: chesty, slim-bellied; sly-looking; wing beats strongish; calls 'teeze' piercingly.

Rock pipit: largest, most robust; wing beats strong, sweeping flight; largest bill; dark legs; tall stance; bold-looking; calls 'sweep' weakly.

Above: three small, brownish birds, difficult to distinguish; moreover, the tree and meadow pipit have overlapping habitats, as may the meadow and rock pipit – so they are not always distinguished by where they happen to be seen.

Without time to note subtle plumage variations, the only way to identify them is by observing their 'jizz' – character as expressed by behaviour and form. The notes above are from the artist's own field observations.

or the jay. Even an experienced birdwatcher would recognize the pitfalls of separating this bird, actually a tree pipit, from the almost identical, small, brownish meadow pipit. The beginner, and quite likely the expert, would use his notebook under these circumstances, carefully recording the main details of the song flight, which happens to distinguish the bird. A glance at a good field guide will reveal that the meadow pipit's song flight starts from the ground and lacks the loud coda at the end.

As the bird has landed within binocular range, some further notes can be taken of plumage and markings. However, as will be seen above, successful

identification need not depend on getting down absolutely detailed plumage notes.

Indeed, the meadow and tree pipit, together with their all-too-similar cousin the rock pipit, illustrate possibly the most important factor in visual identification of birds.

The reality of birdwatching, and of birds, is that there is so rarely the opportunity to make a full mental or written note of plumage. But gathering an *impression* of the bird's behaviour and overall form or build can be just as useful because these two factors add up to the bird's 'jizz', or essential character in the field. Without taking this into

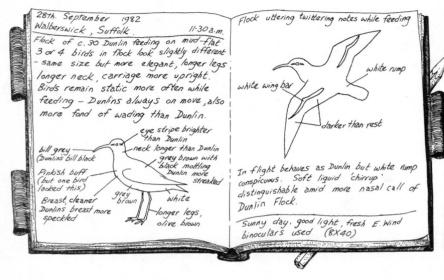

28th. September 1982
Walberswick, Suffolk.   11·30 a.m.

Flock of c. 30 Dunlin feeding on mud-flat 3 or 4 birds in flock look slightly different - same size but more elegant, longer legs longer neck, carriage more upright. Birds remain static more often while feeding - Dunlins always on move, also more fond of wading than Dunlin.

eye stripe brighter than Dunlin
bill grey (Dunlins bill black)
neck longer than Dunlin
grey brown with black mottling Dunlin more streaked
Pinkish buff (but one bird lacked this)
Breast cleaner Dunlins breast more speckled
grey brown
white
longer legs, olive brown

Flock uttering twittering notes while feeding
white rump
white wing bar
darker than rest

In flight behaves as Dunlin but white rump conspicuous. Soft liquid 'chirrup' distinguishable amid more nasal call of Dunlin Flock.

Sunny day, good light, fresh E. Wind binoculars used (8X40)

A well-kept notebook, essential for difficult identifications, and a reminder of days out.

account, birdwatching can indeed be a fruitless and frustrating pursuit.

The heath happens to be one of the few homes of quite a rare species, the Dartford warbler, which has eluded our birdwatcher on several previous visits. With a skulking bird such as this, the best approach is simply persistence and vigilance. Settling down on a knoll commanding a wide view of the gorse, the birdwatcher maintains a constant surveillance while eating his sandwiches. Twenty minutes of sweeping back and forth with the binoculars eventually produces a glimpse of a bird darting into cover. Keeping the binoculars focused for a full minute on the spot where the bird dived in, the observer notices a stirring; and out comes a beautiful grey and chestnut warbler to perch briefly on a dead stem, tail cocked up distinctively.

Other clues

Size, song, diagnostic plumage features, jizz and behaviour are all important clues; three others should also be borne in mind.

First, bill size and shape. This is generally eye-catching in the field, and among small birds particularly is a vital distinction: a thick (seed-eating) bill or a thin (insect-eating) one separates a large number of species.

Second, habitat: some species just do not occur in certain habitats, although outside the breeding season they are encountered in unexpected places. Thirdly, the season: certain species will not be found in some places at certain times of the year; see pages 30–33.

The heath gives way to pasture, beyond which is a sea wall bordering the estuary. Near the foot of the wall there is a deep ditch filled with reeds. By now, some of the first reed warblers should be in, but a walk along the edge reveals nothing – all is silent. Remembering a tip once heard, the birdwatcher claps his hands, and almost at once a male reed warbler breaks into his guttural, repetitive song. Once heard, there is no prob-

Systematic note-taking both of the bird standing and in flight paid off in this case. The mystery species was a curlew sandpiper, whose downcurved bill is a good recognition feature, but did not particularly strike the observer. The white rump, however, did – but only when the bird flew. No other small wader has this feature, except the white-rumped sandpiper, a rare vagrant from North America.

lem in tracing this.

Moving back to the sea wall, the tide is discovered to be well up. Further ahead, a dense flock of waders twists this way and that, like an animated cloud of smoke, then settles on a shingle spit.

In this open area, an approach with the body outlined starkly against the sky is likely to alarm the birds. The best course, under the circumstances, is to descend to rougher ground at the landward foot of the wall and move up under its cover.

About where the flock is estimated to be, there is a stile across a wall. This is an ideal makeshift hide – the stile breaks up the observer's outline, and provides a prop for his telescope. Scanning the flock reveals dunlin, with some redshank in among them. Nearer the wall, running about on the tidal debris, is a small wader. It flies off with a low, flicking wingbeat and a high-pitched call. Once again, recognition (and this is usually the case with fast-moving waders) depends on distinguishing behaviour rather than plumage. The cloud of animated smoke could only have been dunlin; the flicking wingbeat and high-pitched call indicates a common sandpiper.

Having arrived at high tide, it is worth waiting for the water to start falling, because the waders will move back on to the mud to start feeding; and with just a thin strip of mud exposed, the concentration of waders is likely to be higher than usual, giving the chance that some other species will arrive.

Time is nearly up, and the remaining minutes are spent scanning the estuary with the binoculars – better for this purpose than the telescope, with its concentrated field of vision. A line of posts already noticed on previous scans suddenly, almost unconsciously, alerts the birdwatcher. One of the posts has changed shape.

Sure enough, perched on top, eyes fixed on the observer, is a short-eared owl. Even as it is spotted, it takes off to quarter the marsh. As well as everything else, you need to develop a sixth sense to be a birdwatcher.

End of March
Chiffchaffs, singing their name, are among the earliest summer visitors.

April
The first swallows are often noticed over rivers or lakes, but by the end of the month, they can be seen pursuing insects around farms, fields and waterways throughout Britain.

May
Along undisturbed stretches of sandy coast, activity on Sandwich tern colonies is at full swing, with ground displays and fish-carrying flights making a continuous hubbub as breeding gets under way.

Do any one of the walks in this book in July, then repeat it in January, and it goes without saying that the range of birds to be seen will be very different. There is little point in seeking out a swallow or cuckoo in mid-winter or a jack snipe or Bewick's swan in the summer; by then they will be hundreds or even thousands of miles away from Britain.

Breeding birds and 'residents'

Just over 200 species of birds breed regularly in Britain; of these about 60 occur here only as summer visitors (and spend the winter mainly in Africa), while the remainder can be classed as 'resident' – i.e. the species may be found in Britain throughout the year. This does not necessarily mean that these 'residents' stay in one place throughout their lives. Indeed few of them do.

Although some species, such as the house sparrow and red grouse, rarely move more than a few miles from their birthplaces, many others which are thought of as being sedentary often travel long distances. Thus while many British robins or song thrushes, once adult, do not move far, a substantial proportion of young birds (especially from northern areas) move south into France and Spain in their first winter, and many others of the same species from northern Europe come to Britain for the winter or migrate through the country in spring and autumn. Many 'resident' birds are partial migrants, some of the population migrating to south-west Europe, part remaining here: linnet, goldfinch and meadow pipit are examples. Yet others, like the lapwing, attempt to stay in Britain through the winter but move rapidly southwards, out of the country whenever hard weather strikes, and back again as soon as the thaw comes.

Within Britain, a number of species, notably waders, nest on upland moors, but move to estuaries and other lowland areas in winter: the golden plover, curlew, dunlin and twite are examples. And whereas some of our most familiar breeding birds – starlings, blackbirds, rooks, black-headed gulls, coots and others – are essentially non-migratory, vast numbers of the same species come here from northern and central Europe to winter in our rather more equable climate.

Closer to home, many woodland and farmland birds move into gardens to take advantage of food put out specially for them, particularly in cold weather.

A few species which occur in Britain in all months of the year do so because totally different populations are involved: the black-tailed godwits that nest – in small numbers – in England winter mainly in western Africa; those that are here through the winter are Icelandic breeding birds.

Migration patterns

No one is certain how existing migration patterns began or evolved, though all that affect Britain must have developed since the ending of the most recent Ice Age. As the ice retreated northwards, so birds must have been able to extend their breeding ranges to exploit habitats and new-found resources opened up.

There are three main, long-distance migrations that affect British birds. First, the great north–south trek involving our summer visitors – terns, warblers, flycatchers and many others, most of which winter in tropical and southern Africa. Nearly all of these trans-Sahara migrants make their journey at night, though members of the swallow and tern families are exceptions – they move by day. Most follow a broad-front autumn migration that takes them southwards over the Iberian Peninsula, but there are three species – the cuckoo, red-backed shrike and lesser whitethroat, that travel south-east from Britain and cross into Africa over eastern Mediterranean.

The two other main migrations both involve winter visitors to Britain. One,

End of May
Song thrush nesting continues – it is a species with a long breeding season.

June
One of the last summer visitors to arrive, the spotted flycatcher attracts attention by regular aerial sallies for insects from a fence or other favoured perch.

July
Reed warblers delay nesting until the reeds around which they weave their nests are well grown.

August
House martins continue to use their mud nests under the eaves throughout August and into early autumn.

August
Red-necked phalaropes spend winter far out at sea, but during autumn migration may turn up at reservoirs or coastal lagoons, where their exceptional tameness allows close-up views of the dainty shape and behaviour.

September
Curlew sandpiper – a Siberian wader passing through some areas at this time.

October
Redwings begin to arrive in numbers during this month, making full use of the autumn crop of hawthorn berries. Night migrants can sometimes be detected by their flight calls.

from areas lying north-west of Britain, involves a relatively small number of arctic and sub-arctic species, mostly waders and wildfowl. The other is the 'north-west European flyway', involving large numbers of waterfowl, gulls and passerines from northern Europe and north-west Siberia. Although some of these species are mainly nocturnal migrants many, such as lapwings and starlings, migrate by both day and night. Together with chaffinches, which are mainly diurnal, they may be seen arriving from the sea and passing westwards in a procession of large flocks over south-east coasts in autumn. Migration in progress is often a spectacular sight and is particularly worth looking for at places such as Dungeness in Kent, on October mornings with light north-west or west winds.

Non-breeding visitors

As well as the bird species that breed in Britain, another 40 or so occur here regularly as either winter visitors or as migrants, or both. With the exception of two sea birds (the great and sooty shearwaters) which breed in the southern hemisphere and visit British seas in late summer (their winter), all these birds nest in northern latitudes, not just in Europe but in arctic or sub-arctic North America, Greenland and Siberia too. The winter visitors include, for example, knot and other waders from arctic Canada, virtually the whole of the Icelandic population of pink-footed geese, a substantial part of the world population of black-bellied brent geese from Siberia, and many others, especially wildfowl and waders attracted to our relatively ice-free and productive estuaries and other wetlands. 'Exclusive' passerine winter visitors are few, but include small numbers of great grey shrikes from northern Europe and erratic – occasionally huge – numbers of waxwings from the same area which arrive here when their berry food source fails in Scandinavia.

Vagrants

Vagrants are birds that occur in Britain accidentally, normally in autumn (when a lot of immature birds seem to get lost on migration) but occasionally in spring or at other seasons. Some, considering the British Isles are so far from their normal migration routes, occur here with surprising frequency, particularly at isolated coastal sites and islands. Thus every autumn, some dozens of Richard's pipits and yellow-browed warblers – both of which breed in Siberia and winter in southern Asia – turn up in Britain, apparently a thousand or more miles off course from their normal migration. Even some of the long-distance migrants moving between breeding quarters in North America and winter grounds in South America turn up here annually, particularly in western Britain: waders such as pectoral, white-rumped and buff-breasted sandpipers can be found at certain sites in the West Country after westerly gales in September.

As well as the 40 or so accidentals that occur so frequently as to be classed as annual, almost 200 other species have wandered to Britain. New birds are added every year. And it is the hope of finding or seeing one of these extreme rarities – and, who knows, even a species from America, Africa or Asia never before recorded – that spurs on many keen birdwatchers.

Among the best places to find these rarities are Britain's dozen or so coastal bird observatories. These are situated on islands such as Fair Isle and the Isle of May in Scotland or Bardsey in Wales or on exposed headlands such as Spurn and Gibraltar Points, Dungeness and Portland Bill in England. These observatories provide hostel-type accommodation for visiting birdwatchers and can be recommended to anyone wishing to learn more about bird migration or identification. The British Trust for Ornithology, Beech Grove, Tring, Herts., can provide further information.

November
Wintering flocks of geese such as these white-fronts begin to build up in their traditional wintering areas.

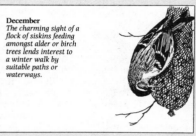

December
The charming sight of a flock of siskins feeding amongst alder or birch trees lends interest to a winter walk by suitable paths or waterways.

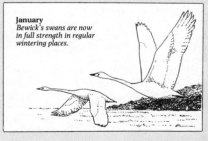

January
Bewick's swans are now in full strength in regular wintering places.

February
The smew, wintering at favoured reservoirs or gravel pits.

March
Fieldfares, soon to return to northern breeding places, are seen on meadows in early spring.

The South-west

The West Country is an ideal region to combine walking with birdwatching. Not only are there the hundreds of miles of the South West Peninsula Coast Path, but also eminently walkable moorland, wooded valleys and heath, together providing a remarkable range of species.

The coastal walks included here, at Trevalga in Cornwall and Portland in Dorset, have the fine scenery and views which are the peninsula's stock in trade; very much part of this magic is the spectacle of breeding sea birds in their cliff and other colonies.

The South-west's geographical position, reaching into the Atlantic, makes it a landfall for rare migrants and vagrants, particularly from North America. The offshore islands of Scilly and Lundy are particularly renowned for such vagrants; those who would not, or cannot, travel so far could be lucky at the Hayle Estuary on mainland Cornwall.

There are still some fine valleys of mixed deciduous woodland, of the sort that are being all too frequently felled and replaced by plantations of alien conifers and they support marvellously rich bird populations. The estuaries, of which the Exe with its flock of wintering avocets is only the most famous, harbour a wealth of waders and wildfowl. And for lonely, wilderness walking, with its share of specialized birds, there are the moorlands of Dartmoor and Exmoor.

Razorbills and guillemots.

Hayle Estuary
2½ miles (4km)
Landranger 203 546363 SW 63

Even at low tide this small estuary allows exceptionally close views of a wide range of densely concentrated waders and wildfowl. And because of its far westerly location it often boasts sightings of rare vagrants from the far side of the Atlantic, particularly North American waders and wildfowl such as the **long-billed dowitcher**, **American wigeon** and **white-rumped sandpiper**. In winter there are **divers** and diving duck on the tidal pool of Carnsew, and in summer, the absorbing sight of terns diving for fish. *Mainly hard paths; RSPB hide and (unmanned) information hut.*

Time and season Excellent all year, but best chance of vagrants during the autumn migration period, and added interest of divers and diving duck in winter. Although the estuary as a whole is rewarding at any time of tide, the best

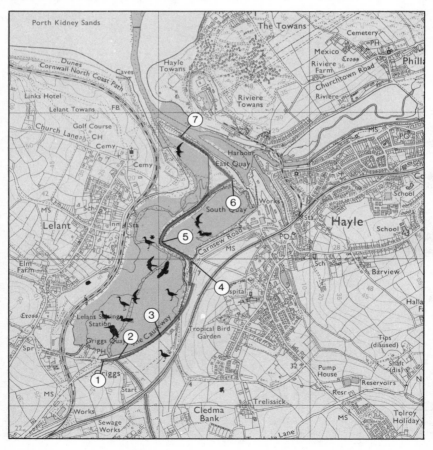

viewing from the hide is within 2 hours of high water.

Start Leave Hayle on the A30 and turn right at the junction with the A3074 towards St Ives. **Car park** of Old Quay House Restaurant almost immediately on right.

① Visit the RSPB information hut and adjacent hide in the restaurant grounds and from the hide ② walk along the estuary edge bordering the A30, in the direction of Hayle. In about 350 yards (320 m) ③ cross road and continue towards Hayle for about ½ mile (0.8 km) then ④ recross to footpath and continue around Carnsew Pool (road curves inland away from estuary). ⑤ Keep to path round edge of pool and at far end ⑥ continue towards the mouth of the estuary. In less than ½ mile ⑦ retrace steps and follow same route back to car park. *In summer it is worth driving to Lelant and following the footpaths across the golf course to see the terns roosting on Port: Kidney Sands.*

The hide gives first-class views of the estuary's birds. Redshank, oystercatchers, lapwings and dunlin are present all year, and shelduck in most months. Autumn and winter bring plenty of wigeon and teal, along with many migrant waders. Some of the scarcer waders such as the little stint and curlew sandpiper crop up regularly; and there are the rare vagrants. Kingfishers sometimes use the posts out in the estuary. High tide is the best viewing time because birds are concentrated on a reduced area of feeding ground, but at low tide there are still excellent, comparatively close views of birds picking about at the edge of the tidal channel.

Scanning the tidal channel a little further up the estuary is usually rewarded with a grey heron. Large flocks of gulls – including Mediterranean as well as the

White-rumped sandpiper.

more common species – use the estuary as a roost. The Mediterranean gull has a black head in summer which makes it look like the black-headed gull, but there the resemblance ends, for the wing tips are white (except in second-year birds). Otherwise the Mediterranean is more like a common gull, but it is stockier, with a more substantial (red) bill and longer legs. Its calls are deeper-pitched than the black-headed's and more shrill than the common's.

A flock of golden plover often roosts on the estuary at low tide from October to March. The mudflats below Carnsew are the main area for curlew.

When the water is high in the estuary waders frequent these fields to the E of the A30.

When the waders on the estuary suddenly fly up in alarm, look for the predator which may have disturbed them – peregrines and sparrowhawks are regular visitors.

All along the Carnsew Pool footpath there are good views of small waders, mainly turnstones and ringed plovers, on the estuary side of the wall.

In summer there may be terns fishing on Carnsew Pool, or roosting on the mud. In winter it holds auks, great northern divers, Slavonian grebes and sea duck such as red-breasted mergansers, goldeneye and even long-tailed ducks.

In summer terns fly in from their roosts on Porth Kidney Sands to feed at the mouth of the estuary.

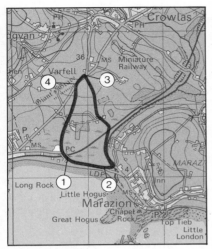

The spotted crake, mostly a non-breeding visitor to the UK, is patchily distributed and exceptionally shy and secretive, more often heard than seen.

Marazion Marsh
2 miles (3 km) Landranger 203
510313

This freshwater marsh, actually a submerged forest, is an exceptionally rich wetland habitat. In spring and autumn it attracts rarities during their migration. *Marsh, pools, reed-beds.*

Spring great northern diver (offshore), garganey, shoveler, gadwall, ruff, hirundines, yellow wagtail; **summer** heron, buzzard, stonechat, warblers; **autumn** spotted crake, greenshank, wood sandpiper and other passage waders; **winter** divers, Slavonian grebe (offshore), water rail, snipe, jack snipe.

Start From Penzance follow the A30 E and after 2 miles (3 km) fork right on to the A394 towards Marazion. **Parking** by the roadside immediately after the railway bridge.

❶ Walk towards Marazion (the marsh can be viewed from the A394). ❷ Turn left on to the unclassified road. After 100 yards (90 m) turn left on to footpath which leads through the marsh. The path crosses the railway, passes the end of a farm drive and continues to the A30. ❸ Turn left on to the main road and ❹ again turn left on to the B3310. Follow this back across the marsh to the railway bridge.

St Ives Island
This is a peninsula rather than an island, situated at the NE corner of St Ives, and one of the best spots in Britain for sea bird passage, especially during onshore northwesterly gales: gannets, shearwaters, skuas, auks, kittiwakes and terns, with some rarities, especially gulls, in autumn; divers and grebes in winter.

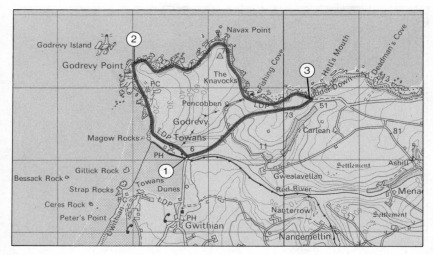

Navax Point
4 miles (6.5 km) Landranger 203 586421

The National Trust owns this and many other stretches of the N Cornish coast; this area, N of Gwithian, supports most of the commoner cliff-nesting birds. *Sea, cliffs, rough grassland.*

Summer razorbill, guillemot, raven, buzzard.

Start Leaving Hayle on the A30 towards Camborne, turn left at the edge of Hayle on to the B3301 and continue to Gwithian. About ½ mile (0.8 km) N of the village the road crosses a river bridge; stop immediately by the narrow track on the left. **Parking** by the side of the road.

① Follow the track and then the public footpath along the cliff edge to Godrevy Point (opposite the lighthouse on Godrevy Island). ② Continue along the cliff top to Navax Point, Fishing Cove and ③ Hell's Mouth, where the footpath meets the B3301. Walk back along the road to ①.

The neck-nibbling routine which is part of razorbill courtship behaviour, along with head-shaking, when the bill is opened to reveal its yellow interior.

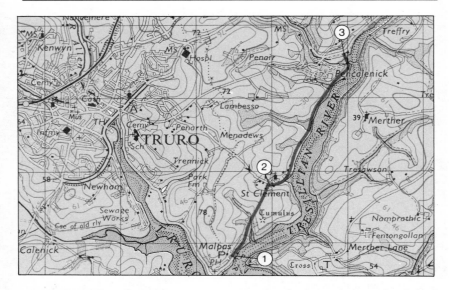

Truro and Tresillian Estuaries
4 or 6 miles (6.5 or 9.5 km)
Landranger 204 845428

The sheltered, wooded estuaries of the Rivers Fal, Ruan, Truro and Tresillian form an important feeding area for waders and wildfowl: the receding tide uncovers large areas of mud, particularly in the narrower channels and side creeks. The National Trust owns several stretches of the foreshore and leases 3 miles (5 km) along the River Fal to the Cornwall Naturalists' Trust. *Mudflats, saltmarsh.*

Spring waders; **autumn** black-tailed godwit, curlew sandpiper, green sandpiper, greenshank, spotted redshank; **winter** black-tailed godwit, greenshank, pintail, red-breasted merganser, wigeon, teal, shoveler.

Start Leave Truro S on the unclassified road to Malpas (the Truro Estuary can be viewed all along this road). **Parking** in Malpas.

① Take the footpath from the end of the unclassified road in Malpas to St Clement, which the path approaches by way of a cul-de-sac. Continue to the main street ②, turn right and walk to the end of the street. A track leads from here to Pencalenick along the Tresillian River. Follow the track until ③ it meets the A39. Retrace to ①.

> Hawke's Wood, just outside Wadebridge, a 9-acre (3.5-ha) reserve belonging to the Cornwall Naturalists' Trust, supports a varied population of birds. It is not open to the general public, but members of any of the county naturalists' trusts may visit free of charge.

Ducks, all male, seen on these estuaries. Wigeon, pintail, teal and shoveler are surface-feeders. The shoveler's bill has a 'sieve' for filtering out food particles.The merganser's is serrated for grasping slippery fish securely.

Wigeon

Pintail

Teal

Red-breasted merganser

Shoveler

Trevalga
2½ miles (4 km)
Landranger 190 081900 SX 08

This walk provides the best opportunities on mainland Cornwall to see **puffins** during the breeding season, April to mid-July. They, and other auks, are visible from the coast path on Long and Short Islands, tall stacks close inshore. Spectacular views of the north Cornwall coast, and, in summer, a wonderful variety of wild flowers and butterflies. An excellent introduction to the delights of the 268-mile (431-km) Cornwall Coast Path, which runs from Marsland Mouth near Bude to Cremyll on the Tamar. *Mud after rain.*

Time and season April to mid-July, after which the auk breeding season is over;

from then on the sea birds are seen mainly offshore on passage, with the closest views during onshore gales.

Start From Tintagel take the B3263 towards Boscastle. At Trevalga turn left for the church. **Parking** near church.

① From the church follow footpath through farm gate and down the combe towards the coast. On joining the coast path ② turn left. Continue along the coast path, stopping to inspect Short Island and Long Island. Long Island, seen from ③, provides the best bird-watching because of its height and closeness to the shore. Continue along the coast path about ¾ mile (1 km) and after crossing Rocky Valley ④ turn inland to walk up the valley footpath to the road, where ⑤ turn left. Continue

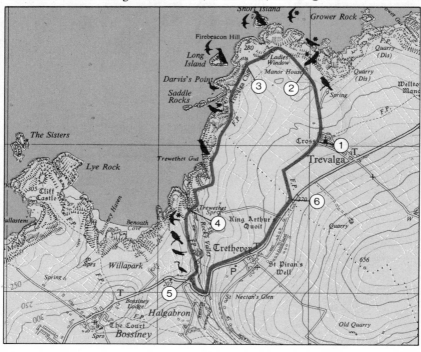

along road rather over ½ mile (0.8 km) until reaching ⑥ the footpath sign indicating Trevalga church. Follow the path back to ①. *The walk can be extended in either direction along the coast path; going S may be slightly more rewarding.*

High loading makes the puffin's wings whirr furiously, especially on landing – here with sand eels for the young in the burrow.

Look for warblers and finches in the scrub along the path.

Buzzards and ravens – which breed in the cliffs – are likely to be seen anywhere on the walk.

Numbers of sea birds are likely to be seen just offshore all along the coastline. Look for kittiwakes (black wingtips) and fulmars, which glide along the cliff faces, performing superb aerobatics, on long, rigidly held wings.

Long and Short Islands are splendid auk breeding grounds. Look for the puffins near their burrows on the grassy slopes on the sides of the stacks. There are guillemots and razorbills, too: the former look browner than razorbills in flight and nest in larger groups. Razorbills tend to be more scattered.

Fair numbers of shags nest on the islands. Herring gulls are common, and there are a few of their relatives, the lesser black-backed gulls, which have slate-grey wings paler than those of the much larger great black-backed gulls.

Oystercatchers nest along the rocky shore: listen for their piping calls and look for them along the tideline. When roosting they have a habit of standing shoulder to shoulder, all facing in the same direction.

Jackdaws are much more common and numerous than ravens – smaller in size and with a grey nape.

Razorbills again.

The shelter of Rocky Valley makes it suitable for whitethroats and other warblers, and finches such as linnets. Also look for cuckoos and kestrels. Sometimes herons nest in the woods near the road.

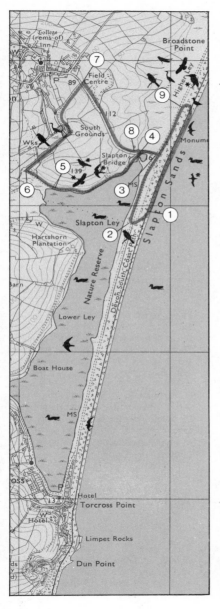

Slapton Ley
3 miles (5 km)
Landranger 202 829440 SX 74/84

Slapton Ley is a large freshwater lake behind the long, shingle ridge of Slapton Sands. The Higher Ley – the northerly part – has a sizeable area of reed marsh which holds substantial populations of warblers in summer, including **Cetti's warbler**, a recent arrival, of which there are about 200 pairs nationwide. The Lower Ley supports a wealth of wildfowl in winter and breeding **great crested grebes**. Offshore there are sometimes large numbers of divers and grebes, including **Slavonian** and **red-necked**. Rarities such as the **bluethroat** occur during migration. The area is a nature reserve managed by the Field Studies Council. *Field Study Centre open in summer and at other times by request; Bird Observatory (Devon Birdwatching and Preservation Society) is worth visiting if manned – usually during weekends and autumn migration; mud after rain.*

Time and season All year.

Start From Kingsbridge take the A379 to Torcross and follow the road along the shore, passing Slapton Lower Ley to the left. **Car park** in 1¼ miles (2 km), behind the beach (before the junction with the road to Slapton village).

① From car park cross to shore of Lower Ley ② and walk N to the T-junction. ③ Follow the road towards Slapton, crossing the bridge between the 2 lakes and ④ turn left through the gate and take the footpath round the side of the Ley. The path curves ⑤ up the little valley. In 350 yards (320 m) ⑥ turn right with path through farmland and continue to road near Field Centre, where ⑦ turn right. Follow the road towards the sea, visiting the Field Centre and, just before the bridge ⑧, Observatory. At the T-junction turn left and follow the shore of the Higher Ley N for about ½ mile

(0.8 km) and ⑨ cross road to return to car park along beach. *The walk can be extended in either direction along the shores of the Higher or Lower Ley.*

The reed and scrub fringe of the Lower Ley holds numbers of reed and sedge warblers in spring and summer.

Look for great crested grebes all year round; in winter check for other grebes, including Slavonian. Winter wildfowl flocks include goldeneye and the occasional long-tailed duck.

Inspect the small bays and reedy pools along the shore of the Lower Ley for water rails – regular in winter; and crakes, including the spotted crake.

Ravens, buzzards and kestrels may be seen all round the walk; peregrines in winter.

This valley of coastal farmland is one of the likeliest places in Britain for the easily overlooked cirl bunting (range confined to southern England, main population S Devon). Its song, still heard in July and August, usually from a tall tree, is similar to the yellowhammer's but lacks the final phrase. Herons frequent the wet fields near the valley bottom.

The reed and willow scrub of the Higher Ley is a prime habitat for both breeding and migrant warblers. Listen for the powerful, short burst of song from Cetti's warbler. The bird is an extreme skulker, but if you are lucky enough to get a glimpse of it, identification is made relatively easy by the combination of rich, dark brown plumage and a long, rounded tail. Reed and sedge warblers are common in summer. In winter listen for the 'pinging' calls of bearded tits. There are numerous cuckoos in spring. Herons and the occasional bittern crop up in winter. Marsh harriers and even ospreys are possible during migration periods. Kingfishers all along the Ley.

Cetti's warbler is best located by song. The tail is often depressed during perching. Behaviour in vegetation can seem quite wren-like, with frequent tail-cocking.

Small waders on the shoreline, notably turnstones, ringed plovers and dunlin.

Large flocks of gulls roost on the beach; check for rarities, including Mediterranean and little gulls.

Small groups of divers occur regularly offshore in winter, mainly great northern and red-throated. Sea duck include common scoter; during onshore gales watch for uncommon species like arctic skuas and Manx shearwaters.

The Lower Ley is a gathering place for large flocks of swallows and swifts prior to migration.

Large rafts of wildfowl, including pochard, tufted duck, teal, wigeon and occasionally ring-necked duck, are seen on the Torcross end of Lower Ley and the beach is a safe roost for large gull flocks.

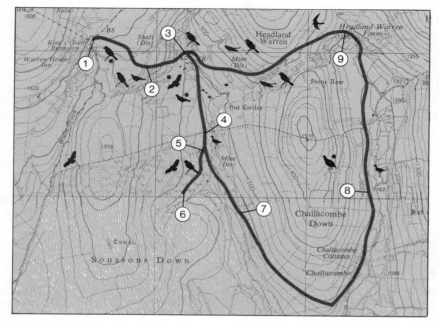

Headland Warren
4 miles (6.5 km) Landranger 191 686811
SX 68/78 and SX 67 and SX 77

An all-round Dartmoor walk, with grass and heather moorland together with a large conifer plantation. Typical breeding birds of the former are **wheatears, whinchats, ring ouzels, ravens** and possibly **red grouse**. Winter visitors can include **great grey shrikes** and **hen harriers**. In the plantation, breeding species include goldcrests, coal tits and possibly redpolls and siskins. *Rough moorland tracks; the mist comes down quickly on Dartmoor – a call to the local pre-recorded weather forecast is recommended before setting out on this route; do not attempt in poor visibility; mud after rain.*

Time and season Best in spring and early summer; most chance of seeing roosting

hen harriers in late afternoon in winter.

Start From Moretonhampstead take the B3212 towards Princetown. On reaching moorland, continue about 2 miles (3 km) to Warren House Inn on right.

Parking opposite Inn or 200 yards (180 m) back along road.

① Take the track on the right 200 yards N of Warren House Inn. Follow track down towards valley, checking area of old fluvial mining ② before reaching stream in valley where ③ turn right and follow path along valley between 2 areas of woodland towards ④ the plantation marked as Soussons Down. Where the path forks right into the plantation ⑤ follow the right-hand path a few dozen yards to check for woodland species, and ⑥ return to original path, continuing S, crossing valley. ⑦ Follow the moorland track around the S side of Challacombe Down and ⑧ walk N up the next valley to Headland Warren Farm. ⑨ Turn left and follow the track back to the path towards the parking area.

Meadow pipits and skylarks are the commonest birds of the open moorland, but Dartmoor has one of the UK's best populations of wheatears. They range widely over the moor; look for them near rocks and stone walls – the white rump shows clearly as the bird flies off.

The narrow gorges cut by the old mine streams provide a sheltered habitat favoured by ring ouzels, which arrive in early April. This 'moorland blackbird', with its white gorget (throat patch), is rather shy, so watch well ahead for it. Stock doves sometimes nest in the area.

Dartmoor has one of the South-west's largest populations of buzzards and ravens. Buzzards have exceptionally varied plumage, ranging through from pale to dark; their markings are perhaps best described as patchy, and this, with the broad, rounded shape of the wings, is perhaps the best means of identification. Soaring is their most distinctive habit: groups numbering more than two dozen are commonly seen wheeling in great circles, hundreds of yards across. The call is high-pitched, something like a gull's.

The sheltered valley with scattered hawthorns is a habitat for stonechats, whinchats, reed buntings and, in spring and summer, tree pipits. In winter look for great grey shrikes perching on top of the bushes.

The boggy areas in the valley bottoms can be feeding areas for curlew and snipe.

The plantation is worth exploring in spring. Listen for the songs of chaffinches, coal tits, goldcrests. Siskins and redpolls

Ring ouzels – the male, top, basically black, the female brownish – have whitish wing patches and crescent-edged feathers; tail longer, wings narrower than blackbird's.

are occasional. Sparrowhawks sometimes hunt along the firebreaks (gaps in trees) and rides.

Red grouse are thinly distributed on Dartmoor, but they can occur in any area of well-established heather. Probably the simplest way of identifying the bird is its 'go-back' call as it flies off in a flurry.

Look for kestrels hovering over the grassy parts of the moorland.

In spring and early summer check the old mining areas below Headland Warren for ring ouzels. In spring, too, open moorland is likely to give sightings of cuckoos; look for them flying quite low, their pointed wings giving especially long downward strokes.

In winter, Soussons Down is a roost for hen harriers. Typical late afternoon sightings are of the bird gliding in low over the moor, heading for its roost.

DEVON

Lannacombe Bay
6 or 8 miles (9.5 or 13 km)
Landranger 202 818375

This bay, with its promontories of Prawle Point and Start Point, lies at the southernmost part of the Devon coast: a vantage point for watching sea birds during the spring and autumn migrations. In summer, breeding cirl buntings may be seen singing from tall trees on coastal farmland, and later in the year they sometimes form flocks in Start Point car park. This is a magnificent coastal walk, with some splendid views over the Channel, worth the effort of the return journey by foot, or of arranging suitable transport from East Prawle to ①. *Sea, rocky coast, farmland; the route follows the Devon South Coast Path.*

Spring migrants; **autumn** Manx shearwater, Balearic shearwater, fulmar, gannet, guillemot, passerines, other migrants; **winter** stonechat, cirl bunting, finch flocks.

Start From Kingsbridge take the A379 E to Chillington. In the centre of Chillington turn right along an unclassified road and head SE for 1½ miles (2.5 km) in the direction of Beeson to a T-junction. Turn right and follow the road S for 1¼ miles (2 km), bearing left before Kellaton to follow the road towards Start Point. **Car park** on right after 1¾ miles (3 km). **Return to start** from East Prawle is possible by means of inland roads and footpaths via Woodcombe; alternatively combine 2 parties in separate cars, parking one at Start Point and the other in East Prawle, exchanging keys midway.

① From the car walk towards the lighthouse ② at Start Point. Retrace about 200 yards (180 m) and turn left to follow the coast path 4½ miles (7 km) to ③ Prawle Point. Either return by the same route or carry on to join the minor road to East Prawle.

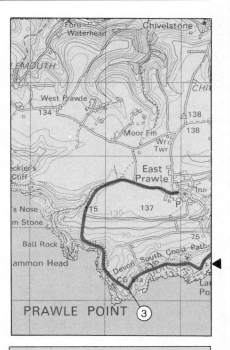

PRAWLE POINT ③

The Forestry Commission's Hartland Information Centre in Torridge Forest gives details of forest walks and picnic places in Devon and Cornwall and contains displays on the birdlife of forest and moorland. The centre is on the A39, 11 miles (17.5 km) NE of Bude.

Woodbury Common is an ideal area for watching a large number of typical heathland birds, including nightjars, tree pipits and stonechats. If making the visit just to see nightjars, go ½ hour before dusk and continue watching until ½ hour afterwards. Patient watching is usually rewarded: see page 56. From Exeter take the A376 S for 2 miles (3 km) via Clyst St Mary, then turn left on to the B3179, passing through Woodbury to reach the common.

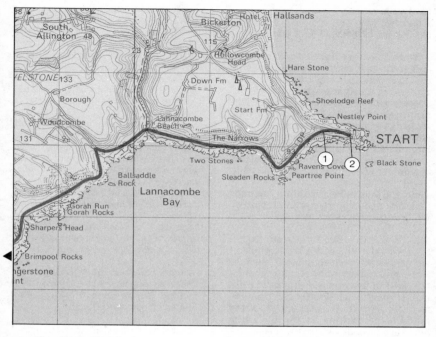

Meadhaydown Wood
4½ miles (7 km) Landranger 191 804883

A public bridleway runs the length of this wood, a nature reserve managed by the Devon Trust for Nature Conservation. The predominantly oak woodland holds healthy populations of tits and finches, and open areas of scrub attract summer migrants. The River Teign further widens the range with waterbirds. *Deciduous wood, mixed scrub, river; free to any nature conservation trust member, otherwise small fee – contact county trust.*

Summer grasshopper warbler, garden warbler, blackcap, willow warbler, chiffchaff, wood warbler, spotted flycatcher; **winter** firecrest, siskin, redpoll; **all year** sparrowhawk, buzzard, the 3 woodpeckers, grey wagtail, dipper, goldcrest,

long-tailed, marsh and coal tits, nuthatch, treecreeper, raven.

Start From Moretonhampstead take the B3212 E. Before Dunsford the road crosses the Teign at Steps Bridge. **Car park** on the right after bridge.

① From car park walk back to bridge. Before the bridge, a public bridleway leads right; follow it 1¾ miles (3 km) to the road ②; retrace to car park.

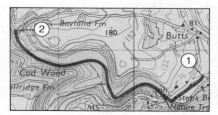

Exe Estuary
4 miles (6.5 km)
Landranger 192 960875 SX 88/98

The walk follows paths along a canal and river wall with excellent views of the Exe Estuary's rich population of waders. At the right season this includes **avocets** and **black-tailed godwits**. The return route gives the opportunity of crossing Exminster Marshes, which although now heavily drained attract large flocks of wintering thrushes and plovers when wet, besides offering views of summer visitors. *Mud after rain.*

Time and season Best within 3 hours of high tide and August–April, but worthwhile during the other months.

Start Take the A379 S from Exeter towards Dawlish, and after Exminster village the left turn signposted 'Swan's Nest' pub. Cross railway and stop in ½ mile (0.8 km), where track widens; trains from Exeter Central to Topsham and foot ferry from Topsham to Exeter Canal bank. **Parking** on track, shortly after tarmac ends (where track is joined by another from left).

① Walk back along the side track for 20 yards (18 m) to ②, where follow the footpath on right across meadow via series of small bridges over ditches. ③ Turn right on to path along canal and continue about 1 mile (1.5 km) to ④ Turf Lock. Cross lock gates and walk upstream a few hundred yards to view estuary. ⑤ Retrace to ④ and continue downstream on river wall to ⑥ where the deep channel comes close to the path. Retrace to ⑦, a stile to the left of the lock entrance. Cross and follow path across fields to ⑧, where turn right to follow path beside railway to road at ⑨, where turn right and return to car. *From ⑥ the walk can be extended by continuing along the river wall to Powderham and returning by the same route – about 2 miles (3 km) there and back.*

Swallows and martins hawk for insects over the meadows and canal in summer.

The reeds between the canal and river support substantial populations of reed and sedge warblers.

Black terns occasionally occur along the canal in August.

From the canal bank large numbers of wildfowl and waders can be seen on the fields – except in summer. During floods and hard weather there may also be white-fronted geese and Bewick's swans. Large flocks of golden plovers, lapwings, snipe, redwings and fieldfares are regular occurrences. At high tide there are plenty of waders from the estuary, especially a large flock of black-tailed godwits, for which the Exe is internationally important; also redshank, dunlin and curlews.

When the flocks of waders suddenly take to the air, look for the bird of prey which might well have caused their alarm; in winter it might be a peregrine.

Short-eared owls sometimes occur in this area; look for them on the low fence posts.

At low tide the waders and wildfowl tend to spread out over the mudflats. In summer, look for family parties of shelduck. Large flocks of gulls roost on the estuary.

November through to early March are the months to see the wintering avocets. At low tide they are often out of sight along the tidal channels; the best chance of seeing them is at mid-tide, when they may be feeding along the shore just upstream from Turf Lock, or at high tide, when they float amongst the gulls slightly further upstream. Don't always expect to see the upturned bill: besides using it underwater in sweeping movements, the avocet up-ends, like a duck.

Diving duck such as goldeneye in the main channel.

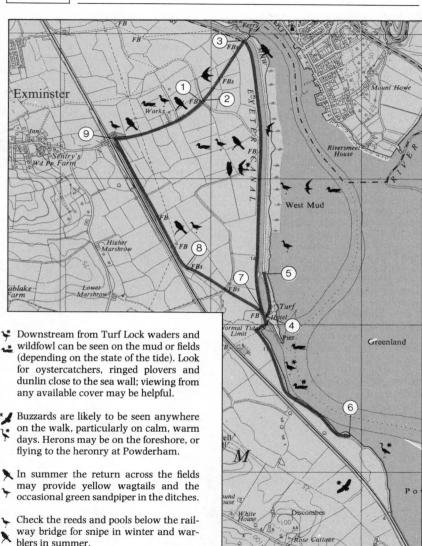

Downstream from Turf Lock waders and wildfowl can be seen on the mud or fields (depending on the state of the tide). Look for oystercatchers, ringed plovers and dunlin close to the sea wall; viewing from any available cover may be helpful.

Buzzards are likely to be seen anywhere on the walk, particularly on calm, warm days. Herons may be on the foreshore, or flying to the heronry at Powderham.

In summer the return across the fields may provide yellow wagtails and the occasional green sandpiper in the ditches.

Check the reeds and pools below the railway bridge for snipe in winter and warblers in summer.

In winter scan the fields to the left closely: numbers of the waders, ducks and passerines mentioned elsewhere on the route can still be seen.

DEVON

Taw-Torridge Estuary
9½ miles (15 km)
Landranger 180 486357

The estuary is a rich feeding ground for
waders and Braunton Marsh is used by
wildfowl. *Mudflats, saltmarsh, dunes.*

Summer common tern, kittiwake;
autumn whimbrel, green sandpiper,
common tern; **winter** peregrine,
wigeon, golden plover, grey plover,
sanderling, greenshank, bar-tailed
godwit; **all year** shelduck, oystercatcher,
turnstone, ringed plover, kingfisher.

Start Braunton. **Car park** near centre.

① From crossroads take minor road S;
turn right at Braunton Burrows sign;
continue to Marstage Farm, following
path between road and river. Soon after
passing farm ②, when the road bears
right, keep to the river. Continue to the
estuary – another mile (1.5 km) – and
③ follow the shore. In about ½ mile (0.8
km) follow the path out to the lighthouse, ⑤. Retrace to ④, fork left and
follow the coast Path 3 miles (5 km)
to the B3231. ⑥ Turn right for Braunton.

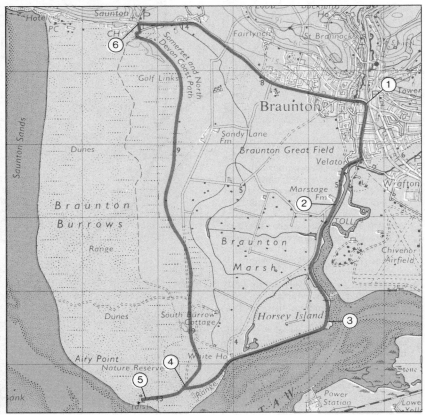

Arne Heath
1 mile (1.5 km) Landranger 195 972877

The Arne peninsula holds one of the largest tracts of lowland heath in Britain, of which 1,100 acres (445 ha) are owned by the RSPB. A traditional breeding ground of the Dartford warbler. The area around Shipstal is open throughout the year, but the rest of the reserve can only be visited by booking in advance to join a conducted walk. *Heath, woods, carr, reedbeds, saltmarsh; tours available on Sundays, Wednesdays, Thursdays and Saturdays from April to August; no smoking on the reserve at any time; nature trail leaflet available from reception area; entry fee for non-RSPB members; mud after rain.*

Summer nightjar, reed warbler, blackcap, Dartford warbler; **winter** grebes, wildfowl, red-breasted merganser, hen harrier; passage waders, including spotted redshank, black-tailed godwit; **all year** shelduck, teal, sparrowhawk, green and great spotted woodpeckers, stonechat, reed bunting.

Start From Wareham take the A351 (Swanage road). In Stoborough, about 1 mile (1.5 km) from Wareham, turn left on to unclassified road to Arne. **Car park** and reception area on right after 2 miles (3 km), before village of Arne. (Small car parking charge to non-members.)

From the car park walk to Arne church. A bridleway begins opposite the church and leads out to Shipstal Point. Return by the same route.

Radipole Lake
½ mile (0.8 km) Landranger 194 676796

Radipole Lake, at the mouth of the River Wey, lies within the town of Weymouth and is of interest at all times of the year. It contains a small population of Cetti's warblers and thousands of yellow and

The black and white pied wagtail, top, and, below, the yellow wagtail, whose plumage is basically yellow, but varies individually.

pied wagtails roost in the reeds during migration. Managed by the RSPB. *Open water, reedbeds, rough pasture, scrub; free entry.*

Summer reed, sedge and grasshopper warblers; **autumn** rails, crakes, little ringed plover, little stint, sandpipers, spotted redshank, greenshank, little gull, terns, including black tern, swallows and martins, wagtails, sedge warbler; **winter** mallard, teal, shoveler, pochard, tufted duck; **all year** little and great crested grebes, cormorant, heron, mute swan, shelduck, other wildfowl, kingfisher, Cetti's warbler, bearded tit, reed bunting; **spring** garganey, terns, swallows, martins, wagtails, sedge warbler.

Start Weymouth, at the terminus of the A354 S of Dorchester; frequent trains and buses – railway and bus both within 5 minutes' walk of the reserve. **Car park** at The Swannery.

A nature trail starting from the Swannery car park leads past the lake, reedbeds and scrub.

Portland Bill
3 miles (5 km) Landranger 194 677686
SY 67/77

The great promontory of Portland extends 6 miles (9.5 km) into the English Channel, giving grandstand views of sea birds in numbers never seen close inshore. It is also an outstanding location for migrants of all types. *There is a bird observatory at Portland Old Light; mud after rain.*

Time and season Fascinating at any time, but the prime periods are the migration months of August–October and March–May.

Start Take the A354 S from Weymouth and follow the signs for Portland. Continue through town, following signs for Portland Bill, turning left at Southwell. Carry on towards the tip of the Bill. **Car park** (main car park) N of new lighthouse.

① From car park walk N, crossing road by Devenish Arms, where ② follow path in front of coastguard cottages and bear left past quarry, rejoining road at ③. Visit Portland Bird Observatory in Portland Old Light ④ before crossing road and ⑤ taking track to left. At top of ridge ⑥ turn right and follow track past barns. When almost at Southwell ⑦ turn right and continue to road, crossing stile on the way. At road ⑧ turn right and in 400 yards (350 m) ⑨ turn left on to path leading to shore, where ⑩ follow cliff path back to Bill and ⑪ return to car park.

Look for migrants on the short grass near the car park. Wheatears and pipits are usual – but surprises may well turn up.

The bushes near the coastguard cottages are shelter for migrating birds; in autumn pied flycatchers are likely and there might be melodious and icterine warblers, as indeed extreme rarities like the sub-alpine warbler.

The gardens viewed from the observatory have been cultivated to provide shelter for migrants; ringing and netting is carried out here and a log recording recent sightings is available on request.

The path now passes through fields where many rare migrants have been seen. Among regular rare passerines are the ortolan bunting and tawny pipit. There are plentiful flocks of linnets and goldfinches. Predators passing through regularly include hobbies, marsh and Montagu's harriers and sparrowhawks. In summer listen for the jangling song of the corn bunting. Cuckoos crop up on their journey S and several members of the crow family will be seen.

The old quarry workings on the coast provide holes and shelter for little owls and kestrels.

In winter, small numbers of purple sandpipers can be seen along the rocky shoreline. They are very easily overlooked, their sooty upperparts (with a faint, purple gloss) merging efficiently with their normal background of weed-covered rocks.

At the Bill spend some time looking out to sea. During migration, shearwaters, skuas, gannets, terns, divers and gulls will be seen in large numbers. In the breeding season, shags, kittiwakes, fulmars, guillemots, razorbills and sometimes puffins can be seen flying to and from their breeding colonies on the cliffs to the W – one of the few breeding auk colonies on the S coast of England. At long range, gannet flight is direct, with some gliding, and of course diving into the sea from a height with wings folded. Razorbills are difficult to separate from guillemots in flight, although in breeding season the difference in bill shape may be discernible. At long range, puffins are also difficult to distinguish from other auks, unlike in close views, when the bill is unmistakable.

Manx shearwaters, left and right, appear almost to flicker as they turn back and forth exposing dark and pale upper- and underparts. The Balearic shearwater (S European race) has dull brown 'armpits'.

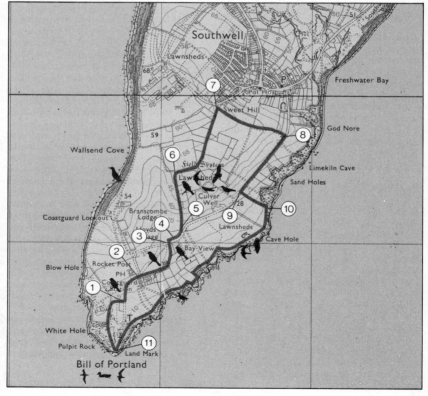

DORSET

Studland Heath
2½ miles (4 km)
Landranger 195 034862
SZO8

This is one of the few remaining areas of lowland heath in Britain, offering exceptional opportunities of seeing **nightjars** and the relatively rare **Dartford warbler**. The route also gives fine views over the tidal shoreline of Poole Harbour for waders, terns, grebes and gulls. The freshwater lagoon of Little Sea harbours flocks of wintering ducks. Part of the walk is through the Studland National Nature Reserve managed by the Nature Conservancy Council. Fire is an ever-present risk; please take extreme care. *Mud after rain.*

Time and season The heath is at its best in summer, Poole Harbour and Little Sea in winter. Dartford warblers are resident; to see nightjars, do the walk late on a summer evening.

Start Follow the A351 from Wareham towards Swanage. Turn left on to the B3351 to Studland and drive through the village towards the ferry, passing toll gate (small fee). **Car park** near South Haven Point.

① Walk across the heath following paths to shore of Poole Harbour. ② Follow the shoreline to Redhorn Quay ③ where turn left, following footpath to road. ④ Cross road and turn right; in about 20 yards (18 m) join the path on the left. Follow path and in about 250 yards (230 m) ⑤ turn right at path junction. Continue across heath for ½ mile (0.8 km) to ⑥. Retrace steps to ⑤ and continue straight ahead on track bordering Little Sea, which gives access to hide at ⑦. Follow track back to road and ⑧ turn right along road back to car. *The walk can be extended from ① by following the path out to Shell Bay, where sea birds may be sighted offshore. Return by same route.*

❴ Black-headed and common gulls on the foreshore; common and sandwich terns hovering above the tideline.

➤ A variety of waders occur on the area between the low and high tidelines – look especially for bar-tailed godwits (the only straight-billed wader, which is brown with a white V on the back) and curlews.

➤ Wildfowl visiting Brand's Bay in winter include brent geese and wigeon. Also look for Slavonian grebes – the latter being smaller than great crested grebes, with a dark, slanted cap.

➤ Look for the Dartford warbler in the tall stands of European gorse (rather than low dwarf gorse). Sightings require patience – this is a skulker – but it will emerge briefly, long dark tail cocked characteristically, likely as not to exclaim at an intruder. The bird is sedentary – it does not even make local movements away from breeding quarters, so it is particularly vulnerable to severe winters. The British population, confined essentially to the heaths of S England, has been almost annihilated on several occasions, the last most notable being the heavy winter of 1963, when numbers were reduced to 10 pairs. Since then it has recovered considerably. Stonechats and linnets are among other small birds on the heath.

➤ If doing the walk from May to August, start listening for the nightjars ½ hour before dusk. The song of the male is weird and unmistakable – a prolonged, dry 'churr' or trill, almost as if made by some piece of machinery, and changing pitch from time to time. Nightjars feed on airborne insects, and you may be lucky enough to see one hawking moths before the light goes. (The hunting call is a 'queek'.) It is worth watching quietly for up to ½ hour after dark: the unmistakable buoyant, wheeling, twisting flight may well be glimpsed against a pale, western sky.

➤ The scrub woodland bordering Little Sea

holds small warblers in summer. Listen for chiffchaffs, willow warblers and reed and sedge warblers on the water margins. Jays are frequent near the woodland edge.

In winter, make use of the hide to scan Little Sea for wildfowl. There are teal, pochard, tufted duck and coot; water rails and snipe may be picking about on the marshy edge.

Offshore sea birds – shearwaters, skuas, gannets – especially during migration periods.

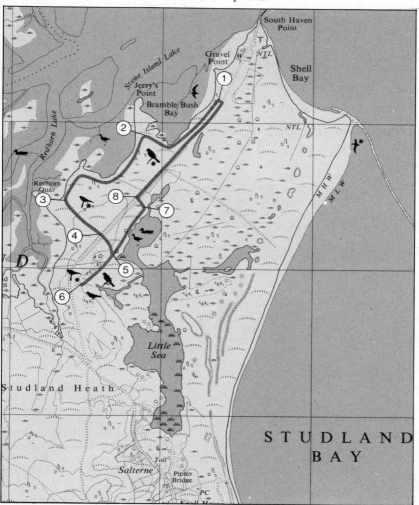

SOMERSET

Hawkridge Ridge and the Barle Valley
$4\frac{1}{2}$ miles (7 km) Landranger 181 870291
SS82/92 and SS83

Valleys of superb mixed woodland like
the Barle were once typical of the West
Country; sadly many are being replanted with fast-growing conifers. In
the breeding season the mature oak and
beech woods have a rich and well-
distributed birdlife, giving real opportunities of seeing – among many others
– **wood warblers, redstarts** and the rare,
patchily distributed **pied flycatcher**.
Variety is given by the small moorland
area on which the route finishes – a
remnant of a once much greater expanse. *Footpaths well marked and maintained by Exmoor National Park; mud after
rain.*

Time and season April–June.

Start Take the B3222 S out of Dulverton
and soon turn right, following signs for
Hawkridge. At Five Cross Ways take the
right-hand of 3 forks and in $\frac{1}{2}$ mile (0.8
km) stop at the signpost on left showing
'Hawkridge $1\frac{3}{4}$'. **Parking** for two or three
cars in clearing opposite signpost on
right; otherwise carefully on wider parts
of road.

① Follow the path signposted Hawkridge and ② go through gate, following
yellow waymark. ③ Cross bridge and
④ turn right, following footpath downstream keeping fairly close to the river.
⑤ Where footpaths split take direction
indicated by Dulverton sign. ⑥ At
Castle Bridge turn left in direction of
Hawkridge sign and ⑦ where paths
split leave waymarked path, continuing
towards Hawkridge. Cross farmland on
the ridge, later passing through the left
of two gates. At signpost ⑧ turn left
towards East Anstey Common and
return on path with yellow waymarks
to ①. Cross road and go through gate
on to East Anstey Common. Continue
straight ahead and in rather under

$\frac{1}{2}$ mile ⑨ turn right and cross common
to road at ⑩ – just over $\frac{1}{2}$ mile. Turn
right to car. *From ⑥ the walk can be con-
tinued downstream towards Dulverton.*

The open scrub and bracken slopes are
classic tree pipit, whinchat, yellowhammer and cuckoo habitats. Watch for
buzzards circling above.

This woodland fringe is worth inspecting
closely for redstarts and spotted flycatchers.

In the woodland listen for the rich trilling
of wood warblers, which are well distributed throughout the valley.

After the footbridge the path reaches an
area of scrub and meadow which is excellent for small warblers, principally willow
warblers and chiffchaffs. (Also look for
the rare marbled white butterfly here.)

Dippers are resident and will be seen all
along the fast-flowing river; most likely
sightings are near turbulent areas and
bridges. The likelihood of seeing grey
wagtails also adds to the enjoyment of the
riverside stretch. Grey upperparts con-
trasting with bright yellow beneath make
identification easy. The long, thin tail is
constantly wagged and the flight pattern
is undulating. In summer the adult male
has a black 'bib'.

Rich, deciduous woodland – the place to
look for pied flycatchers. They nest in
holes in mature trees. Nuthatches and
woodpeckers are likely, too.

The open fields at the top of the ridge
provide a clear view over the valley and
the likelihood of buzzards and ravens.
(Ravens have a harsh, 'krup' call; buzzards have a mewing call.) Also look for
sparrowhawks, circling on thermals.
They have rounded wings and longish
tails, often alternating wing flapping with
long glides.

Look for stonechats and whinchats on the

common; linnets are likely to be seen round the gorse edges.

❮ Kestrels are common, hovering over the moorland. The area is now too confined for there to be much chance of a merlin, although the bird might crop up in winter.

Pied flycatchers, male left, female right.

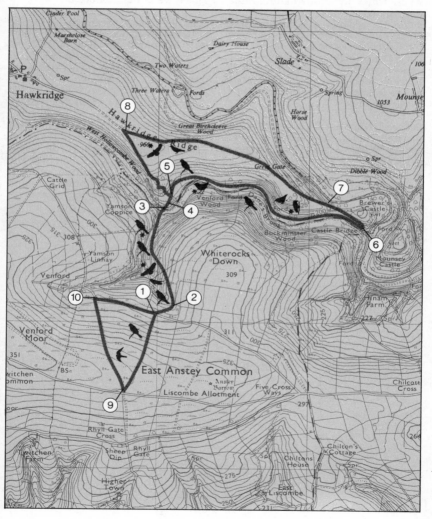

SOMERSET

Chew Valley Lake
7 miles (11 km) Landranger 172
560617

Chew Valley Lake is a man-made reservoir of more than 1,200 acres (486 ha) whose banks are mostly natural rather than concrete. This means that in addition to wildfowl it attracts nesting grebes and a variety of waders. A permit is required for access to the lake shores, but the surrounding roads give adequate views from the S, W and NE; especially Herriotts Bridge and Herons Green. *Open water; permits from the Bristol Waterworks Company.*

All year great crested grebe, little grebe, gadwall, ruddy duck, Canada goose; **spring** waders, black tern; **summer** garganey, shelduck, reed and sedge warblers, yellow wagtail; **autumn** blacknecked grebe, little ringed plover, cur-

lew sandpiper, ruff, spotted redshank, green sandpiper, wood sandpiper, common sandpiper, black-tailed godwit; black tern; **winter** Bewick's swan, wigeon, pintail, shoveler, pochard, tufted duck, goldeneye, smew, goosander, water rail, bearded tit.

Start From Bristol take the A38 SW towards Winscombe. After 5 miles (8 km) turn left on to the B3130 to Chew Magna, then right on to the B3114 to Chew Stoke. **Parking** with care to avoid obstruction in Chew Stoke.

① Follow the B3114 from Chew Stoke towards West Harptree. In 2 miles (3 km) ② turn left on to the footpath which leads to the S edge of the reservoir. Follow track/footpath to the A368, ③, turn left and walk alongside the road for about 1½ miles (2.5 km) into Bishop Sutton, where ④ turn left on to

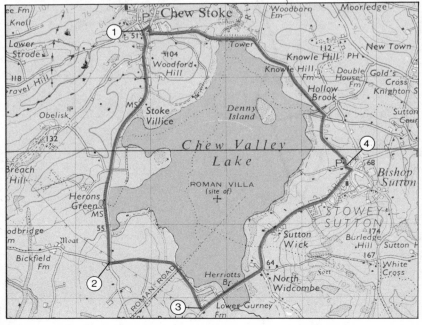

road following the NE side of the lake, continuing to Chew Stoke.

Ebbor Gorge
½ or 1½ miles (0.8 or 2.5 km)
Landranger 182 522484

There is a choice of walks on this National Trust reserve – a short walk through damp woodland and a longer, more strenuous walk (requiring sturdy footwear) involving a scramble up through the Gorge. The longer route, climbing to 800 feet (250 m), gives superb views over the reserve and surrounding countryside. Near the entrance a display centre describes the geology and wildlife of the reserve. *Woods, coppice, scrub, grassland, stone gorge.*

All year typical woodland birds.

Start Leave Wells on the A371 NW towards Cheddar. After 1½ miles (2.5 km) (having passed through Haybridge) turn right on to minor road to Wookey Hole. About ½ mile after Wookey Hole turn right towards Priddy. **Car park** on the right, about ½ mile along this road.

Both routes start from the stone stile in the car park and are waymarked by posts with coloured arrows. Follow the black arrows for the shorter route and the red arrows for the longer one. Keep to these routes and do not leave the paths.

Black Rock
1 mile (1.5 km) Landranger 182
483545

Black Rock Nature Reserve, at the head of the Cheddar Gorge, is owned by the National Trust and managed by the Somerset Trust for Nature Conservation. *Woods, conifer plantations, rough grassland, scree; the walk follows a marked nature trail which is free; leaflet available at start.*

The ruddy duck, also known as a stifftail because of the obvious feature of the male, above, is an oddity breeding in Somerset. It has also spread in recent years to other parts of England, and even into Scotland. A North American species, it became established in the wild after escaping from collections. The bird in flight is a female; the expression on her face is, curiously enough, characteristic.

Summer willow and other warblers; **all year** sparrowhawk, buzzard, kestrel, finches, jay.

Start From Wells take the A371 to Cheddar, where turn right on to the B3135 through Cheddar Gorge to Black Rock Gate. **Parking** for 15 cars at Black Rock Gate.

From Black Rock Gate follow the green arrows. Numbered posts relate to the nature trail leaflet.

South-east England

Ornithologically, the most striking aspect of South-east England is the amount of woodland remaining in such a densely populated region. Kent, Surrey and East and West Sussex are the most thickly wooded counties in England; and as more than one-third of the UK's breeding birds are woodland species, this is of some significance to the birdwatcher.

A number of other, specialized habitats are scattered across the region. There are the wild and beautiful Thames and Medway estuaries; the south coast 'harbours'; the North and South Downs; the remnants of the ancient sandy heaths and the remarkably diverse medieval landscape of the New Forest.

Geographically, South-east England lies on the 'flyways' of birds migrating between northern Europe and Africa. In addition, a number of species reach the northernmost edge of their breeding range here, particularly in the vicinity of the south coast. Londoners, and those who live in the home counties, rarely need drive more than a day to find any type of birdwatching, from the downright unusual to solid, all-year interest.

Mixed waders, Kent

HAMPSHIRE

New Forest
*4½ miles (7 km) Landranger 195 228147
SU 21/31*

The New Forest is an outstanding bird area, with scarce species occurring in its mixed woodland, heath and bog. This walk covers mainly the first and last, with fair opportunities of seeing **redstarts, tawny owls** and **hawfinches** in the woods, plus wetland and heathland species on the open areas. The route takes in some magnificent ancient oak and beech woods; the whole New Forest is managed by the Forestry Commission. *Mud.*

Time and season The breeding season is the best time to visit this area; as in most woodland, a morning walk reveals more than an afternoon one.

Start From the *major* Cadnam roundabout by the M27, take the Landford and Fordingbridge road. In 1 mile (1.5 km) take the second fork left at the Bell Inn. At the next crossroads take the first left marked Fritham, Boldrewood, etc.; in ½ mile (0.8 km) turn right, following the sign for 'Fritham and Eyeworth only'. Keep right at the minor left fork with the dead end sign. In ¼ mile (0.5 km) look for the Royal Oak on right and continue ahead downhill to pond and **car park** on right.

① From car park, facing pond, take gravel track on right into woods. In about 300 yards (270 m) emerge from woods and in a few yards ② strike left across stream (no bridge), making uphill for the woods on the left. At the bottom corner of the enclosure fence plainly seen at fringe of trees, ③ follow the fence into the woods. At the dilapidated 5-barred gate ④ enter the enclosure and follow ahead along the disused track, often barred by fallen trees identifiable by ruts. Exit enclosure by similar gate, and follow same track out of wood. Follow path about ¼ mile (0.5

km) on to open heath (cars visible ahead) and ⑤ on meeting a distinct track turn sharply back to the left. Almost immediately turn right ⑥ along smaller but distinct path, just after whitebeam trees on left and right. Continue into woods and where path becomes indistinct, follow generally right-handed downhill, soon coming to small bank on right and 2 solid posts. Pass between them and continue downhill on grassy track to ⑦ a footbridge. Cross and turn left to follow bank of stream until reaching another footbridge. Turn right here along wide, grassy track, keeping left at the next intersection and soon left again to follow a wide, grassy track bordered by banks. In about 1 mile (1.5 km) track meets a well-defined gravel road ⑧ where turn left and continue 1 mile (1.5 km) to ⑨ a one-bar gate. Turn left to tarred road, where ⑩ turn left for pond and car park.

🪶 Eyeworth Pond has breeding Canada geese, mallard and coot. Check the exit stream for grey and pied wagtails. Gunpowder was manufactured here.

🦆 Curlews, occasionally redshank and snipe are seen on the wet heathland.

🦅 Kestrels over open areas.

🦉 Tawny owls with recently fledged young during June and July can be very noisy here during the day.

🐦 This ancient woodland supports range of passerines from woodpeckers to tits, also stock doves. Redstarts are common. The elusive hawfinch is seen regularly; in summer, look for it in the tree tops, especially oak, locating birds by their sharp 'tick' call, like a robin's.

🐦* Check the gorse and bracken for stonechats, the open heath for meadow pipits and the woodland edge for tree pipits; an opportunity to observe their different song flights.

Wood warblers, blackcaps, spotted fly-catchers and redstarts are scattered through this oak and beech woodland. Listen, and look for the male wood warbler as he issues his intense, trilling song from a song perch below the canopy.

All 3 woodpeckers can be seen or heard.

Cuckoos abound and the bubbling call of the female is frequent in spring.

Nuthatches and treecreepers, together with marsh and other tits, are widespread.

Grey wagtails are often seen from Fritham Bridge.

Goldcrests, coal tits and occasionally siskins in the conifer stands.

The bracken, heath and bog support tree pipits, yellowhammers and willow warblers.

The sparrowhawk can be seen all round the route, hunting, usually fast and low along a woodland edge, or in its soaring display flight.

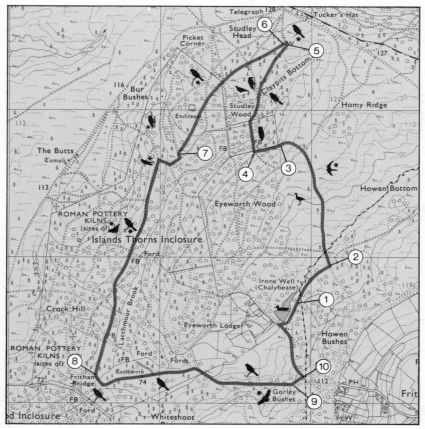

HAMPSHIRE

Langstone Harbour
4½ miles (7 km)
Landranger 197 708058

The great mudflats around Langstone and adjacent harbours attract huge flocks of wildfowl and waders. *Mudflats, saltmarsh.*

Summer garganey, terns, yellow wagtail; **passage** green, wood and common sandpipers, little stint, ruff, whimbrel, spotted redshank, greenshank, passerines; **winter** black-necked and other grebes, brent goose, wigeon, teal, pintail, goldeneye, red-breasted merganser, grey plover, dunlin, knot, sanderling, spotted redshank, greenshank, black-tailed godwit; **all year** shelduck, teal, sparrowhawk, kestrel, oystercatcher, bar-tailed godwit, curlew.

Start Opposite pedestrian precinct in Havant take Stanton Road about ⅓ mile (0.5 km); turn right into Brockhampton Road; continue to bridge over A27, cross and turn right into Harts Farm Way. **Parking** in 100 yards (90 m) on right in Brockhampton Lane.

① Take footpath signposted Solent Way/Emsworth to open harbour. Continue along shore to ② the A3023. Turn right; walk on to Langstone Bridge for views. Return to The Ship Inn and locate path on landward side. Follow it 20 yards (18 m) to row of cottages; turn right, left and right again. Past 'The Watch Tower' turn left on to front. Continue to Royal Oak; pass it on harbour side. At double footpath sign ③ fork right. Continue nearly 3 miles (5 km) to Emsworth, where ④ take train to Havant.

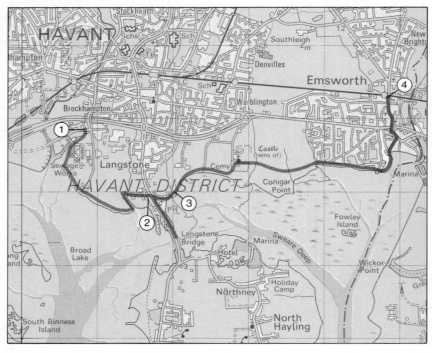

Lower Test Marshes
$2\frac{1}{2}$ miles (4 km)
Landranger 196 364150

The lower reaches of the River Test are managed as a nature reserve by the Hampshire and Isle of Wight Naturalists' Trust. The S half is tidal and the N freshwater. Disturbance is a continual problem and visitors should keep to the footpaths at all times. *River, reedbeds, saltmarsh, water meadows, grassland; free to any conservation trust member, otherwise small fee – contact county trust.*

The kingfisher's short tail is responsible for the odd-looking proportions. The pale blue streak on the back contrasts vividly with the duller tones of surrounding vegetation. Hovers briefly before diving.

Summer sedge and reed warblers; **winter** wigeon, green and common sandpipers, water pipit, bearded tit, siskin, redpoll; **all year** little grebe, lapwing, redshank, curlew, snipe, reed bunting, kingfisher.

Start Going E over the Totton flyover, on the W edge of Southampton, fork left following signs on to M271 (M27). Leave at first exit – about 450 yards (400 m). Exit from roundabout first left. In 200 yards (180 m) turn right, off road, at footpath sign. **Parking** on gravel area by railway crossing.

Cross the railway line with utmost care; go through gate and follow footpath into reserve. Just past the electricity pylon path becomes unclear. Bear left towards trees, where turn right to follow stream. In 50 yards (45 m) there is a sluice, where there is reasonable cover and fairly long views of the river. Retrace to railway crossing and turn left to follow path about $\frac{1}{2}$ mile (0.8 km) to the road. Retrace to the crossing.

The village of Selborne on the B3006 SSE of Alton was the home of Gilbert White, the celebrated natural historian. The surrounding countryside – downs, farmland and some fine beech hangers – is worth exploring by means of quite numerous public footpaths; the bird interest is mainly in summer, and an interesting companion for such an expedition is White's famous *The Natural History of Selborne*.

On the SE edge of the New Forest, the Beaulieu River is of some ornithological interest: little terns, turnstones plus various waders and occasional nightingales in the mainly oak woodland fringing the banks. A well-defined public footpath runs from the village along the W bank to Bucklers Hard. In Beaulieu, access to the path is up the gravel lane to the left when facing the Montagu Arms main hotel entrance. The first views of the river come in about 5 minutes' walking, and the path approaches the river quite closely again in another $\frac{1}{2}$ mile (0.8 km), after the ancient brick building with the tall chimney stack (The Brickyards). The full distance to Bucklers Hard is about 3 miles (5 km), from where there are buses back to Beaulieu. The walk is not recommended on fine summer weekends when the path is heavily congested with visitors to the Motor Museum and Bucklers Hard. Keep to the footpath: access to the river itself is strictly limited.

HAMPSHIRE

Alresford Valley and Downs
$5\frac{1}{2}$ miles (9 km) *Landranger* 185 588332
SU 43/53

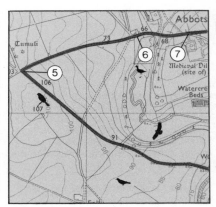

Three major habitats are encompassed
on this walk: the shallow, Old Alresford
Pond, fringed with vegetation and rich
in waterfowl; the clear chalk River Alre
(and tributaries), with dense undergrowth and a plethora of watercress
beds and fish farms; and the open, cultivated downland typical of mid-Hamp-
shire. Most of the route follows the well-
used Wayfarer's Way, an unofficial
long-distance footpath, but is nonetheless extremely productive for water and
farmland birds.

Time and season All year for the Pond
and river valley, but best as a whole in
spring, when morning is the period of
greatest activity.

Start In New Alresford on the A31 take
the B3046 signposted Old Alresford/
Basingstoke. Go down Broad Street and
in 300 yards (270 m) follow round the
bend into an avenue with the Pond on
the right. Drive down through the trees
for 200 yards (180 m); **parking** on the
left side of the road.

① Go to the gate opposite the parking
area to view Old Alresford Pond, then
walk back towards the town. Entering
Broad Street ② double back to the right
into Mill Hill. In 50 yards (45 m) join
the signposted Wayfarer's Walk swing-
ing left between houses and along the
river bank. After crossing the river cut
across the field at ③ to the road. (May
be ploughed out, but there is an excellent view of the valley from the road.)
Continue along road and in about 400
yards (350 m) ④ join the major bridleway which leads over the side of the hill.
Continue across the valley; about $1\frac{1}{4}$
miles (3 km) after starting to climb
again, at the T-junction of paths ⑤
(with others going off just left) turn
sharp right and descend into Abbot-

stone, joining the road ⑥ and continuing on it across the valley to ⑦ – the
top of the hill. Carry straight on leaving
the road, following this bridleway $1\frac{1}{4}$
miles (2 km). Entering Old Alresford ⑧
turn sharp right into Manor Farm. Go
down the road, turning left, then right
back to Alresford Pond.

Dabbling duck are abundant on the shallow waters of the pond: teal, mallard,
shoveler, wigeon and gadwall. Coots,
moorhens and Canada geese are also seen
in plenty. A wide variety of other waterfowl may occur, but few diving duck.

There are plenty of reed warblers around
the edge of the pond; most woodland birds
can be seen in the trees, including great
spotted woodpeckers.

Although seen anywhere in the valley,
herons are most regular here.

There is a large swallow and sand martin
roost in the reeds in autumn.

Sedge warblers and reed buntings are the
most characteristic birds of the dense
riverside vegetation, but also look for
blackcaps, garden warblers, spotted flycatchers, lesser spotted woodpeckers and,
in the yews, goldcrests.

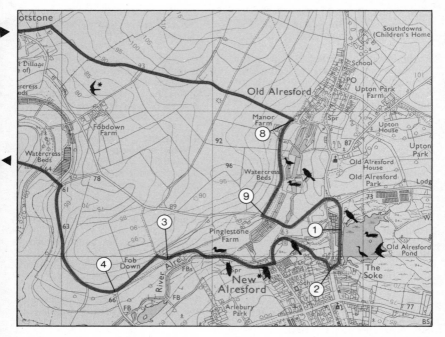

Look for kingfishers all along the river.

Little and tawny owls in the large trees.

Tufted duck and little grebes can be seen on the larger pools in the deeper parts of the river. The little grebe, otherwise known as the dabchick, is shy and tends to dive as soon as it is alarmed. Often the only clue to its presence is the call, an odd, tittering sound, something like high-pitched laughter. Seen from above, the body is almost circular.

Sparrowhawks can be seen hunting.

Rooks and crows on the open fields, together with lapwings, and in spring, golden plover.

The wet meadows support snipe, red-shank and a variety of migrant waders.

Typical farmland birds such as corn buntings, yellowhammers, thrushes and finches.

Kestrels are frequent; occasionally a hobby comes in to harry the hirundine roost in autumn.

There is a good chance of seeing wintering green sandpipers in the watercress beds; also other wader species on passage. Green sandpipers are localised wintering birds in Britain, with a preference for spring-fed watercress beds, which rarely completely freeze over. The bird is more heavily built than the common sandpiper. When flushed, the bird dashes skywards, calling shrilly.

The watercress beds are also a likely spot for pipits, especially water pipits. Look for water rails in winter.

Butser Hill and Queen Elizabeth Forest
6½ miles (10.5 km) Landranger 197
718182 SU62/72 and SU71

At the W end of the South Downs, the route gives opportunities of seeing birds in mature coniferous and deciduous woodland, scrub, on open downs and cultivated land. It is one of the few areas where **golden pheasants** are regularly seen. The walk lies within the Queen Elizabeth Country Park, with trails laid out in woodland managed by the Forestry Commission and downland managed by the Hampshire County Council. *Mud after rain; the Information Centre explains many aspects of the Park.*

Time and season All year, although the woodland is as always best during the morning from late winter to early summer. Downland interesting all year.

Start Going N on the A3 from Portsmouth go through Horndean and in 3 miles (5 km) look for signpost to Queen Elizabeth Country Park, where there is a **car park** (fee).

① From the car park walk S on the road side of the Information Centre and follow the yellow markers of the Holt Trail. Pass through a series of conifers and beech and oak to ② Holt Pond. From here many tracks can be followed to explore the woodland. Retrace with the trail to the Centre, go under the road, and climb the open downland, aiming at the gap between the 2 wooded coombes. At the plateau turn left along the track (away from the radio mast) and ③ right on to the signposted Butser Trail. Continue on trail down, then up towards wooded coombes on Ramsdean Down, then back uphill, going S. At top of Butser Hill swing E, then W to the radio mast track. Retrace to the Centre.

Farmland birds are seen on the edge of Park, especially yellowhammers, also partridges.

This woodland is excellent for warblers; check the sallows (low willows) for early migrants.

Look for the golden pheasant feeding under the conifers. These probably descend from stock introduced from abroad during the last 20 years, although this Asian species has been released in many areas since the late 19th century.

The purring of turtle doves (summer) is a feature of these western hemlocks. It is a beautifully soporific noise. Displaying birds rise with rapid wing beats, then glide down, wings and tail widely spread.

Great spotted and green woodpeckers are common in the older trees and glades.

Golden pheasants feed under the yews.

Willow tits are notable among the wide range of passerines seen here.

Typical farmland birds are seen around the reconstructed farm – greenfinches, chaffinches and pied wagtails.

Kestrels hunt the steep slopes.

Jackdaws, rooks, crows and magpies are a feature here; they like to look for food in the grass cropped short by sheep.

Common gulls feed on the downland in winter.

Green woodpeckers feed out in the open.

Meadow pipits and skylarks are typical open downland birds seen here.

Sparrowhawks are frequent.

These woods, fences, elder patches and open areas are likely spots for migrant wheatears, whinchats, blackcaps, lesser whitethroats and ring ouzels. In winter, redwings, fieldfares and other thrushes abound.

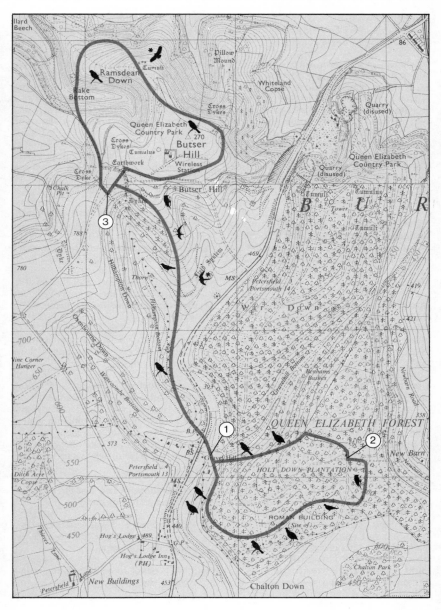

Pagham Harbour
3 or 5½ miles (4.5 or 9 km)
Landranger 197 880976 SZ 89

Pagham Harbour is one of the outstanding areas of S England for variety of birds. This walk provides open views across mudflats and saltings, with hordes of waders, wildfowl and terns, while inland reedbeds, scrub and farmland are homes to a wide selection of finches, thrushes, waders and birds of prey. The harbour is a Local Nature Reserve managed by the West Sussex County Council. *Paths running alongside the mudflats and saltings can be flooded by the very highest tides.*

Time and season An all-year walk, although most wildfowl are present in winter and the range of species is greatest in autumn. The walk by Pagham Lagoon is only worthwhile between October and April.

Start From the A27 Chichester by-pass take the B2145 then the B2166 signposted to Pagham. At Lagness continue straight on the minor road through Nyetimber to Pagham. In Pagham turn right, following the sign to the parish church, and go 200 yards (180 m) past the church; **parking** on the right-hand side of the road.

① From the parking area take the path round Little Welbourne and walk W along the N wall of the harbour. At the T-junction turn left to ② then proceed alongside the saltings to the outskirts of Sidlesham village ③; the path along this section of the walk may become less clear due to tidal erosion. At Sidlesham turn right past the *Crab and Lobster* pub and follow the road to ④. The road turns left, but keep straight on along the path ahead. This crosses a field and in about ½ mile (0.8 km) at ⑤ turn sharp right and proceed S back to the seawall. Turn left and retrace steps as far as ⑥, then turn right and walk alongside the

wall to ⑦. Continue, turning left to walk by Pagham Lagoon to ⑧. Take the path to the left back to the road then turn left to return to the parking area. *The walk can be extended from ⑤ over typical farmland, returning via Nyetimber. Alternatively, from ③ walk a little way along the road ahead, then follow the seawall S towards the Information Centre and Sidlesham Ferry, returning by the same route.*

In winter, little, Slavonian, great crested and occasionally red-necked grebes are found on the harbour. Little grebes are present all year in the dykes.

Reed and sedge warblers are present during summer in the reedy dykes.

Black-tailed godwits, golden plover and ruff feed on the fields to the right.

Herons rest in the fields or on the marshes. Fish are their primary food, but they also eat frogs, small mammals or water birds.

Short-eared owls, occasionally soaring, wheeling and gliding like a buzzard, hunt over the saltings.

On the mudflats, redshank, dunlin, grey plover and curlew are common. Many other species of wader are found towards the harbour mouth, and migrant whimbrel and greenshanks frequent the saltings. At high spring tide, some come into the fields; on falling tides many feed near the seawall.

Pintail, shelduck and teal are common in the centre of the estuary.

Migrant chats and warblers perch conspicuously on fences and bushes on farmland behind the saltings.

All 4 species of dove may be seen around the field edges.

➤ At all times of the year, mixed groups of black-tailed godwits, ruff and golden plover are common on the farmland.

𝄆 Kestrels, and the very occasional merlin, fly over the fields in search of prey.

𝄆 In winter, sparrowhawks, best distinguished from other raptors by their 'flap and glide' flight, hunt over the farmland; also hen harriers.

🦆 In early winter, brent geese are seen on the mudflats morning and evening. Some years they are found on grass nearby, and this indicates a shortage of food (certain seaweeds) on the mudflats. The birds breed in the high Arctic, making nests on sea shores, islands or marshy tundra.

𝄆 Little and common terns feed in the estuary gullies. Sometimes Sandwich and black terns are also present.

🦆 In winter diving ducks, including smew, are to be found on Pagham Lagoon.

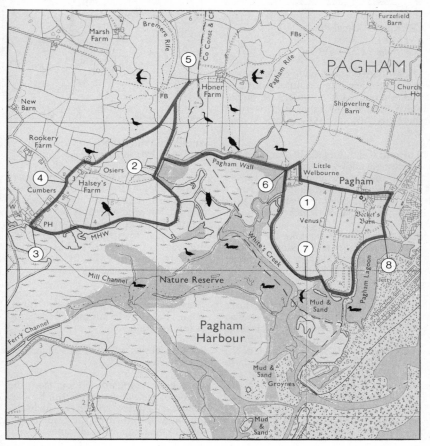

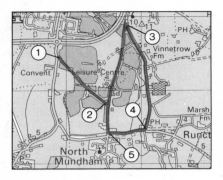

Chichester Gravel Pits
3½ miles (5.5 km)
Landranger 197 869034

These disused gravel pits S of Chichester are of primary interest during autumn and winter, with a variety of ducks. More than 6,000 sand martins roost there in autumn. *Open water, reedbeds.*

Autumn teal, little gull, black tern, sand martin, swallow, sedge warbler, reed warbler and, if low water, a wide variety of waders; **winter** gadwall, scaup, ruddy duck; **all year** great crested grebe, shelduck, pochard, tufted duck, coot.

Start From Chichester take the B2145 S (in the direction of Hunston). **Parking** by the roadside 200 yards (180 m) after crossing the A27, from where the pits are visible.

① Follow the path between the large pool on the left and the small one on the right. Continue between pools on to a track which leads to a T-junction. ② Turn left and follow the W edge of the pools until the track meets a road. ③ Turn sharp right on to the road and follow it 1 mile (1.5 km) to North Mundham, where ④ turn right on to the B2166. After ⅓ mile (0.5 km) ⑤ turn right on to a track. In ¼ mile (0.5 km) fork left at ② and retrace to ①.

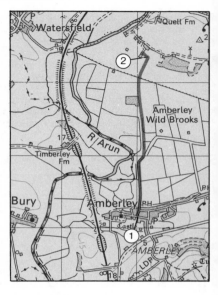

Amberley Wild Brooks
3 miles (5 km) Landranger 197 031133

Until recent years, these water meadows in the valley of the River Arun formed an important breeding and wintering ground for wildfowl and other birds. Winter flooding is now unfortunately much less frequent and the huge numbers of wigeon and teal that occurred until the 1960s are much reduced. *Water meadows.*

Winter wigeon, teal, shoveler, pochard, sparrowhawk; **all year** mute swan, snipe, barn owl; **summer** redshank, yellow wagtail.

Start Amberley, off the B2139; **parking** in the village.

① Take the footpath leading from the N side of the village across the Brooks. Follow it 1½ miles (2.5 km) to the buildings and ② return by the same route. Keep to the footpath at all times.

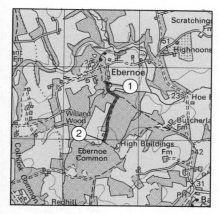

Ebernoe Common
1 mile (1.5 km) Landranger 197 979278

Ebernoe Common is an ancient wood, one of the best examples of what an original 'wildwood', or natural, unman-aged woodland may have looked like. The diversity of birdlife is enhanced by 2 large ponds and areas of open scrub and pasture. This is a nature reserve managed by the Sussex Trust for Nature Conservation. *Woods, scrub, open water; free to any conservation trust member, otherwise small fee – contact county trust.*

Summer warblers, nightingale; **all year** heron, woodcock, kingfisher, green woodpecker, great and lesser spotted woodpeckers.

Start From Petworth on the A283 drive N along the A283 for 3½ miles (5.5 km). Turn right along minor road towards Ebernoe. **Car park** in 1½ miles (2.5 km) beside the church.

① From car park follow the track S into the reserve. Explore the reserve by means of the various footpaths and ② return by the same route.

Great crested grebes, the female incubating a clutch on the floating nest. Courtship displays are elaborate and fascinating.

Cissbury and the South Downs
6 miles (9.5 km) Landranger 198 162095
TQ00/10 and TQ11

This section of the Sussex Downs provides an example of open, mainly cultivated downland with small copses, essentially of hawthorn and elder. **Autumn** and **winter raptors** are a feature, along with a wide variety of **migrants**. The section along Cissbury and Lychpole Hill reveals many **breeding birds** and excellent concentrations of **migrant warblers, chats** and **flycatchers**.

Time and season Probably at its best from April to October, but interesting at all seasons. The scarce raptors tend to be frequent only in 'good' years; morning best for migrant passerines; most times for raptors.

Start Take the A283 N from the Shoreham flyover (signposted Steyning). After 3 miles (5 km) take the left road at a small roundabout and the second left at the next roundabout, signposted Steyning. Continue 400 yards (350 m) and where road bends right take the second left signposted Sompting/The Downs. Continue uphill about 1 mile (1.5 km) and about 400 yards after reaching the plateau, shortly after a sharpish left bend, **car park** on left.

① Turn right on to the road, and where the road bends right, carry straight on along a field edge. In 250 yards (230 m) ② turn left on to a major track which soon drops steeply to No Man's Land. Keep straight on at ③, ignoring path at right angles to the left and also one curving sharply up to the right. In about 1 mile (1.5 km) turn left on to next major track towards Cissbury Ring, leaving the car park at ④ by the track going diagonally left – not along the bottom of the hill. Reaching the top, ⑤, bear left down the slope and ⑥ follow the path along the bottom of Lychpole

Hill. In the valley with the taller trees ⑦ turn sharp left and continue through fields to Beggars Bush where ⑧ pass farm buildings; carry straight on to ①.

Healthy populations of grey and red-legged partridge.

Migrant wheatears occur on fences and open ground – cultivation long ago destroyed their breeding grounds. In autumn, look for whinchats, stonechats and redstarts in the vicinity, including on standing corn.

Reed buntings, yellowhammers, corn buntings and chaffinches are regular in the hedges at the bottom of the valley.

Sparrowhawks are regular. In autumn migrant marsh and Montagu's harriers are seen, also osprey and buzzards. In winter, buzzards, the hen harrier and the very occasional rough-legged buzzard may occur. Lapwings breed and winter here. The occasional migrant dotterel and golden plover is seen.

Kestrels are frequent and hobbies are seen on spring and autumn migration.

The dense scrub on the Cissbury slopes is favoured by migrant willow warblers, chiffchaffs and blackcaps; tree pipits pass through in autumn.

The open patches among brambles, hawthorn and blackthorn are ideal for passage redstarts, whinchats, pied and spotted flycatchers, linnets and whitethroats.

Lesser whitethroats, blackcaps, garden warblers and a variety of tits and finches frequent the densest areas.

Stock, turtle and collared doves are abundant, the last mainly near the farm.

Green woodpeckers are common, and lesser spotted can sometimes be seen during winter in the elder copses.

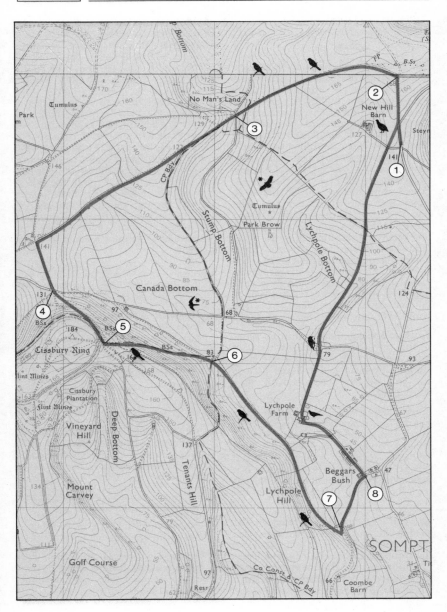

Lullington and Friston Forest
5 miles (8 km) Landranger 199 563014
TQ 40/50

The South Downs, with their remarkable contrasts of vegetation, provide extremely interesting birdwatching. Compared with the Lullington area, few parts of the Downs encompass such a range of different bird communities associated with the various habitats. This walk covers, and illustrates well, the birdlife of open downland, cultivated downland and then a series of increasingly dense scrub areas which have encroached on the ancient downland. In times past, the vegetation was kept down to grass by sheep, but in many areas it is slowly being lost to hawthorn and other bushes. Finally, in dropping down then climbing up through Friston Forest there is a transition from scrub to deciduous, mixed, then coniferous woodland. Lullington Heath Reserve is managed by the Nature Conservancy Council and Friston Forest by the Forestry Commission. *Mud after rain.*

Time and season Excellent at all times of the year, but the widest variety of birds is present during spring and early summer. Winter and passage periods can be good for raptors and migrants respectively.

Start Follow the A27 E towards Eastbourne then head S on the A22. In about ¼ mile (0.5 km) turn right at the crossroads (signpost to Wannock) and follow the Jevington road. At Jevington village, go almost to the S side and just before leaving turn right into a small **car park** set 50 yards (45 m) back from the road.

① From the car park go back to the road, walk N for about 50 yards (45 m), then turn left for the church ②. Here the route joins the South Downs Way. Continue past the church and up along the hedgerow, through the semi-mature woodland, keeping left at ③, and on the

scarp slope up on to the top of the Downs. From ④ go N towards the Long Man of Wilmington. Before reaching this area the path comes to the top of a steep valley slope ⑤. Leave the South Downs Way, turn sharply back, following the path heading SW, and descend along the edge of the valley. On reaching the large crossing path ⑥ turn sharp left and enter the nature reserve. Walk E to the stile ⑦ then double back along the path to the right that runs through heavy scrub. On crossing the scrub area, enter the forest along the broad ride ⑧, pass through the beech plantation and follow the curving path back up through the beech and conifer areas to the open downland overlooking the valley. Descend back across the farmland to Jevington village and the car park.

A wide variety of passerines is present in this attractive village; note the spotted flycatchers and tits.

The steep, well-wooded scarp slope is the home of long-tailed and marsh tits, blackcaps, willow warblers and thrushes.

Cuckoos are to be seen over most of the downland and open scrub.

Kestrels hunt over the whole area and occasionally in summer, hobbies; in winter, merlins can be seen on passage.

The three resident species of dove are abundant, with collared doves tending to be lower in the valley. In summer the soft purr of the turtle dove can be heard almost everywhere.

Red-legged and common partridges occur on the farmland and downland.

On open farmland skylarks, corn buntings and passage meadow pipits abound.

Sparrowhawks may be seen hunting over the slope to the right throughout the year and buzzards and other hawks occur on passage or in winter.

🐦 In the scrub along the paths, the soft 'reeling' of the grasshopper warbler may be heard. Look for the aerial flight of the tree pipit. Also listen for the summery song of the willow warbler – a fluent, descending series of notes.

🐦 The dense scrub in the valley bottom is the home of many pairs of nightingales, blackcaps, garden warblers and a wide range of other songbirds.

🐦 Green woodpeckers may be found feeding on the downland or along the rides, while great spotted woodpeckers can be seen in the older woodland.

🐦 The mixed woodland along this path encourages tits, especially coal tits; also goldcrests and finches.

🐦 The more open scarp scrub here has breeding yellowhammers, whitethroats and linnets.

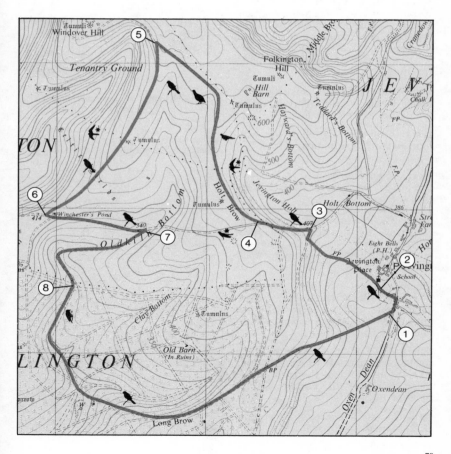

WILTSHIRE

Savernake Forest
2 miles (3 km) Landranger 173
199683

The beech trees surrounding Posterne
Hill picnic site in Savernake Forest are
around 200 years old. A Forest Trail
leads through them, and past young oak
plantations, giving opportunities for
seeing a range of woodland birds, particularly in summer. *Beech forest, plantations.*

Summer turtle dove, nightjar, garden
warbler, blackcap, chiffchaff, wood warbler, spotted flycatcher, redstart, nightingale; **winter** brambling; **all year** green
woodpecker, great and lesser spotted
woodpeckers, long-tailed and marsh
tits, nuthatch, treecreeper.

Start From Marlborough take the A346
SE for 1 mile (1.5 km). **Parking** on left
at Posterne Hill picnic site.

From the picnic site follow the waymarked Forestry Commission trail.

Marlborough Downs
3 miles (5 km) Landranger 173 129746

This chalk grassland is crossed by a
maze of footpaths, chief of them the
Ridgeway long-distance path (marked
Ridge Way on OS map); bird interest is
greatest during the summer. *Chalk
downs.*

Summer quail, hobby, whinchat,
wheatear; **winter** hen harrier, short-
eared owl, golden plover; **all year**
buzzard, skylark, meadow pipit, yellowhammer.

Start From Marlborough take the minor
road which leads NW to Broad Hinton.
After 5 miles (8 km) the road crosses
the Ridgeway Path. **Parking** on the
roadside.

① Follow the Ridgeway S for 1½ miles
(2.5 km) and ② retrace to ①.

*The skylark's song flight seems to sum up the
freedom of the open country the bird inhabits.
Pouring out an unbroken stream of song, it
floats higher and higher; when it is a speck
against the sky, it abruptly plunges towards the
ground, levelling out at the last moment.*

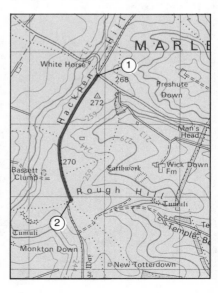

WILTSHIRE

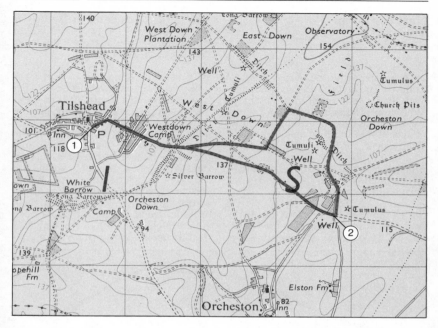

Salisbury Plain
5½ miles (9 km) Landranger 184 035379

Much of the rolling chalk grassland of Salisbury Plain has now been ploughed and grows cereals rather than sheep. Most of the extensive areas of grassland left are in the hands of the Ministry of Defence. There is also some woodland, and hawthorn scrub has much increased recently. This route is representative of all these habitats. Most interesting in summer. *Grassland, scrub, woods; easy walking on quiet metalled road.*

Summer kestrel, quail, turtle dove, garden warbler, whitethroat, lesser whitethroat, willow warbler, whinchat, wheatear; **all year** buzzard, skylark, meadow pipit, yellowhammer, corn bunting.

Start From Salisbury take the A360 N

to Tilshead. **Parking** at the E end of the village in Candown Road.

① Take Candown Road out of the village. After cottage marked '21' fork right. Continue via camp. Stay on metalled road through left and right bends, continuing 3 miles (5 km) to junction ② after derelict buildings. Turn right along concrete track. After plantation on left bear right with main track. At end of beech copses fork left. Soon rejoin road; retrace to ①.

Coate Water, on the SE edge of Swindon, holds warblers in summer and small numbers of wildfowl during winter; black terns occur on migration.

81

Lambourn Downs

10½ miles (17 km) Landranger 174 343851

A long walk on the Berkshire/Oxford-shire border within quite easy reach of London. The first third is on the Ridge-way Path and takes in the famous Whitehorse Hill and Wayland's Smithy, the neolithic barrow or burial ground. Wayland was smith to the Saxon gods. *Chalk downs.*

Summer/passage turtle dove, wheatear; **winter** golden plover; **all year** kestrel, corn bunting.

Start From Newbury follow the A4 W and soon branch right on to the B4000 in the direction of Lambourn. From Lambourn continue on the B4001 N across the downs for 4½ miles (7 km) to where the Ridgeway crosses the road. **Parking** at the roadside.

① Follow the Ridgeway Path N for 4 miles (6.5 km) – it is well defined. By the sign to Wayland's Smithy ② turn left at the crossing of tracks. Continue, passing belts of plantation, almost exactly 2 miles (3 km) and ③ turn left at the crossing of tracks (marked by a small pile of medium-sized boulders seen on right). Continue to the left bend and use the stone to climb the fence, which obstructs the right of way leading ahead across the field. This may be ploughed, or under crops; aim for the broad track seen straight ahead. Join track by stile near corner of copse; turn right and con-

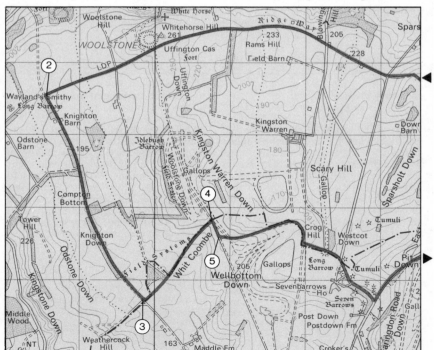

tinue on track, soon uphill. At top ④ turn right (do not pass wooden railings or walk on the gallop). Continue, fence immediately to right, to the wooden rail about 150 yards (140 m) ahead. Just past it ⑤ turn left to join grassy track leading downhill. Follow it through right curve; 100 yards (90 m) after it straightens, turn left. Pass end of beech copse; continue to road. Turn right. In ½ mile (0.8 km), at right bend, turn left on to track. Follow it to ⑥ the B4001. Turn left – one mile (1.5 km) to ①.

Maidenhead Thicket
1½ miles (2.5 km)
Landranger 175 856811

On summer evenings this area of woodland, owned by the National Trust, is a likely place to hear nightingales. *Woods.*

Summer tree pipit, garden warbler, blackcap, whitethroat, lesser whitethroat, willow warbler, chiffchaff, nightingale; **all year** green woodpecker, great and lesser spotted woodpeckers, nuthatch, treecreeper.

Start From Maidenhead follow the A4 W to the outskirts of the town, where there is a roundabout junction with the A423 and the A423(M). Take the third exit, the A423, and after ¼ mile (0.5 km) turn left into Maidenhead Thicket along a gravel drive. **Parking** by the roadside.

From the gravel road, close to the A423, follow the footpath running SW for ½ mile (0.8 km) to the A4. At the road follow a second footpath back into the Thicket, heading approximately N for ½ mile (0.8 km) until it reaches the gravel road ½ mile (0.8 km) W of the A423. Return E along the gravel road to the start.

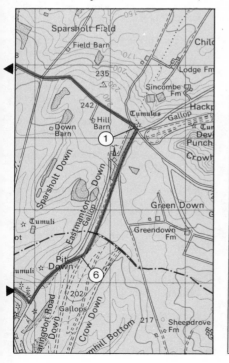

Considerable areas of Windsor Great Park are open to the public and provide pleasant, varied walking along the numerous rides and footpaths. The park contains an impressive starling roost, while the ponds support an established population of mandarin ducks and other wildfowl. There are woodland birds in plenty during summer, and a chance of seeing hobbies. The Great Park is just S of Windsor; free parking all along the A332 running through it.

Theale Gravel Pits lie alongside the Kennet and Avon Canal at Theale, attracting a variety of wildfowl, especially diving duck, mainly in winter. Access is along the towpath on the S side of the canal, approached via the minor road leading S out of Theale; Theale lies close to M4 exit 12.

Virginia Water
5½ miles (9 km) Landranger 175 980688
SU 86/96

Few areas so close to London can provide as varied a birdwatching walk as this. The old woodland, scrub and parkland set around a large lake provide the opportunity of seeing most **woodland** and several **wetland species**. The selection of **tits, finches, woodpeckers** and **warblers** is particularly impressive; and here is an excellent opportunity of seeing the **mandarin duck**, a recently introduced colonist. *Mud after rain.*

Time and season Visit as early as possible in the morning, when the woodland birds are most active, and there is least human disturbance. An all-year route; finches are the obvious feature in winter, warblers in summer.

Start Just N of the Wheatsheaf Hotel on the A30, almost opposite the junction with the B389, where there is a large **car park** (fee).

① Go through the gates in the fence at the back of the car park and make for the lake, where turn left and follow the shore. In 400 yards (350 m), reach ② the waterfall; it is worth walking right up to it. Retrace to where the path curves down to the right and follow the path alongside or near the lake. Turn sharply back E at the far end and in 900 yards (820 m) ③ follow the track across open parkland. Unless short of time, do not take short cuts by crossing the bridges except at the Totem Pole, ⑤. Make occasional short detours into the woodland to follow up interesting calls. Otherwise it is best to remain near the shore to obtain broad views. *From ④ an alternative is to walk through the wood NE towards the Obelisk Pond, crossing parkland, returning via the Totem Pole.*

🦆 Tufted duck are present all year, and joined by pochard for the winter. Also present: mallard, great crested grebes, coots and other water birds.

🦆 The mandarin duck has its British centre here. It came from the Far East and was originally released in the country about 1930. The mainly pinkish-chestnut male is colourful, but the greyish female is better camouflaged. They may be seen on the lake edge, but more usually in small groups resting under or on overhanging branches. Sometimes they gather on the grass to the E of the Moat. And you might glimpse birds flying to nest holes high in mature trees.

🐦 Reed and sedge warblers are seen in the small reedbeds fringing the lake.

🐦 Grey wagtails, always drawn to fast-flowing water, are particularly fond of the waterfall area.

🐦 Great and lesser spotted woodpeckers are frequent, the latter especially in the alders and birch.

🐦 The birch and alders are also attractive to redpolls, siskins and willow warblers, while in the dense understorey of rhododendron there are blackcaps and garden warblers – at the appropriate season.

🐦 Look for crossbills, goldcrests and coal tits in the mature pine trees.

🐦 Kestrels are regular, and in autumn there may be the occasional hobby; look for the black moustachial stripe.

🐦 Green woodpeckers on the open areas, where they like to feed.

🐦 An exceptionally wide variety of tits, finches, warblers, thrushes and the occasional hawfinch are present.

🐦 Nuthatches and treecreepers on the mature trees.

🐦 Sparrowhawks are seen regularly.

Mandarin duck: right, the male, with wing fans and side whiskers; left, the female.

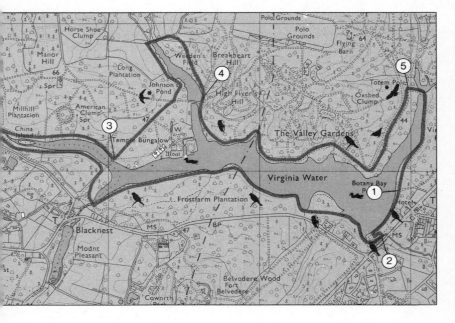

The characteristic birds of Surrey's gorse and bracken heathland: in the middle distance is a sparrowhawk.

Frensham Common
2 miles (3 km) Landranger 186 848406

A partly wooded common with a large and a smaller pond, excellent for passerines at all times of the year. *Heath, ponds, woods, scrub.*

Summer tree pipit, garden, willow, wood and reed warblers, whitethroat, lesser whitethroat, redstart, nightingale; **autumn/winter** buzzard, great grey shrike; **all year** stonechat, woodpeckers.

Start From Haslemere take the A287 N (in the direction of Farnham). Two miles (3 km) N of Churt, after passing Frensham Great Pond, there is a **car park** on the left.

From Frensham Great Pond walk N to the wooded area, cross the A287, and walk through the woods to Frensham Little Pond. Cross the Common back to the car park.

There are numerous walks over Great and Little Bookham Commons, which are together designated an SSSI and owned by the National Trust. They are grassland and scrub, wooded with oak, and there are several old fishponds. These varied habitats support a fair selection of birds, and more than 500 flowering plants. The Commons, each with ample parking, lie 2½ miles (4 km) W of Leatherhead.

The handsome male yellowhammer is the only yellow British bird with a rufous rump. Its song is unmistakable – 'a little bit of bread and no cheese'.

Alice Holt Forest
1¾ miles (3 km) Landranger 186 813413

A relic of an extensive royal hunting ground, Alice Holt Forest is now Forestry Commission property with deciduous and coniferous trees up to 160 years old. There is a Visitor Centre ¼ mile (0.5 km) SE of Bucks Horn Oak. *Woods, stream, meadow.*

Summer garden warbler, blackcap, willow warbler, chiffchaff, spotted flycatcher; **winter** siskin; **all year** kestrel, great and lesser spotted woodpeckers, goldcrest, long-tailed tit, coal tit, nuthatch, treecreeper, redpoll.

Start From Farnham take the A325 (Petersfield road) S for 3 miles (5 km) to Bucks Horn Oak and turn left on to the Batt's Corner road. The Forestry Commission picnic site and **car park** are on the right after ½ mile (0.8 km).

Follow the waymarked trail from the picnic site.

Male linnet: the only small brownish bird in Britain with a grey head and crimson forehead and breast.

Staines Reservoirs
3 miles (5 km) Landranger 176 045730

On the W edge of London, these 2 large reservoirs with a causeway between them provide excellent winter bird-watching. Wildfowl are the main interest. *Open water.*

Summer yellow wagtail, swifts; **passage** black-necked grebe, common sandpiper and other waders, little gull, black tern, common tern, wheatear, whinchat; **winter** goldeneye, goosander, also (especially in hard weather) divers, scaup, red-breasted merganser, smew; **all year** great crested grebe, pochard, tufted duck.

Start From Staines take the A3044 N from the roundabout; frequent trains to Staines. **Parking** beside the reservoir.

Continue up the A3044 to the causeway between the 2 reservoirs. Follow this to the B378, turn left, and continue for ¼ mile (0.5 km) to where a footpath on the left leads alongside a cemetery back to the reservoirs. Follow the path around the N side of the N reservoir to rejoin the B378. Turn left and continue to the A3044. Retrace to the car.

Male stonechat, which has a habit of perching conspicuously, is unmistakable, too, especially in summer plumage – black head, white neck patches, chestnut beneath. Its song, like the yellowhammer's, is completely distinctive: like 2 pebbles being knocked together.

Bay Pond
¾ mile (1 km) Landranger 187 352516

More than 100 species have been recorded in this wetland reserve at the foot of the North Downs owned by the Surrey Trust for Nature Conservation. *Open water, swamp, farmland.*

All year great crested grebe, heron, wildfowl, kingfisher, grey wagtail.

Start From Croydon take the A22 S towards East Grinstead. After 6½ miles (10.5 km), in the village of Godstone, look for the White Hart Hotel. **Parking** opposite the hotel, on the green.

Take the footpath on the right-hand side of the hotel and follow it along the S edge of Bay Pond. Return along same path.

Cliffe Pools
6½ miles (10.5 km)
Landranger 178 736768

There is plenty of interest on these pools adjacent to the Thames, surrounded by marshland and created by the extraction of clay for cement making; wildfowl are the main feature. *Open water, mudflats, marsh.*

Winter divers, great crested grebe, little grebe, many wildfowl, including white-fronted goose, goldeneye and scaup, hen harrier, short-eared owl; **passage** black tern, ruff, wide range of other waders; **all year** shelduck, pochard, tufted duck, redshank.

Start Cliffe, at the terminus of the B2000 N of Rochester; **parking** in the village main street.

① At the N end of the village main street, turn left and continue towards the radio mast and pools. On reaching the water's edge ② turn right and walk around the perimeter of the pools, past the coastguard cottages and out to the sea wall – nearly 2 miles (3 km). ③ Turn left along the sea wall, and follow it along the W edge of the pools, then back towards the village. Bear right ④ at the works and continue to the minor road, ⑤, where turn left. After the pub ⑥ turn right to follow the SE side of the pools back to ①.

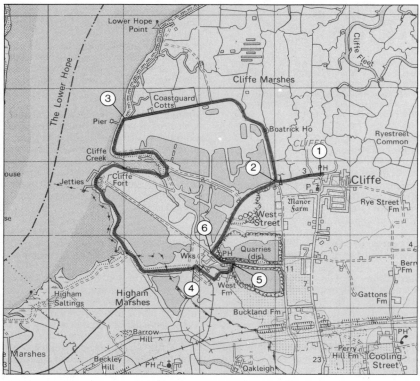

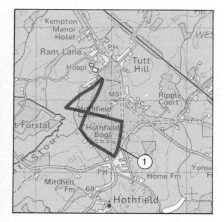

On a gloomy winter evening the short-eared owl can seem like a great moth. Hunting flight is slow and uncertain, low over the ground, with rolling and hovering often preceding the strike. The head is noticeably rounded, and the underwing pale with a pronounced patch. This is the owl most likely to be seen by daylight.

Hothfield Common
2 miles (3 km) Landranger 189 969459

Hothfield Local Nature Reserve is designated an SSSI and managed by the Kent Trust for Nature Conservation. A total of 63 species has been recorded. *Woods, heath, bog; free to any conservation trust member, otherwise small fee – contact county trust.*

Summer sedge, garden and willow warblers, blackcap, whitethroat, chiffchaff, spotted flycatcher, tree pipit; **winter** redwing, fieldfare; **all year** green woodpecker, nuthatch, treecreeper, yellowhammer, reed bunting.

Start From Ashford take the A20 NW and in 2¼ miles (3.5 km) turn left on to an unclassified road – the second turning directed to Hothfield. Then take the first right. **Parking** on right after 300 yards (270 m) and on the left after 400 yards (350 m), near football ground.

① Enter the Common at the Kent Trust for Nature Conservation notice board opposite the first parking area. In a few yards a concrete post marked with an arrow points the way along a nature trail – a double loop as shown.

Dungeness is, of course, the site of a nuclear power station; it is also an excellent place for birdwatching: protruding far out into the Strait of Dover, migrants use it as a landfall. The flooded gravel pits, areas of gorse and brambles, and the sea water warmed by the power station's cooling system, all add to the variety of the area and the richness of its birdlife. The minor road from Dungeness to Lydd and from Lydd to Camber enables the shingle area to be viewed by car.

Terns breed on islands in the flooded gravel pits, where black terns occur on migration, and many duck, including smew, overwinter. Look out, too, for wintering hen harriers, rough-legged buzzards and other raptors. On October mornings watch for thousands of starlings, chaffinches and other diurnal migrants arriving from Cap Griz Nez against light NW winds.

Shell Ness
6 miles (9.5 km) Landranger 178
045695 TR06/16

It is worth travelling far to see the spectacle of **massed waders** on the shell banks and saltings of this easterly point of the Isle of Sheppey. During autumn, especially in strong N winds, there are huge **sea bird movements**. The grassland is also a valuable habitat, with **breeding waders**. *Mud after rain.*

Time and season Interesting all year and most times of day.

Start From Leysdown on Sea on the Isle of Sheppey carry straight on along the sea front to Muswell Manor. **Parking** just past Muswell Manor Country Club.

① Walk along the track below the sea wall towards Shell Ness; glance over the wall occasionally. Stop at ②, the end of the wall, to scan the sea or mud. In summer, or at high tide, do not go past the buildings at the end. Retrace 400 yards (350 m) and turn left along top of sea wall. Continue about 2 miles (3 km) and ③ follow the path uphill. ④ Turn right and in 250 yards (230 m) right again on to path which descends. Follow it across the marshes to ①.

Wheatears and whinchats occur as migrants along the fences; also warblers.

Large, roosting flocks of oystercatchers, bar-tailed godwits, knot and sanderling at high tide (on mud at low tide). At highest tides they may fly to roost on adjacent fields. In winter there may be brent geese. In September, shelduck display and breed on the inland fields.

Large autumn sea bird movements include gannets and skuas; in winter, divers.

Migrating common, little and Sandwich terns, also kittiwakes are seen off the beach or resting on it.

Two further wader roosts.

Wigeon and shelduck on the estuary.

Breeding redshank and lapwings on fields.

Kestrels, occasional merlin or peregrine.

Breeding yellow wagtails and meadow pipits.

The hen harrier and other large raptors may be seen in winter.

Short-eared owls, with their flicking wing beats, may be seen over the fields.

Yellow wagtails and meadow pipits again.

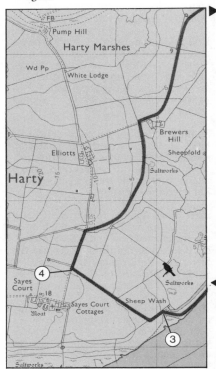

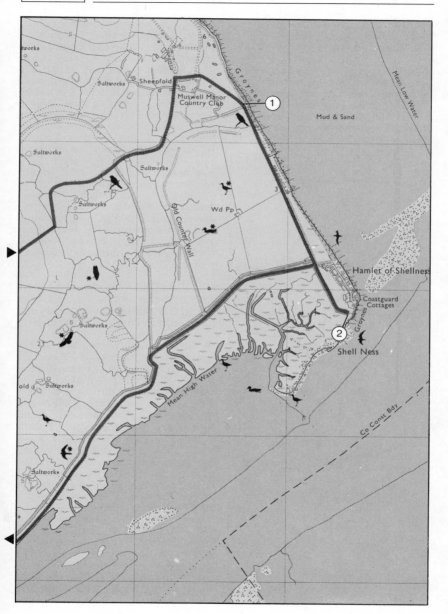

Saltworks
Sheepfold
Muswell Manor
Country Club
① Mud & Sand
Mean Low Water
Saltworks
Saltworks
Old Counter Wall
Wd Pp
Saltworks
Hamlet of Shellness
Coastguard
Cottages
Saltworks
② Shell Ness
old Saltworks
Mean High Water
Co Const Bdy
Saltworks

91

Northward Hill and Halstow Marshes
1½ or 7 miles (2.5 or 11 km)
Landranger 178 784751

This RSPB reserve, closely bordering a housing estate, contains Britain's largest heronry, of which views are obtainable from an observation platform in an oak tree. It also faces out across the North Kent marshes towards the Thames Estuary. After a short walk through the woods, taking in the observation platform, the energetic can follow a footpath out across the marshes to the estuary and back. The Saxon Shore Way, marked on the map, is part of a 140-mile (225-km) waymarked route running from Gravesend to Rye tracing the ancient coastline of Kent. It gives numerous opportunities for sea and estuary watching; route card available from Kent Rights of Way Council. *Woods, scrub, marsh, mudflats, estuary.*

Summer heron, turtle dove, garden warbler, blackcap, whitethroat, lesser whitethroat, nightingale; **passage** waders; **winter** brent goose, white-fronted goose, pintail, wigeon, long-eared owl, short-eared owl, hen harrier, merlin, knot, curlew; **all year** shelduck, redshank, little owl, great spotted woodpecker.

Start From Rochester take the A228 NE towards the Isle of Grain. After 3 miles (5 km) turn left on to a minor road to High Halstow. **Parking** at village hall.

① Access to the reserve is from the housing estate, Northwood Avenue, via a path leading to the reserve entrance. At the RSPB notice board ② follow the main path and soon turn right ③ where a sign directs 'viewpoint'. Continue to ④ the observation platform. Spend some time viewing the heronry. Return to the main path and continue W for nearly ¾ mile (1 km) to ⑤ a stile leading to farmland. Retrace to ②; for the shorter walk, return to the start. To continue, carry straight on, following the edge of the wood E then N, joining a farm track. Follow this out towards the estuary, passing Decoy Farm and Swigshole. Turn right ⑥ at the fork and follow the track to the sea wall, where ⑦ turn left. Continue along the wall to Egypt Bay, turning S with the wall. Soon a footpath leads inland from the wall; follow it back to the track at ⑥ and retrace to ①.

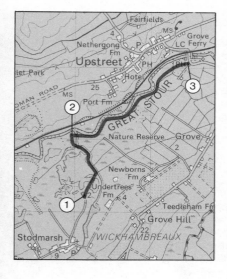

Stodmarsh
3 miles (5 km) Landranger 179 221610

Stodmarsh is an interesting wetland area created accidentally by subsidence due to coal mining. There is a scarcity of wetland habitats in this part of Britain, and its proximity to the continent has led to the establishment of 2 rare warblers, Cetti's and Savi's. *Open water, reedbeds; now an NNR.*

Summer garganey, redshank, common tern, Savi's, grasshopper and reed warblers; **winter** wigeon, sparrowhawk, hen harrier, ringed plover, snipe, water pipit, siskin; **passage** osprey, marsh harrier, ruff, green sandpiper; **all year** bittern, teal, gadwall, shoveler, pochard, tufted duck, water rail, lesser spotted woodpecker, Cetti's warbler, bearded tit, willow tit, redpoll.

Start From Canterbury take the A257 E towards Sandwich. In 1 mile (1.5 km) turn left on to an unclassified road to Stodmarsh. In the village pass the Red Lion and then turn left along a lane leading to the reserve **car park**.

① From the car park follow the lane which, after a stile, becomes a track running along the top of Lampen Wall. Continue along the wall until ② it meets the River Stour. It is possible to continue another 1¼ miles (2 km) by turning right and following the river, but the path tends to be overgrown with reeds, nettles and thistles, especially in summer. At the road bridge ③ return by the same route.

Heronries are almost always situated in trees; very occasionally they are found on cliffs or in reedbeds. A typical grey heron colony has rather less than 200 nests. It is usual for the first egg to be laid in March, and the clutch usually contains three to five. Nesting birds have a repertoire of raucous sounds.

Wales

The valleys of South Wales are intensively industrialized, but most of the Principality is relatively unchanged by the activities of man. It affords extensive areas of countryside immensely rich in birdlife: the hills and valleys, clear rivers, mud-rich estuaries, ancient woodlands, new forests, cliff-girt coasts and rocky islands produce a remarkable, almost infinite variety of birdwatching opportunities in an intricate juxtaposition of habitats not duplicated elsewhere in Britain.

Being on the western side of the British Isles and benefiting from the mild Atlantic influence, the estuaries and inland waters are important wintering places for many thousands of waders, wildfowl and other birds which move away from the frozen countries of northern and central Europe. The Anglesey lakes and the great estuaries of the Dee, Dyfi, Burry and Severn are principal among these.

The western headlands and offshore islands, apart from holding big colonies of breeding sea birds, have long been renowned as migration points. Dinas Head, St David's Head and The Great Orme are among the foremost of these classic places for watching sea bird passage.

Almost nowhere in Britain are birds of prey as numerous as in Wales – a sure indication of the general richness of the countryside. Here, the buzzard, not the kestrel, is the commonest raptor, occurring in greater numbers than anywhere in the country. Sparrowhawks and peregrines are also numerous; red kites, hen harriers and merlins less common, but often seen by visitors.

Hen harrier and young

95

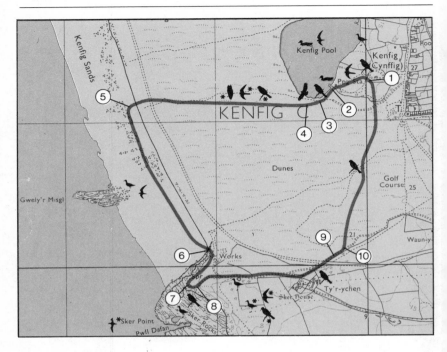

Kenfig Pool and Dunes
3½ miles (5.5 km)
Landranger 170 801813 SS78/88

This area is one of the few survivors of what was formerly a marvellous range of coastal habitats in South Wales. There is every chance of an impressive range of **wildfowl**, **passage waders**, **predators** (including **merlin**) and **vagrants**, all at appropriate seasons or under the right conditions. The Pool and Dunes are a nature reserve administered by the Mid Glamorgan County Council and walkers are encouraged to call at the reserve centre for up-to-date information on recent sightings. *Reserve open daily; the hide is open each Sunday, or other days as advertised in the Centre, otherwise request loan of key (deposit) from the Centre; standing water in winter and after rain — appropriate footwear essential.*

Time and season All year.

Start The Reserve is ½ mile (0.8 km) W of the M4, from which it should be approached by leaving the motorway at junction 37 (Pyle). **Car park** at the reserve centre.

① Take the path immediately adjacent to the Centre, leading towards the Pool. In 150 yards (145 m) take the right fork (signposted) towards the Pool. ② At the Pool bear left and follow the margin. In about 200 yards (180 m), where sallow bushes crowd either side of the path, ③ follow the board walk which leads off to the right to a hide screened by bushes. Spend time in the hide. Return to the original track, continue about 50 yards and ④ leave the path (which follows round the edge of the Pool) to follow the well-trodden and clearly defined path which leads straight across the dunes towards the sea. In about ½ mile (0.8 km) at the beach ⑤ turn left and walk along the beach or tide edge for ½ mile (0.8 km). Arriving at Sker Point and Rocks, make for the emergency telephone on a conspicuous post where ⑥ the rocks and dunes meet. Follow the edge of the grassland round above the rocks towards ⑦ the Point, passing through a dilapidated gate in the fence. At the Point look inland, immediately behind, to locate ⑧ the broad gravel track. Follow this across the old fence towards the derelict Sker House. At the house stay on the same sandy track, continuing along the farm wall and across a corner of the golf course. Just before the track ends at a barbed wire gate there is a stile ⑨ in the fence on the left. Cross to the golf course and turn right to follow the fence, again on a well-defined sandy track. In 200 yards, at the kissing gate in the fence on the right, ⑩ turn left. Back to the kissing gate, locate a poorly defined footpath leading directly across the green and into rough dunes. The path is not easy to make out, but walk directly away from the gate; in about 300 yards (270 m) the reserve centre comes into sight. Continue to ①.

In late summer and autumn, passage waders are seen most readily on the E shore of the Pool; to search this area turn right when first reaching the pool edge and walk towards the old boathouse; return the same way. In autumn and winter, when wildfowl numbers are highest, walk right round the Pool. From Sker Point it is possible to continue along the coast SE towards Porthcawl; return via ⑧.

In the bracken- and scrub-covered dunes there are stonechats, yellowhammers, linnets, reed buntings and (summer) whitethroats and willow warblers. Skylarks, meadow pipits, kestrels on open areas.

Coots, moorhens, mute swans, great crested grebes, tufted duck and mallard should always be present on the Pool,

along with the 5 commoner gull species. In winter add pochard, teal, shoveler, gadwall, goldeneye and little grebe. Whooper and Bewick's swans are fairly frequent. Garganey are regular in spring.

The E shore is best for passage waders in late summer and autumn, notably common and green sandpipers plus dunlin.

In addition to the main species on the Pool, hope to see the following from the hide: hen harrier (winter), water rail, reed bunting and (summer) reed and sedge warblers. Hide excellent in winter.

Pipits, skylarks and kestrels on the open dune grassland meadow; this is also the best area for seeing the short-eared owl and merlin.

Oystercatchers, ringed plovers and the common gull species on the beach, also sanderling (autumn) and often dunlin.

Rock pipits on Sker Rocks; early wheatears in March. Search hard for purple sandpipers and turnstones.

Gannets, Manx shearwaters and fulmars regularly pass close inshore during summer, especially in the early morning. Numbers of terns on passage, especially common and Sandwich.

Approach the tiny Sker Pool cautiously. Improbably, it has an impressive list of vagrants, particularly after bad weather.

In the fields towards Sker House there are winter flocks of lapwings, curlew, golden plover and starlings. Good chance of a merlin in winter. Stay on the path.

This area is notable for finch flocks – chaffinch, greenfinch and linnet. At the feed bins near Sker House look for tree sparrows and yellowhammers. Stonechats, whitethroats, dunnocks and the grasshopper warbler are likely in the rough vegetation on the dunes.

Taf Fechan
⅓ *mile (0.5 km) Landranger 160 037076*

This partly wooded nature reserve less than 2 miles (3 km) NW of Merthyr Tydfil contains a 20-point nature trail following the course of Taf Fechan, a tributary of the River Taff and the main feature of the reserve. Trail leaflets from Merthyr Tydfil Borough Council, Town Hall, Merthyr Tydfil, Mid Glamorgan, who jointly manage the reserve with the Glamorgan Naturalists' Trust. *Woods, grassland, river, scrub; open to the public.*

All year buzzard, kingfisher, great spotted woodpecker, grey wagtail, dipper, nuthatch, treecreeper, raven.

Start Approach Merthyr Tydfil on the A470 from Brecon. **Parking** either in Cefn-coed-y-cymmer on the outskirts of Merthyr Tydfil or in the town itself. The reserve is reached from beneath the road bridge (A470) over the Taf Fechan, between Cefn-coed-y-cymmer and Merthyr.

From the road bridge follow the trail along the E bank of the Taf Fechan, passing under the A465 road bridge and continuing 1½ miles (2.5 km). At the next road bridge cross the river and return along the W bank.

Worms Head
5½ *miles (9 km) Landranger 159 415882*

Situated within the Gower Coast National Nature Reserve, which is part-owned by the National Trust, this long, rocky promontory provides an ideal vantage point for sea-watching. The causeway leading to the Head is under-water at high tide, but remains un-covered for 5 hours, beginning 3½ hours after high tide. The nearby Coast Guard Station will provide details of local tides. *Sea, rocks; there is a real danger of being cau on the causeway during a rising tide, permit required to visit parts away from the footpath during nesting season.*

Summer fulmar, razorbill, guillemot, puffin, kittiwake; **passage** Manx shear-water, skuas, terns; **winter** common scoter, purple sandpiper.

Start From Swansea take the A4118 W along the Gower Peninsula to Scurlage. Here turn right on to the B4247 to Rhossili; **parking** in the village.

Follow the cliff-top bridleway from Rhossili to Kitchen Corner. Take the footpath which continues from here to Worms Head; return by the same route.

Whiteford Burrows
4 *miles (6.5 km) Landranger 159 446933*

A National Nature Reserve at the entrance to the Burry Inlet supporting nationally important populations of 14 species of wildfowl and waders. *Sand dunes, saltmarsh; permit required to visit areas away from public footpaths and way-marked routes.*

Passage terns, whimbrel and other waders; **winter** divers, grebes, brent goose, wigeon, pintail, shoveler, eider, hen harrier, grey plover, turnstone, knot, sanderling, black-tailed godwit; **all year** shelduck, oystercatcher, redshank, turnstone.

Start Leave Swansea W on the A483, turning left on the outskirts of the town on to the A4216 and then right on to the B4295, which terminates at Llanrhidian. From Gowerton to Llan-rhidian this road gives good views over the Burry Inlet (Loughor Estuary). At Llanrhidian, continue W on the minor road to Cheriton, where there is **parking** on the roadside, after the church.

Follow the footpath leading down Frog Lane and across the saltmarsh to a track which runs along Whiteford Burrows to Berges Island. Return by same route.

Peterstone Wentlooge
6 miles (9.5 km) Landranger 171
273811

A flat expanse of grazing and mudflats on the Severn Estuary, managed as a wildfowl refuge by the Gwent Trust for Nature Conservation. It is the best site in Gwent for rarities – gulls, terns and waders. Part of the area can be viewed from the B4239. *Sea, mudflats, salt-marsh, pasture.*

Winter white-fronted goose, wigeon, pintail, golden plover, grey plover, knot, greenshank, green sandpiper, short-eared owl; **passage** whimbrel, avocet (both occasional); **all year** heron, shelduck, redshank, curlew.

Start From Cardiff take the A48 E for 5 miles (8 km) to Castleton. Turn right here on to a minor road through Marshfield to the B4239. **Parking** on roadside in vicinity of the T-junction.

① A footpath starts at the B4239, close

The deciduous woodland of Coed-y-Bedw Nature Reserve supports a rich woodland bird population. Access is via the Taff's Well junction of the A470, taking the Pentyrch road (B4262) out of Taff's Well. Free to members of any naturalists' trust, otherwise apply to Glamorgan Nature Centre, Fountain Road, Tondu, Bridgend, Mid Glamorgan, CF32 0EH (06560 724100).

On the N outskirts of Cardiff are 2 reservoirs – Llanishen and Lisvane – which provide excellent birdwatching in winter, with a wide variety of wildfowl, grebes and divers; there are always large numbers of tufted duck, pochard and gulls, plus the occasional rarity. Easily reached by road or rail from the centre of Cardiff.

to the T-junction, and runs along a lane to the sea wall. At the sea wall ② turn right and follow it 2¾ miles (4.5 km) to ③, the breakwater. Return by same route.

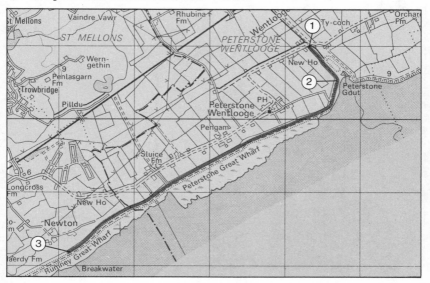

Llanthony Valley
3½ or 3 miles (5.5 or 5 km)
Landranger 161 305222 SO22 and SO32

If ever there was an all-round bird-watcher's walk, this is it. The route takes in open moorland, conifer plantations, deciduous woodland, pasture and a splendid, fast-flowing rocky river. Expect to see a correspondingly wide range of species, with the frequent **redstarts** and the excellent vantage point for viewing **dippers** as highlights. Magnificent views from the track along the top of the ridge separating the Honddu and Grwyne Fawr valleys. *Some obstruction from overgrown branches between ④ and ⑥; mud.*

Time and season Worthwhile all year, but the route offers a significant number of summer visitors; meadow pipits leave the hills in winter.

Start From Llanfihangel Crucorney, W of the A465, turn left on to the B4423 into the Llanthony valley. Continue 1¼ miles (2 km) past the turn to Forest Coal Pit and on to the Queen's Head Inn and trekking centre (where there is a large house martin colony). Turn left at the Inn and in about 200 yards (180 m) right through large entrance. **Parking** area in the plantation.

① From parking go back to the metalled road and walk uphill, continuing for a little over ½ mile (0.8 km), ignoring left turns to Cwm Coedycerrig and Gaer Farm. Pass through the gate ② on to open moorland. Detour, if wanted, to ③ the hill fort; path circling it is a right of way. Continue along the track for about 850 yards (775 m) to ④ the stone-built house on the right. Either continue to ⑤ (see note at end) or,

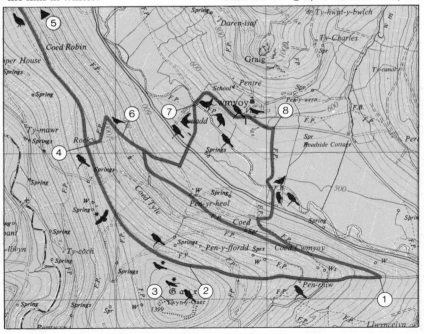

immediately before the house, turn right off the track down the bank and over the gate, keeping close to the garden wall. After 20 yards (18 m) cross the stile into the wood. Follow the narrow path down through the wood to ⑥ the broad track. For the shorter walk, turn right and continue on same track to ①. For the full route, cross to other side of track, turn right and in just 6 yards (5 m) descend some steps on the left into the beech plantation. Follow the stony track, crossing the stile into the field. Continue to road. Cross and climb the fence; walk down past Neuadd Farm to where the narrow road crosses the river. ⑦ Over the bridge, follow the road up to the village; continue along the lane down-hill past Cwmyoy Farm and ⑧ turn right through the gate signposted 'Queen's Head 1 km'. Walk down to the river, keeping to the hedge on the right of the field. Cross the footbridge and walk up to the road. Cross and take the track opposite the cottages. After the gate, turn up to the stile at the edge of the wood. Cross and take the woodland track to join the broad track. Turn left and continue to ① – car shortly in sight. *From ④ the walk can be extended along the ridge track to ⑤ the cairn, Garn-Wen, and back by the same route.*

Listen for the thin, high-pitched calls and the 'zitti-zitti-zitti' song of the goldcrest. Coal tits, also in the conifers, have a rather similar call. Blue and great tits also occur in the roadside trees.

Cuckoos will be heard all along the route, but especially on the hills – at the right season. Their shape is hawk-like, best seen as they fly over open moorland.

A harsh 'cronk' draws attention to the raven, the huge crow with a wedge-shaped tail. Carrion crows are frequent.

Redstarts are frequent: look for the red tail as the bird flies along before you. Willow warblers are common at the woodland edge and on the bracken-covered slopes with scattered trees. Chiff-chaffs prefer the denser plantations. Thrushes feed on the rowan berries in August. Ring ouzels a possibility.

Buzzards soaring over the valley.

Meadow pipits are the most abundant bird of the open hills, but look for the similar tree pipit. These favour areas with scattered trees and they sing as they descend in a 'parachute' display flight to the top of a tree. A flash of white rump tends to be all that is seen of a wheatear as it flies away. Watch out for them perched on hummocks, and for whinchats (pale eye-stripe) on the tops of bracken or small bushes, giving out a scolding 'tac tac tac'.

Red grouse occur on the hills, preferring heather-clad areas rather than whortle-berry (bilberry). The pheasants, common in the valley, are reared artificially.

Woodpigeons roost and nest in the thick cover of the larch and spruce.

Swallows nest in the farm buildings, and pied wagtails in their vicinity.

Dippers and grey wagtails frequent the river and can often be seen from the bridge, together with kingfishers. King-fishers sometimes feed as far up as Llanthony.

Blackcaps nest in the hedges and pour out their lovely, melodious song in May. Magpies and rooks are common.

Pied flycatchers nest in holes in the river-side alders. The smart black and white males are most conspicuous in late April and May. Spotted flycatchers also nest along the river.

Nuthatches, treecreepers and all 3 wood-peckers nest in holes in the alders, as do great, blue and marsh tits. Siskins and redpolls feed on the seeds in the alder cones in the late winter.

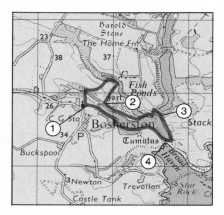

Bosherston Pools
2¼ miles (3.5 km)
Landranger 158 966947

The fish ponds at Bosherston were created artificially in the 19th C. by damming 3 narrow limestone valleys. The ponds are covered with water-lilies in summer, and are best for birds in winter, when they attract a wide range of passage and wintering wildfowl. The reserve is owned by the National Trust and managed jointly with the Nature Conservancy Council as part of Stackpole National Nature Reserve. *Open water; further information including leaflet from The Warden, NCC Office, Stackpole Home Farm, Pembroke.*

Winter pochard, goldeneye, mallard, teal, heron, kingfisher, with grebes, gadwall, goosander, smew and red-breasted merganser occasional.

Start From Pembroke take the B4319 S turning left after 5 miles (8 km) on to a minor road to Bosherston; **car park** in the village beside the church.

The reserve sign below Bosherston car park displays a map showing the main footpaths encompassing the W lake and extending N along the main lake.

① Follow the public footpath beginning in the car park, following it to the edge of the lake. Turn left to the end of the causeway. Cross the causeway and ② follow the path and signs to the central arm of the lake and a second causeway. Cross this and follow the path down to the bridge. Cross this and ③ continue with path alongside the lake and down to the shore. Return along the path ④ through the woodland on the W side of the lake and return to the car park.

St David's Head
3½ miles (5.5 km) Landranger 157 734272

Along a particularly beautiful section of the Pembrokeshire Coast Path, providing outstanding opportunities for sea-watching. *Sea, cliffs, heath.*

Summer Manx shearwater, storm petrel, kittiwake, razorbill, guillemot, puffin; **passage** skuas, terns; **all year** fulmar, gannet, shag, peregrine, buzzard, stonechat, reed bunting, chough.

Start From St David's take the A487 (Fishguard road) NE for ½ mile (0.8 km) and then turn left on to the B4583. Follow this for 2 miles (3 km) to its end, where there is a **car park**.

From the car park follow the Pembrokeshire Coast Path N around St David's Head. After 2 miles (3 km) turn inland along a public footpath which leads back to the B4583.

Cwm Rheidol
2½ miles (4 km) Landranger 135 697796

The Central Electricity Generating Board use the large catchment area of the Afon Rheidol to generate 86 million units of electricity annually. The scheme was carefully designed to preserve or improve the character of the steep-sided, wooded valley, and an 11-point nature trail has been created around the river, close to one of the dams. Trail guides are available at the CEGB Reception Centre. *Open water, woods, scrub.*

Summer common sandpiper, sand martin, grasshopper warbler, garden warbler, blackcap, willow warbler, chiffchaff, wood warbler, pied and spotted flycatchers, wheatear, redstart; **winter** Bewick's swan, goosander, fieldfare, redwing, brambling; **all year** tufted duck, sparrowhawk, buzzard, kestrel, stock dove, green and great spotted woodpeckers, meadow pipit, grey wagtail, dipper, goldcrest, stonechat, longtailed tit, coal tit, nuthatch, treecreeper, raven.

Start From Aberystwyth take the A44 E for 4¾ miles (7.5 km) to Capel Bangor and then turn right to a minor road to Dolypandy. The road follows the N bank of the Afon Rheidol for 3½ miles (5.5 km) to the CEGB Reception Centre at the W end of the reservoir; **parking** at the Centre.

From the Reception Centre follow the nature trail anticlockwise around the reservoir. Away from the road, the trail is marked by yellow-topped posts.

Castle Woods
2⅖ miles (4 km) Landranger 159 627225

Castle Woods, surmounted by the ruins of Dynevor Castle, are a nature reserve belonging to the West Wales Naturalists' Trust. There is a fair range of woodland birds. The castle itself is not open to visitors. *Woods; keep strictly to the paths.*

Summer garden warbler, blackcap, whitethroat, chiffchaff, wood warbler, pied flycatcher, redstart; **all year** sparrowhawk, buzzard, kestrel, green woodpecker, great and lesser spotted woodpeckers, goldcrest, long-tailed, marsh, willow and coal tits, nuthatch, treecreeper, jay, raven.

Start Approach Llandeilo from the S on

The storm petrel's fluttering feeding flight, when it seems to almost walk on the water, regardless of the height or ferocity of the waves. Except when driven ashore by the most violent weather, it only comes to land to breed, using holes in rocky coastlines.

the A483. Cross the river on the S edge of the town and then fork left by the church, directed to Carmarthen (A40). After 400 yards (350 m) the road joins the A40 (on the right) and immediately after this junction, on the right next to the ambulance station, is a **car park**. There is a railway station in Llandeilo.

From the car park cross the road and enter Penlan Park via the footpath behind the old school. After 300 yards (270 m) the path enters South Lodge Woods, the first part of the nature reserve. Continue on past Llandyfeisant Church, Gwaith Go-Back Pool, through Castle Wood to Dynevor Castle. (The first castle on the site is said to have been begun in 876. The ruins comprise the keep, a drum-tower and some of the curtain wall.) The way is marked at intervals by Badger Footprint signs. Note particularly that when crossing fields the path follows the fence lines. Return to the car park along the same route.

Dinas Island
*3 miles (5 km) Landranger 157 005398
SN 03 and SN 04*

The range of birds to be seen on this headland (an 'island' in name only since prehistoric times) is remarkably wide at any time of year; several of the most exciting birds – **choughs, ravens, peregrines** and **fulmars** – are resident. The scenery is magnificent, with dramatic cliffs all round and a beautiful cove either side of the island. The walk is in the Pembrokeshire Coast National Park and starts and finishes at a welcoming café-pub. *Mud after rain.*

Time and season All year, but added interest of migrant passerines in spring and autumn; crowded in summer months.

Start Take the narrow lane from Dinas village near Fishguard to Pwll Gwaelod cove – about 1¼ miles (2 km). **Public car park** by the Sailor's Safety.

① Walk up the tarmac road past the Sailor's Safety towards the island. On the first hairpin bend ② bear left along the waymarked path, heading out along the cliffs. Carry on to ③ the trig. point on Dinas Head – about 1 mile (1.5 km), then continue to ④ Needle Rock – another ½ mile (0.8 km) or so – and in a further ½ mile (0.8 km), the cove of Cwm-yr-eglwys. When the path reaches the tarmac road ⑤ turn left and follow the road. In 100 yards (90 m) ⑥ take the footpath on the right leading along the top side of the boat park on the green. Continue on this path straight across the small caravan park and through ⑦ an old metal gate. Continue along the marshy bottom about ¾ mile (1 km) back to Pwll Gwaelod.

Ravens, choughs, herring gulls and cormorants, in summer together with house martins and swifts, are likely to be seen in and above Pen Castell.

Linnets in abundance; worth listening for the 'reeling' call of the grasshopper warbler. Dunnocks and wrens frequent the steep, bracken slopes.

Rest by the right angle of the fence and look across the cliffs to Pen-clawdd. There is a real likelihood of seeing a peregrine: although its numbers are increasing in its natural habitats, such as this rugged coastal area, elsewhere it is a rare bird. Separate it from other falcons by its bulky body, robust build, heavier moustachial stripe and pale grey rump.

Cormorants and herring gulls nest along the cliffs. Plenty of stonechats along the path; choughs are frequent.

In spring and summer, skylarks perform their song flights in the cliff-top fields. Lapwings, starling flocks and some curlew in autumn/winter. Large finch flocks feed on the stubble in autumn.

From the trig. point there are wide views over the sea of passing auks, gannets, gulls and skuas, especially in autumn. There are usually oystercatchers on the low cliff below Dinas Head. The rocky outcrop 40 yards (35 m) beyond the trig. point is a safe viewing spot.

Abundant linnets; also whitethroats (spring and summer) and stonechats.

Pause by the stile where the path turns steeply downhill opposite Needle Rock. Guillemots and razorbills breed on the seaward side of the cliff. Herring gulls, jackdaws and feral pigeons are usually present. Fulmars nest on the nearby cliffs, laying only a single egg each year. In spite of this, fulmar numbers are increasing, possibly because the birds feed extensively on waste offal produced by commercial fishing. The comparatively long lifespan of 25 years also contributes. The nestlings are well equipped for survival, capable of propelling an extraordinarily foul-smelling jet of stomach oil several feet at anyone who approaches too close.

Where the path passes through black-thorn and hawthorn scrub, listen and look for the common passerine species – thrushes, tits, blackcaps and (spring and summer) the garden warbler. Bullfinches and goldfinches may be seen on the open banks.

The path now follows the marshy bottom of Cwm-Dewi, with woodland and gorse and bracken either side. Woodland birds include buzzards, woodpeckers and jays. Yellowhammers and magpies on the banks; grasshopper warblers, sedge warblers and reed buntings in the marsh; water rails in winter; plenty of migrant passerines in spring and autumn.

Fulmar: the long, narrow wings are held stiffly in the gliding position; particularly adept at using currents close to the cliff.

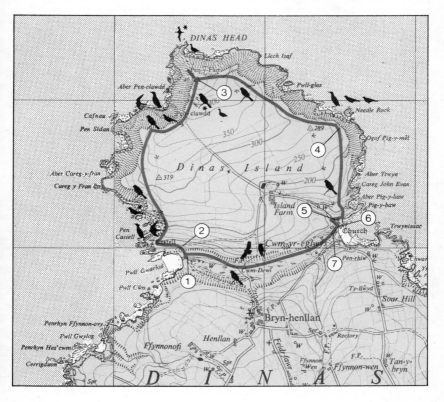

DYFED

Cors Caron
*3 miles (5 km) Landranger 146 and 135
695630.*

A National Nature Reserve of nearly
2,000 acres (800 ha), Cors Caron is one
of the finest raised bogs in Britain, providing excellent birdwatching. *Peat bog,
river.*

Summer curlew, grasshopper warbler;
winter whooper swan, wigeon, pochard, goldeneye, hen harrier; **all year**
sparrowhawk, buzzard, water rail,
snipe, redpoll.

*Identifying the 3 falcons common to several of
the walks in this section is possible on
behaviour alone. The kestrel is an habitual
hoverer; the peregrine flies with distinctively
fast, 'winnowing' wing beats followed by glides;
the merlin is the only falcon of such an
obviously small size that habitually hunts near
the ground.*

Start From Lampeter take the A485 NE
to Tregaron, from where the B4343 towards Pontrhydfendigaid runs along
the SE edge of the bog. Excellent views
of the bog may be obtained from this
road for the first 2 miles (3 km). **Parking**
by side of this road at 687618 or the lay-
by at 695630.

From the lay-by cross the stile on to the
disused railway line and follow it N for
1½ miles (2.5 km) to the NCC observation tower, which is open to the public.
Return by the same route. Permits are
required for other parts of the reserve.

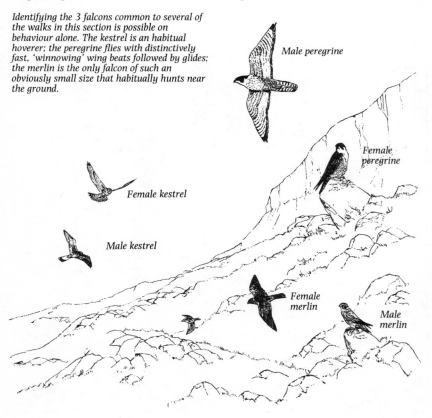

Male peregrine

Female
peregrine

Female kestrel

Male kestrel

Female
merlin

Male
merlin

Strumble Head
4½ miles (7 km) Landranger 157 903399

The cliffs at Strumble Head provide excellent views of nesting sea birds during the summer, and are a fine vantage point for sea-watching in the autumn. *Sea, cliffs, scrub.*

Summer blackcap; **passage** skuas, terns; **all year** (but primarily summer) fulmar, cormorant, peregrine, herring gull, kittiwake, razorbill, guillemot, stonechat, reed bunting, chough.

Start From St David's follow the A487 NE to Mathry; in 1½ miles (2.5 km) turn left on to a minor road to St Nicholas and continue to Strumble Head; **parking** by the roadside after Caer-lem.

Continue along the road from Caer-lem to a track on the left which leads out to Strumble Head and the cliff-top path. Turn left on to the cliff path and follow it round the Head to the Youth Hostel. A footpath leads away from the cliffs, past the Youth Hostel and back to the Caer-lem road. Turn left on to road and return to start.

Ynys-hir (Dyfi Estuary)
1½ miles (2.5 km)
Landranger 135 683964

The mild winters of the W Wales coast bring large numbers of waders and wildfowl to its estuaries, of which the Dyfi is one of the most outstanding. It is a National Nature Reserve part leased and part owned by the Nature Conservancy Council. Adjoining the National Nature Reserve is a reserve managed by the RSPB, which offers an interesting variety of habitats. *Estuary, marsh, saltings, woods, farmland; hides; open all year Sun and Wed, 10–5, also Sat and Thurs from April to Sept; entry fee to non-members; report to the reception centre; mud.*

Summer common sandpiper, nightjar, grasshopper, sedge and wood warblers, pied flycatcher, redstart; **winter** white-fronted goose, teal, wigeon, pintail, goldeneye, bar-tailed godwit, hen harrier, peregrine, merlin; **all year** shelduck, red-breasted merganser, oystercatcher, curlew, sparrowhawk, buzzard, great and lesser spotted woodpeckers, goldcrest, coal tit; **passage** whimbrel, greenshank, sanderling and a wide variety of other waders.

Start From Machynlleth take the A487 S to Furnace. Turn right in the village to the RSPB reserve with **car park**.

Follow the nature trail.

Skomer Island is the largest and, from the point of view of birds, probably the best of the Pembrokeshire islands. It is a National Nature Reserve managed by the West Wales Naturalists' Trust, and reached by boat from Martin's Haven. There are large breeding colonies of razorbills, guillemots, puffins, Manx shearwaters, fulmars, kittiwakes and storm petrels and a variety of species is attracted on migration. A 4-mile (6.5-km) nature trail is laid out around the island and visitors must keep to this. The boat visits the island daily (except Mon) from mid-April to mid-Sept; but visitors should check in advance – 043788 241.

During the breeding season, try following the Pembrokeshire Coast Path from St Govan's Head to Stackpole Head – about 2½ miles (4 km). The limestone cliffs and the isolated stacks hold colonies of razorbills, guillemots and kittiwakes, crowded together on the narrow ledges. Choughs may also be seen here, and birdwatchers may like to start their walk with a visit to the ancient St Govan's Chapel, built on the cliff face, ½ mile (0.8 km) W of St Govan's Head. Follow the B4319 S from Pembroke and turn left along the road leading via Bosherston to the Head.

Dinas Hill, Gwenffrwd
2 miles (3 km) Landranger 147 788471
SN 74

High densities of **breeding summer visitors** can be seen on this route, which makes use of the nature trail (with a raised boardwalk) on the RSPB's Gwenffrwd Reserve. There are exceptional opportunities for seeing woodland birds. The locality is famed for its spectacular landscapes – deeply etched river valleys and steep hillsides – as well as its connections with the Welsh folk hero Twm Shon Catti. *Mud after rain.*

Time and season Rewarding all year, but summer is a popular focus.

Start The information centre at Nant-y-ffin (788471) on the left of the road between Rhandirmwyn and the Brianne Reservoir, just past the tiny church of St Paulinus. **Car park** at Nant-y-ffin.

① Pick up the start of the trail from the corner of the car park. Follow the raised boardwalk 500 yards (450 m) to its end ② and turn right towards the river. Cross the open ground and rejoin the trail at the far end as ③ it climbs the side of the rocky Tywi gorge. Continue on the clearly defined path circling Dinas Hill. After nearly 1 mile (1.5 km) remain inside the wood when ④ the metalled road passes close by; continue another ⅓ mile (0.5 km) to rejoin the boardwalk at ②. Retrace to the car park.

From the car park, watch the hillside and crags above for ravens, kestrels and buzzards; possibility of a peregrine.

The boardwalk starts alongside an attractive small stream where grey and pied wagtails are often present, especially in the early part of the day before the larger numbers of visitors walk through.

Pied flycatchers and redstarts (summer) and several tit species, including long-tailed, plus treecreepers and nuthatches are numerous in the alder, oak and hazel woodland around the boardwalk.

When the path reaches the river, look upstream to the open ground, where the common sandpiper is regular in summer and herons are often seen on the riverside or among the yellow flags; also grey wagtails.

Stock doves breed in the crags above the river gorge. Woods and parkland, preferably with plenty of old timber, are the usual breeding places of this hole-nesting pigeon, but it will use cliffs (including sea cliffs) or even occasionally deserted buildings. Best distinguished from the wood-pigeon by lack of white patches on wings, and from the rock dove by its pale grey rump. The black borders to the trailing edges of the wings are distinctive, too; but none of these marks are particularly eye-catching in the field. Look for dippers on or in the river.

Grey wagtails at this confluence of the Rivers Tywi and Doethie, known as the Junction Pool – a famous fishing pool. Check the river carefully for goosander.

As you move away from the roaring of the river, the comparative silence of the wood should make you aware of the sounds of woodland birds. The whole way from here back to the boardwalk there is (in summer) an abundance of pied fly-catchers, redstarts, wood warblers and willow warblers; residents include several tit species, nuthatches, treecreepers and jays. The tree pipit is another summer visitor.

Pause at the seat where the metalled road comes into view. There is a great range of woodland birds here (see above), but also watch the opposite hillside for buzzards, ravens and even a possible red kite: Dinas Hill was a famous nest site for this bird, but has been unused for many years.

A deeply forked tail is the classic kite identification feature, but when the bird soars it is not so evident. The tail can usually be seen swivelling as the bird uses it for steering. Pale wing patches are prominent. The species has declined through much of its European range and is something of a speciality to Wales.

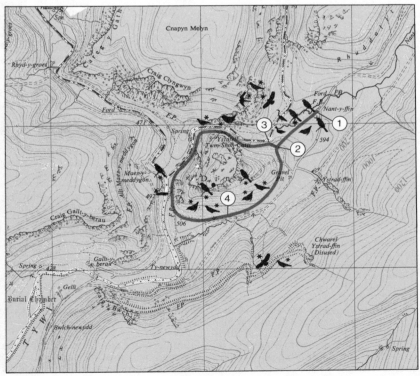

Wyndcliff Woods
1 mile (1.5 km) Landranger 162 524973

This is a nature trail created jointly by the Forestry Commission, the Gwent Trust for Nature Conservation and the Nature Conservancy Council, giving a walk up to the Eagle's Nest viewpoint and back, with an alternative return via the 365 steps, constructed in 1828. The Eagle's Nest gives splendid views across the Wye and Severn Valleys. *Woods.*

All year buzzard, green woodpecker, great and lesser spotted woodpeckers, goldcrest, long-tailed, coal and marsh tits, nuthatch.

Coal tit: white cheeks and nape, black crown.

Start From Chepstow follow the A466 (Monmouth road) N for 3 miles (5 km), past the B4293 junction and ½ mile (0.8 km) N of St Arvans to a left turn sign-posted to Wyndcliff and leading to the Forestry Commission's Upper Wyndcliff picnic site. **Parking** at picnic site.

Follow the waymarked 7-post nature trail from the car park.

Aberithon Turbary
¼ mile (0.5 km) Landranger 147 016575

A 14-acre wetland site managed by the Hereford and Radnorshire Naturalists' Trust. *Bog, reedbeds, meadow; open to members of county naturalists' trusts; non-members should contact the local trust office, 0432 56872.*

Summer water rail, sedge, reed and willow warblers, chiffchaff, wood warbler, pied flycatcher; **autumn** swallow roost; **winter** teal, wigeon, fieldfare, redwing, siskin, redpoll.

Start From Rhayader follow the A470 S to Newbridge on Wye. Continue a further ½ mile (0.8 km) and then turn right on to a minor road to Brynwern. In 100 yards (90 m) **parking** on roadside verge near farm drive.

Enter the reserve through the gate (which must be left shut to contain grazing stock). Walk straight ahead, following the left-hand boundary of the reserve, to the fence at the far side of the reserve. Return by the same path.

Daudraeth Illtyd
2¼ miles (3.5 km)
Landranger 160 976263

A variety of upland habitats with typical birdlife on this nature reserve managed by the Brecknock Naturalists' Trust. *Heath, bog, pools, streams, grassland; wetter parts of the reserve can be dangerous.*

All year grey heron, buzzard, lapwing, snipe, meadow pipit, whinchat, linnet, raven; **summer** redstart, wheatear; **passage** curlew, redshank, green sandpiper (occasional); **winter**, teal.

Start From Brecon take the A470 SW towards Merthyr Tydfil, but after 3½ miles (5.5 km), at Libanus, turn right on to a minor road to the National Park Mountain Centre, where there is a **car park**.

From the Mountain Centre continue on the road for ⅓ mile (0.5 km) to where a track on the left crosses Traeth Mawr.

Marsh tit, left, combination of glossy black crown, nape and chin are diagnostic; best distinguished from willow tit by voice. No confusing a nuthatch, right.

Follow this until it meets another track, turn right and after 500 yards (450 m) right again. Continue on this track for ¾ mile (1 km) to where it joins a minor road. Turn right to the car park.

Glaslyn and Bugeilyn Lakes
4½ miles (7 km) Landranger 135 or 136 837953

Two beautiful natural lakes in a remote part of Powys. *Open water, river, moor.*

Summer common sandpiper, whinchat, wheatear, ring ouzel; **winter** red-breasted merganser, goosander, hen harrier, short-eared owl; **all year** little grebe, great crested grebe, tufted duck, red kite, buzzard, merlin, red grouse, golden plover, curlew, snipe, meadow pipit, grey wagtail, dipper, raven.

Start From Llanidloes take the B4518 NW to Staylittle. In 1¼ miles turn left along a minor road through Dylife; 3¼ miles (5.5 km) beyond Dylife **parking** beside a track on the left.

① Follow the track on foot to Glaslyn lake and then continue to ② Bugeilyn lake. Return by the same route.

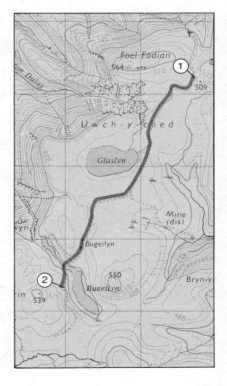

111

Clywedog Reservoir Trail
2½ miles (4 km)
Landranger 136 932867 SN 98

This nature trail established by the Trent Water Authority (which administrates the reservoir) combines particularly impressive scenery with a range of interesting **hillside, woodland** and **water birds**. *One steep climb.*

Time and season Excellent all year.

Start Leave Llanidloes on the B4518 going N and in about 2 miles (3 km)

turn left on to the minor road sign-posted Clywedog Reservoir. Follow the road past the viewing place and continue uphill for another ½ mile (0.8 km) to the white Dieldre chapel house on right. **Parking** on the roadside pull-ins.

① Go through the gate past Dieldre chapel house and cross the stile into the first field. The whole course of the trail is waymarked from here by small yellow arrows. Follow the left side of the field down the slope passing through the woodland edge until meeting a T-junction above the reservoir edge,

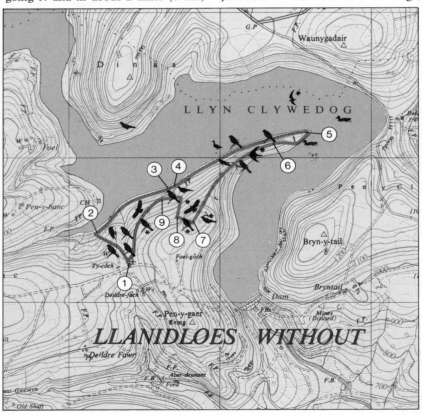

where ② turn right and pass through the old birch wood and across the field beyond it. After ③ crossing the stile at the far end of the field, turn left, ignoring the 'short cut' sign. The path skirts a larch wood, recrosses the fence ④ after about 100 yards (90 m) by way of another stile and then follows the reservoir edge across open ground and scattered woodland to ⑤ the point of the rocky promontory. Turn right and shortly follow the path up the promontory's spine. Pause and rest at the first level stretch ⑥. Continue along the spine right up to the plantation of ancient, scattered larch (first-rate views the whole way). ⑦ Turn right through the far end of the larch plantation and go downhill to the open field the other side. ⑧ Turn right at the Severn–Trent notice board and continue downhill on the path, eventually passing through another larch plantation. As the path emerges from the larch, ⑨ turn left on to the main track. Follow it diagonally across the slope back to ①.

Look forwards from the path to the damp gully across the field and expect to hear or see redstarts (summer), magpies or reed buntings.

As the little wooded gully develops to the left, look for tit flocks; willow warblers (summer); redpolls in the alders and birches (winter) and thrushes on the mass of rowan berries (autumn and early winter).

In winter tit flocks are regular in the birch wood; in summer look for pied flycatchers, wood warblers, willow warblers and redstarts; all year, great spotted woodpeckers.

As the path crosses the open field look in the sky for buzzards and ravens, numerous here. Ravens nest on Dinas Hill: they start building the nest as early as midwinter, and the eggs – four to six in number – are laid in February. Young are fed at first with insects, but soon graduate

to pieces of meat – carrion forms a major part of the diet. Ravens' legendary intelligence has been demonstrated in some interesting studies of captive birds. They seem to have adapted bird actions and behaviour, especially in courtship and threat, particularly well to their needs, using, for example, the impressive bristling of the throat feathers to communicate comparatively subtle information.

There are wood pigeons, goldcrests, coal tits and wrens in the larch plantation.

Cormorants are regular on the reservoir, as are the common sandpiper (summer) and pied wagtail on its stony edge. In autumn and winter there is a large gull roost – mainly black-headed. The bracken slopes above you abound with families of tits, dunnocks and redstarts at the end of the breeding season; cuckoos.

Tree pipits, whinchats and willow warblers breed in the amenity plantation above the path; tit flocks in winter.

From the point, pause and scan the reservoir in both directions. Goosander are regular, breeding in substantial numbers. Also expect mallard, tufted duck, pochard and great crested grebe. Wildfowl are often tucked in close to the banks or resting on the shore.

In heavy summer weather, swifts dash to and fro across the ridge at head height. On the planted slopes either side of the ridge there are breeding whinchats, whitethroats, tree pipits, willow warblers (numerous), chaffinches and magpies.

In and around the larch plantation look for ravens, buzzards, meadow pipits and redstarts – at the appropriate season.

Meadow pipits and skylarks are numerous on the open fields; goldfinches and linnets feed on the mass of thistles in summer and autumn.

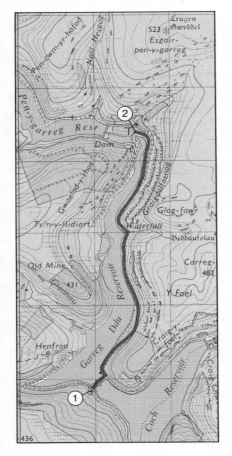

Elan Valley
5 miles (8 km) Landranger 147 909638

The Afon Elan, in the Cambrian Mountains, has been dammed to form a series of 4 reservoirs. The valley is wooded and surrounded by moorland, providing varied habitat for birds. *Open water, woods, moor, rocky outcrops.*

Summer tree pipit, wood warbler, pied flycatcher, whinchat, wheatear, red-start, ring ouzel; **winter** goldeneye, sparrowhawk, siskin, redpoll; **all year** goosander, buzzard, peregrine, marsh tit, dipper, grey wagtail, raven.

Start From Rhayader take the B4518 SW for 2 miles (3 km), then take the right fork along a minor road and turn left after 1¾ miles (3 km) across a causeway between Garreg Ddu and Caban Coch. **Parking** by the chapel at the end of the causeway.

① From the car park re-cross the causeway and follow the minor road N up the valley as far as ② the bridge over the Afon Elan. Return by same route.

Talybont Reservoir
4 miles (6.5 km) Landranger 161 104206

A 300-acre (120-ha) reservoir, where the main interest is wintering wildfowl, but with natural banks and surrounding plantations also attracting passage waders and passerines. Managed by the Welsh Water Authority under an agreement with Brecknock Naturalists' Trust. *Open water, sedge, plantations.*

Summer common sandpiper, yellow wagtail, grasshopper warbler, reed warbler; **winter** mallard, wigeon, pochard, tufted duck, goldeneye, goosander, siskin; **passage** ruff, spotted redshank, greenshank; **all year** cormorant, dipper, redpoll.

Start From Brecon take the A40 SE for 2 miles (3 km) before turning right on to the B4558. After 2¾ miles (4.5 km) turn right on to a minor road to Aber Village, where there is an information centre. Continue through Aber Village to the reservoir. Roadside **car park** halfway along the reservoir.

From car park walk to both ends of the reservoir.

Coedydd Maentwrog and Llyn Mair
¾ *mile (1 km) Landranger 124*
653414

A fragment of the natural oak woodlands of North Wales, managed jointly as a National Nature Reserve by the National Trust, the Nature Conservancy Council and the North Wales Naturalists' Trust. Across the road from the reserve is Llyn Mair (Mary's Lake), which attracts whooper swans in winter. *Woods, meadow, marsh, stream, lake; open to the public.*

Summer wood warbler, pied flycatcher, redstart; **winter** whooper swan, pochard, goldeneye; **all year** little grebe, mallard, buzzard, green woodpecker, great and lesser spotted woodpeckers, coal tit, nuthatch, hawfinch.

Start From Ffestiniog take the B4391 and then the A496 SW to Maentwrog. Join the A487 and, after ½ mile (0.8 km), turn right on to the B4410. There is a small NCC **car park** after ⅔ mile (1 km), opposite Llyn Mair, and a railway station on the edge of the reserve at Tan-y-bwlch.

If arriving by car, follow the 11-point nature trail from posts 1 to 7 to posts A to D. If arriving by train, start at post A, at D move on to post 1 and continue via post 7 back to the station.

Sighting a hawfinch is not easy, but if seen, the massive bill, used for cracking nuts and fruit stones, is unmistakable. Look for its bounding flight fairly high among branches.

Morfa Mawddach Railway
1 to 8 miles (1.5–13 km)
Landranger 124 695185

Snowdonia National Park Authority and the RSPB have jointly established a bird observation post and information centre in a disused signal box on the Morfa Mawddach railway line which was closed in the 1960s. Visitors can walk along the railway line in both directions, and there is also a trail for the disabled. *River, estuary, woods.*

Summer garden warbler, blackcap, wood warbler; **winter** wigeon, peregrine; **all year** cormorant, little grebe, shelduck, red-breasted merganser, sparrowhawk, buzzard, water rail, oystercatcher, redshank, curlew, snipe, stonechat.

Start From Dolgellau take the A493 W for 2¼ miles (3.5 km) to the bird observatory, where there is a **car park**.

From the car park either follow the railway line E for ½ mile (0.8 km) towards Dolgellau and then return, or follow the line W, along the Afon Mawddach Estuary, for up to 4 miles (6.5 km) to Arthog, and then return.

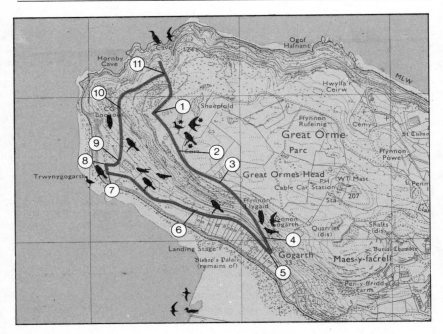

Great Orme
2½ miles (4 km)
Landranger 115 755845 SH 78/88

The Great Orme is a formidable cliff-girt limestone promontory jutting out into the Irish Sea N of Llandudno. Expect to see **breeding sea birds**, **shore birds**, **farmland** and **heathland species**. The area is administered as a country park by Aberconwy Borough Council; a nature trail (leaflet available) covers part of this route. *Mud after rain.*

Time and season All year.

Start From Llandudno follow the Marine Drive (a one-way privately owned toll road) about 2 miles (3 km). After passing the lighthouse, take the first turning on the left and drive up the concrete road. **Car park** (western) in 300 yards (270 m).

① From the car park follow the route markers uphill across the open heath. Pass the cairn ② on the crest of the hill and continue beside the stone wall for another ¼ mile (0.5 km) until ③ reaching the Monk's Path. Follow the waymarks downhill across the slope – a well-defined path. On reaching the Marine Drive at the bottom of this slope ④ turn left; and in 100 yards (90 m) ⑤ sharp right on to an unadopted road. Follow this about ½ mile (0.8 km) and after passing through ⑥ the gate on to open heath, continue on the (wartime) road, keeping to the lower track until arriving just above the rocky shore. ⑦ Where the track turns at right angles to the right, detour a few yards to the left to the shoreline to obtain the best sea views. Continue up the track another 50 yards (45 m) and ⑧ turn right again on to another dilapidated concrete road. In 100 yards (90 m) ⑨ turn left on to footpath across the heath and head diagonally uphill towards the Coast Guard Lookout seen on the cliff-top. On reaching the Marine Drive again by way of the Coast Guard Lookout ⑩ turn left along the drive and continue about ¼ mile (0.5 km) to ⑪ a gap in the wall on the left opposite the turning to the car park. Go through to the cliff-edge viewpoint – heeding the warning signs – to inspect the sea bird colonies far below. Retrace to ①.

Little owls usually appear squat and rounded, with heavy barring on the underside.

The open, sheep-grazed grassland here, and the whole way to the Monk's Path, is a likely area for migrant birds in spring and autumn. Dotterel pause here briefly in mid-April most years; snow buntings are fairly regular near the cairn from Nov to April. In autumn there are large flocks of redwings and fieldfares; also goldfinches, ring ouzels and the occasional yellow wagtail. House martins, swifts and swallows hawk the area in summer; wheatears nest in the dilapidated field walls; meadow pipits and skylarks breed on the open ground.

Scan the rocky area on your left as you descend the Monk's Path. A little owl is regular here; there are jackdaws and often kestrels.

From the Marine Drive, look out to the sewage outfall (marked by a yellow buoy and often by the water's different appearance to the surrounding sea). Herring gulls, lesser black-backed and black-headed gulls regularly congregate there in large numbers. It is also a rewarding spot for winter wildfowl. Great crested grebes, and not infrequently red-throated divers and the occasional Slavonian grebe, come close inshore at high tide. The last has splendid breeding plumage – twin golden crests and red breast and flanks – with the winter appearance, basically black, white and grey, a complete contrast.

Goldeneye, red-breasted mergansers and common scoters are regular. Cormorants occur all year. Shelduck are frequent in summer. Gannets and terns pass by.

The scrub-covered slope above the road is a likely spot for resident species such as blackbirds, song thrushes, robins, wrens, chaffinches, greenfinches and tits. Thrush parties feed on the hawthorn berries in autumn.

Where the scrub gives way to more open bracken and gorse, cuckoos, whitethroats (summer), stonechats and linnets are regular. Ravens breed on the Great Orme and may be seen anywhere round the walk, but this is an especially likely spot.

Look on the rocky shore for oystercatchers, curlew, turnstones, redshank, and in winter purple sandpipers; the latter are inactive and easily overlooked. Rock pipits are plentiful.

In late summer this is a gloriously colourful piece of heath, with a carpet of western gorse and heathers. Expect stonechats again on the slopes.

Look carefully for the little owl again in the rocks below the Coastguard Lookout.

The sea bird colonies are a long way below, but the traffic of auks and kittiwakes in and out of the cliffs is easily seen. A few fulmars float to and fro in front of the cliffs and herring gulls breed on the ledges.

Holyhead Mountain, Anglesey
$4\frac{1}{2}$ *miles (7 km)*
Landranger 114 211818 SH 28/38

This walk, on an RSPB reserve, over-
looks some of the most dramatic coastal
scenery in Wales, with a backdrop of
maritime heathland rising to the rocky
summit of Holyhead Mountain. There
are fine views of **sea birds** on the cliffs,
and **choughs** are a particular feature. In
August the heath is ablaze with purple
and yellow. *One section in the last mile
tends to be overgrown with gorse.*

Time and season All year, but May and
June are particularly rewarding for activity among breeding sea birds on the
cliffs. Spring and autumn migrations
bring a variety of species, best seen in
early morning.

Start From the termination of the A5 in
Holyhead Harbour, follow the signposts
to South Stack. **Car park** by the RSPB
reserve sign on the left side of the road
leading to the headland.

① From the SW corner of the car park
walk to the cliff-top and turn right along
the cliff-top path to Ellen's Tower ②,
where continue uphill to the South Stack
Café. Turn left on to the road and continue as far as the car park above the
South Stack lighthouse steps, where ③
turn right and follow the cliff-top path
to the stone observation post. Continue
along the ridge towards the WT Station
④, passing to the right of it. Follow the
path which slants up to the depression
N of the mountain's summit. Pass
through a wall and the remains of the
old signalling station ⑤ before descending towards North Stack with its Fog
Signal Station ⑥. Retrace steps about
150 yards (140 m) and carry straight
on along the major track heading in the
direction of Holyhead Harbour. At tele-
graph pole no. 15, turn right along a
track which is indistinct at first. Continue along this path, going right at the

fork, until reaching the fields with the
dry stone walls, where ⑦ the path
descends. Turn right at the cross-tracks
and continue between further dry stone
walls towards prominent TV mast. Leave
mast to left and continue past Twr
quarry ⑧. Continue straight on across
another intersection of tracks aiming for
⑨ another prominent mast. Near the
mast turn left at the junction of tracks
and continue to the road; turn left to ①.

Linnets and stonechats breed in the gorse.

Ravens, choughs and kestrels are often
seen along this stretch of cliff. There is
a good chance of a peregrine, as on other
cliff sections.

The view from Ellen's Tower (RSPB Information Centre open May–Sept, 11–5)
is outstanding for breeding sea birds from
mid-April to mid-July, notably guillemots,
razorbills and puffins.

Spectacular migratory flocks occur in
October and November. The birds are
chiefly chaffinches and starlings going W
to Ireland. Lapwings can make spectacular movements in hard weather.

This is a fine vantage point for watching
shags and fulmars flying to and fro from
nesting sites on the cliffs of Gogarth Bay.
Shags are fairly easy to separate from
cormorants at range because they are
basically all dark; cormorant has white
at base of bill and in breeding season on
each thigh.

Another likely spot for choughs, feeding
on the heath or soaring in noisy flocks
over the mountain.

Wrens and stonechats nest in small numbers in the heather.

Sea bird passage can be impressive here
from May to Sept. Gannets and Manx
shearwaters pass close inshore when
there are strong winds at sea.

Woodcock and short-eared owls are seen on the mountain during the autumn, especially in late October and November.

Bramble and gorse thickets along the track from this point provide cover for migrant passerines, particularly goldcrests and warblers; breeding whitethroats.

Choughs are glossy black all over, and simply distinguished from other crows by the downcurved, red bill and red feet. Quite easy to distinguish from a jackdaw because it is larger, and has no grey on the nape of the neck.

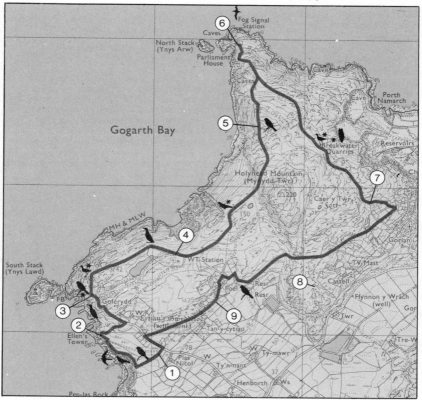

GWYNEDD

Broad Water
8 miles (13 km)
Landranger 135
608034

The Afon Dysynni widens out, just behind its mouth in Cardigan Bay, to form a shallow tidal pool which attracts relatively small numbers of wildfowl and waders, particularly in winter. *Open water, mudflats, marsh.*

Winter mallard, wigeon, pintail, red-breasted merganser, peregrine, golden plover, grey plover, turnstone; **all year** cormorant, teal, buzzard, grey wagtail.

Start Bryncrug, 2¼ miles (3.5 km) NE of Tywyn on the A493; **Parking** in Bryncrug.

① From the A493 road bridge over the Afon Fathew, join the footpath which follows the S bank of the Fathew. Walk W to the Afon Dysynni, then ② turn left and follow the Dysynni 2 miles (3 km) to Broad Water. Continue along the footpath to ③ the railway. Return by the same route.

A large flock of dunlin has a characteristic, elongated shape, and it moves almost like smoke, rising, falling and wheeling. As the birds turn, their pale underparts contrast with the dark upperparts to give a flickering effect. Adults in breeding season can be identified by the black belly patch alone.

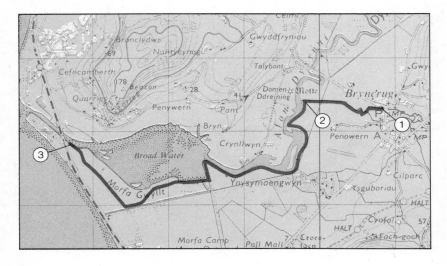

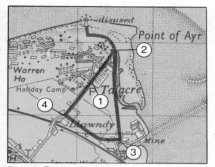

Point of Ayr, Dee Estuary
3 miles (5 km) Landranger 116
123845

The Dee Estuary, one of the most important areas in Britain for wildfowl and waders, is a rich feeding ground at low tide. At high tide one of several roosting sites for densely packed flocks of waders usually occurs near the Point of Ayr. Spectacular birdwatching. *Mudflats, saltmarsh.*

Passage little stint, curlew sandpiper, spotted redshank, greenshank, whimbrel, skuas, Sandwich, common, arctic and little terns; **winter** red-throated diver, great crested grebe, pintail, wigeon, teal, scaup, scoter, goldeneye, red-breasted merganser, peregrine, grey plover, turnstone, purple sandpiper, knot, sanderling, bar-tailed godwit, snow bunting; **all year** shelduck, mallard, oystercatcher, lapwing, dunlin, redshank, curlew.

Start From Rhyl take the A548 for 6½ miles (10.5 km) via Prestatyn, then left along a minor no through road to Talacre. **Parking** at the end of the road.

① Follow the footpath running from the end of the minor road directly out to the Point of Ayr ②, then follow it left to the lighthouse. From the lighthouse retrace to ② and then follow the sea wall S for ¾ mile (1 km) to ③. From

here turn right and follow the footpath back to the minor road at ④. Turn right and follow road to Talacre.

Coed Cilygroeslwyd
¾ mile (1 km) Landranger 116 126553

Exceptionally well-mixed woodland of ash, yew and hazel, owned by the North Wales Naturalists' Trust; notable features are woodcock and hawfinches. *Woods, quarry; free to members of any naturalists' trust, otherwise small fee – contact county trust.*

Summer tree pipit, garden warbler, blackcap, lesser whitethroat, willow warbler, chiffchaff, wood warbler, pied flycatcher, redstart; **winter** fieldfare, redwing, brambling; **all year** woodcock, sparrowhawk, buzzard, kestrel, tawny owl, 3 woodpeckers, long-tailed tit, marsh tit, willow tit, nuthatch, treecreeper, hawfinch.

Start From Ruthin take the A494 S for 2 miles (3 km), then turn left; **parking** by the roadside in this lane.

Walk to the stile opposite the lane on the other side of the A494. Cross and follow the footpath through the wood for 250 yards (230 m) to a stone wall and fence which mark the boundary of the reserve. Cross the stile here and follow the path N through the reserve for ¼ mile (0.5 km) to Bron Eyarth. Continue to follow the path around the quarry and then turn S again, forking right after 250 yards (230 m) and continuing S to the reserve entrance.

Clocaenog Forest, with some interesting woodland birdwatching, is owned by the Forestry Commission, who have provided a Visitor Centre at Bod Petrual, housed in a converted keeper's cottage and containing an exhibition showing the area's ecology.

Middle England

Rich, farming landscape is the popular conception of this region, and it does predominate in the southern counties, notably Hereford and Worcester and Gloucestershire. To the west, there are, in addition, some important woodlands – the Forests of Dean, Wyre and Mortimer. The Peak District is the dominant feature of the northern part, while in the east there are the flatlands of Lincolnshire and the Wash. Right at the heart of the region is the densely populated county of West Midlands. The spectrum of birdlife is correspondingly wide, from the ring ouzel and black grouse of the Peak District's uplands to the rare black redstart, which nests locally in urban derelict land in West Midlands.

Apart from the meres of Shropshire and Cheshire, natural open water is in short supply. However, reservoirs and gravel pits abound, and these have become valued habitats. Although increasing under pressure from activities such as angling and sailing, the variety of waterfowl to be seen at such sites is still wide, with rarer grebes and divers turning up regularly.

On the coasts, the Severn and Dee estuaries and the Wash offer some of the largest concentrations of wintering waterfowl to be found anywhere in the country. And for migration enthusiasts, there is Gibraltar Point, south of Skegness, remarkable for migrant and vagrant passerines in autumn.

Grey heron

Only adult redshank have red legs; the young's are orange-yellow. In flight, white triangles on rump and wings are diagnostic.

Severn Ham, Tewkesbury
1½ miles (2.5 km)
Landranger 150 889326

A small wetland area lying between the Severn and Avon on the W edge of Tewkesbury. *River, grassland.*

Summer redshank, curlew, kingfisher, yellow wagtail, reed and sedge warblers; **all year** skylark, corn bunting.

Start Approaching Tewkesbury from Gloucester on the A38, pass the Abbey (on right-hand side) and immediately turn left. **Parking** in St Mary's Street, near the Abbey.

From parking go down Mill Street opposite the Abbey and ① cross the footbridge. Follow path straight across Severn Ham to the Severn and ② turn right to follow footpath along river, and as it returns along connecting waterway to the Avon where ③ return to ①.

Slimbridge
1½ miles (2.5 km)
Landranger 162 723048

The New Grounds at Slimbridge are the headquarters of the Wildfowl Trust, best known for its collection of 2,300 captive birds, including all 6 kinds of flamingo,

representing 131 of the 148 species of wildfowl found worldwide. However, the area also attracts large numbers of wild waterfowl, including, in winter, flocks of 3,000–4,000 white-fronted geese. Up to 600 Bewick's swans may be present. The reserve is at its best Oct–March, with peak numbers of wild birds in Jan and Feb. *Open water, saltmarsh, mudflats; entry fee – but free to members of the Wildfowl Trust: in 1982 an extensive new system of hides was opened at the reserve, overlooking an area previously out of view of visitors.*

Winter white-fronted goose, Bewick's swan, teal, wigeon, pintail, shoveler, pochard, peregrine, merlin, golden plover, grey plover, turnstone; **all year** shelduck, oystercatcher, redshank, bar-tailed godwit, curlew, sparrowhawk; **spring and autumn** whimbrel, greenshank, ruff and other waders.

Start From Stroud take the A419 W. At Stonehouse take the left fork signposted M5 along the A4096 and continue, via the roundabout which forms junction 13 of the M5, to the roundabout junction with the A38. Turn left here and follow the A38 for 3 miles (5 km). Then turn right on to an unclassified road to Slimbridge, pass through the village and bear right after a sharp left bend. Continue along this road over the canal bridge to the Wildfowl Trust. **Car park** on the right, just before the entrance to the reserve.

Best views of wild birds may be had from the hides overlooking The Dumbles on the NW and SW side of the reserve.

Forest of Dean
1¾ or 2¾ miles (3 or 4.5 km)
Landranger 162 615120

The Forest of Dean is a fragment of the forest that once covered all of the West Midlands. There are many Forestry Commission picnic sites, including the

Speech House picnic place set under oak trees in one of the older parts of the forest. Many people do not realize that the Forest of Dean is an area of great variety, and this can be best seen by following the Speech House trail beginning at the picnic place. The numerous habitats provide opportunities of seeing a wide range of woodland species. The RSPB's Nagshead reserve is within walking distance. *Mature oakwood, plantations, stream.*

Summer turtle dove, nightjar, grasshopper warbler, garden warbler, blackcap, whitethroat, wood warbler, pied flycatcher, spotted flycatcher, whinchat, redstart; **winter** water rail, fieldfare, redwing, brambling; **all year** sparrowhawk, buzzard, woodcock, kingfisher, green woodpecker, great and lesser spotted woodpeckers, grey wagtail, dipper, stonechat, nuthatch, hawfinch, raven, crossbill.

Start From the A40 3 miles (5 km) W of Gloucester turn S on to the A48 (Chepstow road). After 7 miles (11 km) turn right on to the A4151 and in a further 3 miles (5 km), past the sharp right turn, continue on the B4226 through Cinderford. The picnic place with **parking** is on the right, 1¾ miles (3 km) after Cinderford, E of Speech House Hotel.

Follow the waymarked forest trail.

Edward Richardson Reserve
¾ *mile (1 km) Landranger 163 215007*

A reserve comprising 2 disused gravel pits and attracting a variety of water birds. The S section is open to the public and has a nature trail. The N section, containing the largest of the pits, is not open to the public, but can be viewed from the hide at the 9th post of the nature trail. *Open water, scrub; waterproof footwear recommended; keep strictly to the path.*

Summer sedge and willow warblers; **all year** little grebe, great crested grebe, mallard, pochard, tufted duck, sparrowhawk, coot, kingfisher, reed bunting.

Start From Lechlade take the A361 N for ½ mile (0.8 km) then turn left along a track leading to Rough Grounds Farm. **Car park** on left.

Follow the 9-post nature trail from the car park around the S part of the reserve, finishing at the hide at post 9, opposite the car park.

Woodcock roding.

Below Monmouth, the River Wye runs through a beautiful valley with wooded slopes on both sides before flowing into the River Severn. The A466 from Monmouth to Chepstow follows the course of the river, with many pleasant walks along the river starting from this road. Dippers and grey wagtails are frequent, and in summer warblers and nesting buzzards frequent the woods.

Chedworth SSSI, a reserve of the Gloucestershire Trust for Nature Conservation, is open to the general public. Actually a section of disused railway line through wooded countryside, it harbours a rich bird population, mainly passerines, with woodcock, sparrowhawks and kestrels. Access is by the road from Compton Abdale (off the A40 SE of Cheltenham) to the disused airfield at Chedworth. There is parking on the left, immediately after the railway bridge. For a circular walk, continue through the reserve to the Roman villa and return by the public footpath to the W of the reserve.

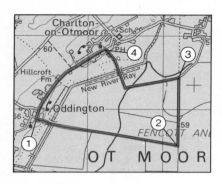

The bars on the neck are unique to the turtle dove. Identification is further simplified by the chequered appearance of the orange-buff upperparts, and the black tail with white edge.

Ot Moor (or Otmoor)
3½ miles (5.5 km)
Landranger 164 554148

A truly flat, open stretch of marsh NE of Oxford, where periodic flooding creates a rich feeding ground for wildfowl and waders. *Marsh.*

Summer curlew, redshank, grasshopper warbler, yellow wagtail; **winter** wigeon, pintail, short-eared owl; **all year** teal, shoveler, snipe.

Start Leave Oxford on the A43 in the direction of Bicester and in 4 miles (6.5 km) turn right on to the B4027 to Islip. In Islip turn left to Oddington. **Parking** in the village.

① Follow the track which leads E from Oddington, crossing the River Ray and continuing across Ot Moor for 1 mile (1.5 km). ② Turn sharp left to follow the course of a Roman road. At T-junction, ③, turn left and continue for ¾ mile (1 km) recrossing the River Ray and entering Charlton-on-Otmoor. ④ Turn left to follow road to ①.

Chinnor Hill
1½ miles (2.5 km)
Landranger 165 766005

Before scrub and woodland took over, this area – a Berks, Bucks and Oxon Naturalists' Trust reserve – was chalk grassland. The variety of cover supports an interesting range of species throughout the year. *Woods, scrub, grassland; free entry.*

Summer quail, turtle dove, garden warbler, blackcap, lesser whitethroat, willow warbler, chiffchaff; **winter** great grey shrike (occasional), fieldfare, redwing; **all year** corn bunting, yellowhammer, linnet.

Start From Princes Risborough take the A4129 and B4009 to Chinnor. In the village the road bends sharp left at a junction with the B4445 and then sharp right. Go straight over this crossroads on to a minor road towards Bledlow Ridge. In ¼ mile (0.5 km), after hairpin bend, turn left to the reserve. Bear right after ¼ mile (0.5 km). **Car park** after a further ⅓ mile.

From the car park a path cut in the escarpment leads down to Bledlow Cross. After ½ mile (0.8 km) this levels out and continues to Hempton Wainhill. Here 5 paths meet. Take one immediately to the right, following it along the edge of Wainhill Wood and across a stretch of heath to the car park.

A long-tailed tit emerging from its delicately constructed nest. The bird's tail, accounting for over half its whole length, together with pink, white and black plumage are unique among British birds. The colouring is not however distinguishable at any distance.

The Hodgemoor Wood Walks in the Chilterns are Forestry Commission routes of ¾, 1 and 1½ miles in length (1, 1.5 and 2.5 km) through attractive mixed woodland, including an area of ancient coppice rich in bird- and insect life. The walks start from Hodgemoor Wood Picnic Place, which is in Bottrell's Lane, the Chalfont St Giles road, off the A355, 2 miles (3 km) N of Beaconsfield.

Church Wood, Hedgerley
½ mile (0.8 km) Landranger 175 973873

For the beginner, the wide variety of species to be found on this RSPB reserve provides an excellent introduction to woodland birds. *Mixed, deciduous wood, hazel, oak and beech.*

Summer turtle dove, garden warbler, blackcap, willow warbler, spotted flycatcher; **all year** sparrowhawk, woodcock, stock dove, tawny owl, green woodpecker, great and lesser spotted woodpeckers, long-tailed tit, marsh tit, willow tit, coal tit, nuthatch, treecreeper, tree sparrow.

Start Leave Slough N on the A355. At Egypt turn right on to the minor road to Hedgerley. In Hedgerley turn right before the pub along a private track. **Parking** on the side of the track before the field gate. Do not obstruct the gateway.

Follow the marked paths round the wood.

Grangelands and Pulpit Hill
2½ miles (4 km) Landranger 165 825057

A reserve managed by the Berks, Bucks and Oxon Naturalists' Trust and comprising farmland, which has been uncultivated for over 30 years, and a former rifle range. Nearly 50 species breed in and around the reserve. *Chalk downland, scrub, beechwood.*

Summer quail, turtle dove, garden warbler, blackcap, lesser whitethroat, willow warbler, chiffchaff; **winter** great grey shrike (occasional), fieldfare, redwing; **all year** corn bunting, yellowhammer, linnet.

Start From Princes Risborough take the A4010 NE for 1¾ miles (3 km) to the outskirts of Great Kimble; trains to Little Kimble, ½ mile (0.8 km) from ①. **Parking** in the lay-by.

① From the lay-by follow the track – a bridleway – SE. The track peters out but the bridleway continues to the minor road. Before reaching the road, ②, about ½ mile (0.8 km) from the end of the track, fork right on to a footpath. Follow this about 250 yards (230 m) and ③ turn right on to the road. In 100 yards (90 m) turn right on to another bridleway. Follow this back to the A4010, where ④ turn right and walk 500 yards (450 m) back to ①.

BUCKINGHAMSHIRE

The Grand Union Canal
3½ miles (5.5 km) or 5½ miles (9 km)
Landranger 165 905144 SP91 and SP81

The canal towpath gives singular opportunities of seeing waterside birds at close quarters, especially **sedge** and **reed warblers**. Though not especially rare, they are often difficult to glimpse in broad belts of reed or around larger areas of water.

Away from the canal, the route is through arable farmland with the unusual feature of pollarded black poplars. Pollarding (cutting off branches for fuel or fodder) tends to produce cavities in older trees, and these are ideal nest sites for **owls** and **stock doves**. The mainstay of such sites used to be elms, which have been wiped out, along with their bird populations, by Dutch elm disease.

Time and season Late evening, to twilight, or dawn, for the owls (although the little owl is relatively diurnal). Sedge and reed warblers are summer visitors.

Start From the A41 ½ mile (0.8 km) E of Aston Clinton take the B489 to Wilstone. Continue through village and shortly stop at humped bridge. **Parking** by bridge close to verge.

① From bridge walk straight ahead along road. In 40 yards (35 m) turn left and continue along lane. At T-junction ② turn left for Puttenham (signposted). Continue through village and turn left at right-angled bend. In ½ mile (0.8 km) reach ③ a bridge. Go down to footpath by crossing stile at side of bridge. Continue W along the canal towpath. In about 2 miles (3 km), at bridge no. 11 (not on map – numbers are at crests of arches), retrace steps. At ③ carry straight on under bridge. In just over 1 mile (1.5 km), at next bridge, return to road and car. The walk can be extended by continuing along towpath as far as Aylesbury – about 1 mile; but ②–③ is the best stretch: after bridge 11 the reedbeds dwindle.

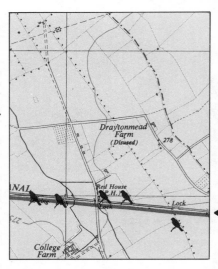

🔻 Little grebes all along canal.

🔻 Where streams and canal intersect, pause to watch for kingfishers. They may fish along the canal, but they nest in earth banks of streams through farmland.

🔻 Mistle thrushes appreciate the cover given by pollard foliage.

🔻 Stock doves are seen perching in, or flying around, the black poplars.

🔻 Tawny, barn and little owls: tawny and little owls may be seen perching on the tree stumps or telephone wires, from which they hunt. Barn owls quarter the ground in flight from dusk onwards, looking like huge, white moths. Little owls are also seen flying from perch to perch with a deeply undulating flight path.

🔻 Hobbies: flight outline like a huge swift.

🔻 Reed buntings in or near the reedbeds, or low over the fields.

🔻 Yellow wagtails nest here.

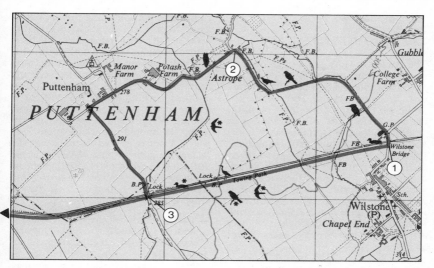

Spotted flycatchers around the dilapidated outhouse; pied wagtails on the lock house lawns.

Sedge warblers are skulkers, but not so much as other warblers. Closely observe the densest parts of the sedge when walking past. Footfall is enough to disturb one or more birds. May also be located by their song.

The best way to sight the reed warblers is to keep walking slowly, eyes on the reeds. The occasional disturbed bird will fly out over the water, returning after a circuit to hide deep in cover. Or, locate them by song: reed warblers often start singing if you clap your hands.

Water rails, moorhens, coot and tufted duck along the canal; in hard weather, water rails are sometimes seen well out of cover out on the ice.

Herons; skylarks over the open fields; goldfinches on the hawthorns (occasionally pruned); kestrels hunting over the open country.

Black poplars have brown-grey bark and their leaves in summer are grey-green; pollarded tree on right.

HEREFORD & WORCESTER

Malvern Hills
2¼ miles (3.5 km)
Landranger 150 766382 SO 63/73

The Malvern Hills are designated an Area of Outstanding Natural Beauty and are heavily visited both at weekends and holiday periods. The walk, approached from Castlemorton Common, an important area of low-lying wet scrubland, follows footpaths and tracks across a relatively quiet part of the Hills. Partly covered in mixed broadleaved woodland, including oak, beech, hazel, holly, yew and rowan, the area gives way to open scrub and hawthorn and attracts a rich variety of birdlife all year round. *Mud after rain and mud on climb through wood. Sheep graze the Common: drive carefully and keep dogs under control at all times.*

Time and season Excellent at all times. Spring is best for stonechats, ring ouzels, wheatears and good views of all woodland birds, and wintertime for buzzards, ravens, fieldfares and redwings. In spring, evening walks on the Common may be rewarded by grasshopper warblers.

Start From Great Malvern, take the A449 S towards Ross-on-Wye and at Little Malvern fork left on to the A4104 towards Upton upon Severn. At Welland crossroads turn right on to the B4208 and in about ¾ mile (1 km), at the sign for Castlemorton village, fork right on the minor road leading across Castlemorton Common. Continue for 1½ miles (2.5 km) to reach a large area on the right suitable for **parking**.

① From the parking area turn right, walk along the minor road for about 450 yards (400 m) and ② turn right to ascend the tarred track into the wood. At the old quarry ③ the track runs into a footpath. Continue straight ahead along the path through the wood until reaching a gate ④. Then follow the right-hand path, keeping the boundary fence to the left. In about 600 yards (500 m) the path emerges from, then runs alongside, News Wood. Soon after the path re-enters the wood, at ⑤, turn sharp right and follow the narrow path that leads directly uphill and joins other paths at the hill ridge ⑥. Take the path to the right, closest to the ridge and leading down the hill, descending gently to the Common and parking area. *Eastnor Park may be entered via the gate at ④. Follow the path straight ahead for about 500 yards (450 m) to the Obelisk, returning along the same route. The herd of red deer in the park is best observed from a distance and by standing quite still.*

➤ The jay has a harsh screeching call and is most easily spotted from outside the wood, where it remains high in the canopy searching for acorns. Look out for its white rump and blue and white markings on wings.

➤ In wintertime, roving tit flocks meander through the woods all along the route searching for food. Locate them by listening for their contact calls. Stand still and watch as they cross the pathway. Look out for treecreepers and goldcrests among the great, blue and long-tailed tits.

➤ Redstarts, with chestnut tails, are occasionally seen in spring. Wrens remain low in the vegetation, but can be located by their loud, scolding call. Yews are likely places to look and listen for goldcrests and coal tits.

➤ Woodpeckers excavate nesting holes in rotting wood. There are some examples along the path. Disused holes may be taken over by nuthatches, or even wasps and bees.

In spring, listen for the drumming of the great spotted woodpecker in the woods. The male has a red nape and red marking under the tail. Green woodpeckers give a loud, laughing call and can be identified by green plumage and yellow-green rump in flight.

Redwings and fieldfares, winter visitors, join resident thrushes to feed on the hawthorn berries alongside this path.

Ravens and buzzards may be spotted in winter, soaring on outstretched wings. Rooks and crows are present all year.

Yellowhammers sing in the scrub areas around the woods. In spring, the reeling song of grasshopper warblers can be heard on the Common out to the left, particularly in the evenings.

Kestrels frequently hover over the open hillsides in search of prey.

In early spring, ring ouzels occasionally break their northward journeys to feed in the area. They are distinguished from blackbirds by the white gorget or neck patch, and pale wing patches. Wheatears and stonechats may also be present during spring.

In late summer, listen for the gentle, twittering song of house martins, which gather in large numbers to feed on insects above the woodland edge and over the hills. Sure identification is by the all-white underparts, together with the white rump, which is conspicuous in flight. The upper-parts are dark blue, but they appear black except at close range.

Grey head and rump, the reddish-brown back and dark tail separate the fieldfare from all other species. Flocks look ragged.

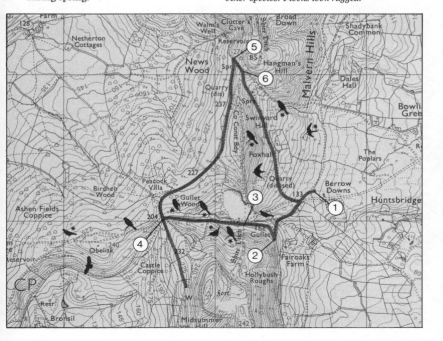

131

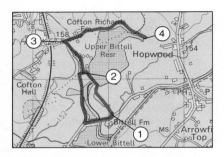

Bittell Reservoirs
3 miles (5 km) Landranger 139 021745

Two large reservoirs on the outskirts of Birmingham with numbers of wildfowl and some waders. *Open water*; the reservoirs are sometimes known as Barnt Green Reservoirs.

Winter wigeon, teal, goldeneye, snipe; **all year** great crested grebe, tufted duck, pochard.

Start Leave Birmingham S on the A441 (Redditch road). Two miles (3 km) from the outskirts of Birmingham, at a roundabout, take the fourth exit, the B4120, towards Barnt Green. Before entering the village turn right on to a minor road which follows the W edge of the Lower Bittell Reservoir and then crosses it on a causeway. **Parking** on the wide grass verges along this road.

① 200 yards (180 m) from the causeway turn left on to a footpath which leads to the SW edge of the Upper Bittell Reservoir. Follow the footpath to ② a track and continue N on this track ③, turning right after ⅓ mile (0.5 km) towards Cofton Richards Farm. Continue past farm on to footpath following N edge of Upper Bittell Reservoir. Where ④ the path leaves the water's edge, retrace to the farm, and turn left at ③. Return along track which leads to the W end of the causeway. Cross the lower reservoir via the causeway to ①.

The Knapp and Papermill
2 miles (3 km) Landranger 150 752522

This reserve, belonging to the Worcester Nature Conservation Trust, has an unusually large range of habitats for its size, supporting nearly 100 bird species together with about 400 flowering plants, 250 fungi, and 250 moths and butterflies. This kind of variety is one of those happy accidents of the English countryside, all the more interesting because it has been protected. The papermill, no longer in evidence, was a water-driven fuller's mill for making paper out of rags. The reserve wardens live at The Knapp House, and may be able to supply further information about the reserve. It is designated an SSSI. *Woods, orchard, garden, grassland, marshy fields, wide stream.*

Summer yellow wagtail, wood warbler; **winter** siskin, redpoll; **all year** mallard, moorhen, kingfisher, green woodpecker, great and lesser spotted woodpeckers, grey wagtail, dipper, goldcrest.

Start Leave Worcester SW on the A4103. In 3 miles (5 km) turn right and after 200 yards (180 m) left to Bransford, continuing along this road towards Alfrick Pound. After 2½ miles (4 km), before reaching Alfrick Pound, the road crosses Leigh Brook. **Car park** on the right, just before the bridge.

There is a circular nature trail around the reserve, beginning at The Knapp House. From the car park cross the bridge and walk up the hill. The Knapp House is on the left after about 150 yards (140 m).

Wyre Forest
¾ to 3 miles (1 to 5 km)
Landranger 138 743738

This is Forestry Commission property including some old natural oak and other deciduous trees in addition to the usual conifer plantations. The mixture supports a larger-than-usual variety of typical woodland birds. The Visitor Centre tells the story of the forest and describes its wildlife. *Woods*.

Summer wood warbler, pied flycatcher, redstart; **all year** sparrowhawk, kingfisher, grey wagtail, dipper, hawfinch.

Start From Kidderminster take the A456 W to Bewdley, then continue for 3 miles to the Forestry Commission Visitor Centre, picnic site and **car park**.

A waymarked forest walk starts from the picnic site and 2 colour-coded extensions give a maximum length of 3 miles.

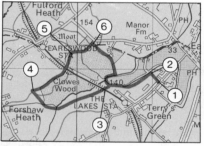

Clowes Wood
3 miles (5 km) Landranger 139 111737

A nature reserve of deciduous woodland owned by the Warwickshire Trust for Nature Conservation. *Woods, meadow, open to members of any county naturalists' trust, but non-members may use the route below, which follows public footpaths.*

Summer turtle dove, garden warbler, blackcap, whitethroat, willow warbler, chiffchaff, wood warbler, spotted flycatcher; **winter** siskin; **all year** woodpeckers, long-tailed tit, coal tit, treecreeper, nuthatch, redpoll, jay.

Start From Birmingham centre follow the A34 S in the direction of Stratford-

upon-Avon, but on the outer edge of the city turn right on to the B4102. After 2½ miles (4 km) turn right and then left to Terry's Green; The Lakes Station is ⅓ mile (0.5 km) from the start of the walk. **Parking** in Terry's Green.

① Take the footpath from the centre of Terry's Green leading NW towards Earlswood Lakes. Continue to the lakes, ② turning left along the S edge of the lakes. ③ Cross the railway line and continue along the S side of Clowes Wood. Follow the path ④ around the N side of Clowes Wood and recross the railway line by the footbridge. Follow the path another 300 yards (270 m) and ⑤ turn right into the wood. Continue to the road, where ⑥ the path turns SE back towards the lakes. Follow it to the SW tip of the lakes and retrace to Terry's Green along the original footpath.

Oversley Wood is a tiny remnant of Shakespeare's famous Forest of Arden. It is a mixture of natural woodland and Forestry Commission plantation, and some areas of coppice are said to date from Roman times. A mile-long (1.5 km) trail has been created by the Forestry Commission and in summer there are a variety of nesting birds. The wood lies immediately SE of Alcester, 6 miles (9.5 km) W of Stratford-upon-Avon.

Despite its location close to Birmingham, the variety of wetland habitats at Kingsbury Water Park attracts numbers of wildfowl all year. The park provides an information centre, hides and nature trails and is easily located by following signs from the A4097 NE out of Birmingham.

Only a few miles from Birmingham and Coventry, Hartshill Hayes Country Park is an area of park and woodland with a variety of breeding birds and interesting mixed flocks of passerines in winter. Follow signs from the A47 (Nuneaton–Birmingham road).

Stoke Floods
1¼ *miles (2 km) Landranger 140*
373792

A wetland reserve with varied birdlife on the edge of Coventry; winter wildfowl are the highlight; managed by the Warwickshire Nature Conservation Trust. *Open water, reedbeds, grassland; free to any conservation trust member, otherwise fee – contact county trust.*

Summer common sandpiper, common tern, spotted flycatcher, sedge warbler, blackcap, willow warbler, chiffchaff, yellow wagtail; **winter** greylag goose, teal, shoveler, pochard, shelduck, fieldfare, redwing; **all year** little grebe, great crested grebe, heron, Canada goose, ruddy duck, kestrel, water rail, snipe, great spotted woodpecker, meadow pipit, grey wagtail, stonechat, long-tailed, willow and coal tits, treecreeper, reed bunting, bullfinch, tree sparrow.

Start From the centre of Coventry take the A46 NE 1¼ miles (2 km) to a roundabout. Take the second exit and continue to a T-junction where turn right and immediately left. The reserve can be reached by any of the roads running E through the housing estate; **parking** on the E side of the estate.

From the housing estate walk E to the lake beside the River Sowe. Walk around the lake, then follow the path N along the river for ½ mile (0.8 km). Return by the same route.

Newbottle Spinney
1 *mile (1.5 km) Landranger 151*
515366

Newbottle Spinney is a fine area of mainly deciduous woodland which is managed as a nature reserve by the Northamptonshire Trust for Nature Conservation, and is open to the public at all times. The very varied population of woodland birds produces a splendid

Generally solitary, the common sandpiper is likely as not seen perching on some low object. In flight, wings appear bowed and flickering; shrill call.

dawn chorus. *Wood.*

Summer garden, willow and wood warblers, chiffchaff; **all year** barn, little and tawny owls, green woodpecker, great and lesser spotted woodpeckers, long-tailed, marsh, willow and coal tits, nuthatch, treecreeper, tree sparrow.

Start From Banbury follow the A41 S to the outskirts of Adderbury and then turn left on to a minor road to Kings Sutton. Turn left in Kings Sutton towards Charlton and after ¾ mile (1 km) turn left again on to the Newbottle road; trains to Kings Sutton, 1¼ miles (2 km) from the reserve. **Parking** on the right after 250 yards (230 m).

From the car park cross the road and follow the ride which leads clockwise around the edge of the wood, meeting the road again ¼ mile (0.5 km) further on. Cross the road again and take the ride on the left, which leads S through the wood towards the Charlton road. Before reaching the road, the ride veers right and enters a car parking area. A ride on the right leads from this car park back to the start of the walk.

Flitwick Moor
1¼ miles (3 km) Landranger 153 046354

Extraction of peat from this marshland area in the past has left a variety of habitats with different water levels which are now controlled by dams and sluices. The rich flora totals nearly 200 species, while insects and birds also occur in great variety. Parts of the Moor are owned or leased by the Bedfordshire and Huntingdonshire Naturalists' Trust as a nature reserve. *Marsh, meadow, woods; keep strictly to the public footpaths.*

Summer tree pipit, grasshopper, sedge, reed and garden warblers, blackcap, whitethroat, lesser whitethroat, willow warbler, chiffchaff; **winter** water rail, siskin; **all year** green woodpecker, redpoll.

Start From the A418 travelling S from Bedford, turn left in Ampthill on to the A507 (in the direction of Baldock). Turn right in Maulden, the next village, and continue to Folly Farm, opposite Jewson's Industrial Estate. Go down the farm road. **Car park** on the right, at the end of the track.

Follow the footpath from the car park across the wooded moor to a footbridge over the mid-drain. In 100 yards (90 m) enter a meadow and turn right. Follow the path across the meadow, turning right again and entering the wood before recrossing the mid-drain. At the reserve boundary the footpath turns left and leads back to the road. Turn right on to the road, back to Folly Farm.

The Lodge, Sandy
*¼, ½ or 1¼ miles (0.5, 0.8 or 2 km)
Landranger 153 188478*

The headquarters of the Royal Society for the Protection of Birds are housed in the Lodge, a Listed Building, and surrounded by 100 acres (40 ha) of woodland and heath. *Woods, scrub, heath,*

The flooded. disused gravel pits at Felmersham are a reserve of the Bedfordshire and Huntingdonshire Naturalists' Trust. The lakes, surrounded by grassland, scrub and hedgerows, attract a variety of water birds all times of the year, plus a number of warblers during the autumn. The reserve is not open to the general public, but access is free to members of any of the County Naturalists' Trusts. The entrance is on the Felmersham–Sharnbrook road, W of the A6 about 5 miles (8 km) N of Bedford.

Maulden Wood, part of Ampthill Forest, is a Forestry Commission wood of oak and pine with a rich bird population. There is a 1½-mile (2.5-km) nature trail through the wood, waymarked by the Commission, starting from the lay-by on the A6, 1 mile (1.5 km) N of Clophill.

open water; open all year Mon to Fri 9–5 and from Easter to Christmas on Sat; hides, picnic area, Reception Centre and Shop; free to members of the RSPB, otherwise fee.

Summer sand martin, tree pipit, garden warbler, blackcap, willow warbler, chiffchaff, spotted flycatcher; **winter** brambling, siskin, redpoll, crossbill; **all year** kestrel, green woodpecker, great and lesser spotted woodpeckers, goldcrest, coal tit, long-tailed tit, nuthatch, treecreeper.

Start From Sandy on the A1 turn E on to the B1042. Cross railway bridge on the outskirts of Sandy and after 1 mile (1.5 km) turn right up the drive signposted The Lodge. **Car park** at The Lodge.

There is a choice of 3 waymarked nature trails through the reserve.

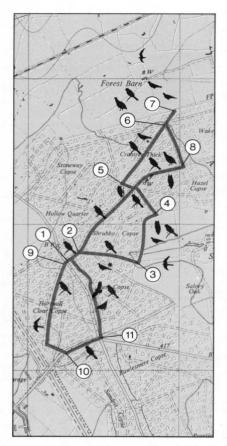

Salcey Forest
2 or 3 miles (3 or 5 km)
Landranger 152 792517 SP75

This is true mixed woodland, with oak a dominant species, and it is segmented by rides, so although the cover is dense in parts, most of the woodland birds can be seen at the forest edge along the rides. Salcey Lawn, at the centre, is no longer used for deer chases and its ancient oaks provide shelter for woodpeckers, owls and jackdaws. The range of passerines is quite wide, with **nightingales** and **spotted flycatchers** as specialities. Controlled by the Forestry Commission and managed in part as a reserve by the Northants Trust for Nature Conservation. *Mud after rain.*

Time and season Late spring and summer for visiting birds; summer evenings for woodcock and nightingale; first light for dawn chorus. Generally, morning watching is the most rewarding.

Start Leave Northampton S on the A508, turning left ½ mile (0.8 km) from the outskirts and passing through Wootton and Quinton; 2 miles (3 km) from the latter enter forest (both sides of road). In 200 yards (180 m) **parking** in the picnic area on the left.

① Join the main forest track (by lavatory block) and head E through the gate. In 25 yards (20 m) turn right ② on to the grassy track and continue to its end ③ – the large open area of Salcey Lawn. Turn left, following narrow trail along W side of Lawn, in forest edge. Take ④ the first main track on the left, pass pond on left, cross over main forest track (stone surface) and continue through beech avenue. In a few yards turn right ⑤ on to bridle track with its cherry tree border and continue to ⑥, the 5-way intersection of trails. Carry on across on to the narrow path – the second on the left – and continue to where it stops at farmland, ⑦. Retrace to ⑥ and take the second ride on the left which soon rejoins the main forest track, ⑧. Turn right and continue back to ①. For longer walk, cross the road from the lavatory block and ⑨ follow the main track into the forest, keeping left. Continue almost to its end (just before the M1) and turn left. On reaching the Hartwell road ⑩, turn left and left again at the road junction ⑪; carry on back to ①, visiting other car park areas on the way.

In Britain, the nightingale sings from deep cover; elsewhere – for example Mediterranean countries – it may perform openly.

Nightingales in this vicinity; warblers include blackcaps, chiffchaff and willow.

Mixed parties of tits in autumn include long-tailed and coal. Goldcrests are abundant. Numerous warblers are heard in summer, with garden warblers and whitethroats commonest. Tunnels in undergrowth made by muntjac deer.

Woodpigeon are common throughout the forest. Turtle doves are easily located in summer by the double purring call.

Kestrels hunt near the forest edge. Sparrowhawks possible; hobbies present in summer, but rare.

Tawny, little and occasionally barn owls use the old oaks. Little owls are sometimes seen on exposed branches in daytime. Stock doves and starlings also inhabit the old trees; redstarts occasionally.

Many finches, thrushes and tits come to the pool in early morning.

The holes in the beech trunks are made by woodpeckers. Early on spring mornings listen for the drumming of the great and lesser spotted – the latter's sounding less powerful than the former's.

The cherry avenue bridleway is attractive to thrushes and finches, especially chaffinches. Jays may also be glimpsed.

Pheasants and partridges on the farmland; skylarks in summer; search the fields for wheatears in autumn and early spring.

Crows and woodpigeons feed on the fields and return to the forest to roost.

Gulls fly over on winter evenings to roost at distant reservoirs; some overhead in daytime are passage birds and often accompanied in autumn by lapwings.

Pheasants, reared in captivity, are released in the woodland and are particularly numerous in autumn. Look for spotted flycatchers sallying forth for insects from perches at the forest edge.

Tawny owls are heard at night and occasionally seen at dusk crossing a ride.

The tree pipit, an uncommon summer visitor in this area, has an impressive 'parachuting' display flight in spring. Woodcock can be heard uttering the low croaking call that goes with their roding flights in summer.

Tree pipits in clearings; finches, tits and jays in the canopy or feeding on ground.

Kestrels in this area quarter the M1 verges for prey.

The low, damp thickets are nightingale terrain. The song is more obvious in late evening when other birds are less vocal; in late summer they are silent.

Regular feeding of birds from parked cars has made birds such as nuthatches, greenfinches and tits hand-tame. Watch them from the car park, using the car as a hide. Fieldfares and redwings are seen on the bushes in winter. Watch for sparrowhawks flying over the road.

Pitsford Reservoir
4 miles (6.5 km)
Landranger 152 755680 SP 66/76

Three principal habitats are visited by this combined route: the reservoir, with **gulls, waterfowl** and **migrants**; old parkland, with ancient oaks used by **jackdaws, starlings, stock doves, owls** and **woodpeckers**; and farmland, both arable and pasture, with such typical species as **yellowhammers, dunnocks** and **skylarks**. A bonus is the occasional **hobby**. *Some mud; the path SE of Pitsford may be ploughed in part.*

Time and season Winter for largest concentrations of wildfowl, and late evenings in winter for gulls; spring and autumn for terns and migrating hirundines. The village and farmland birdlife is richest in summer.

Start Pitsford, just off the A508 4 miles (7 km) N of Northampton town centre; regular buses from Northampton. **Parking** by roadside near the Griffin pub – opposite the bus stop.

① From the pub continue towards the village crossroads and ② leave on the road signposted 'Reservoir Car Park'. On the outskirts of the village, use the footpath on the right, running parallel to the road. At the hilltop ③ enter the reservoir car park and skirt the perimeter fence clockwise, rejoining the road at the lower gate ④. Turn left along the road, cross the causeway and enter Moulton Grange parkland over the cattle grid. Follow the road to the intersection ⑤ and then retrace to Pitsford village crossroads, ②, where turn left heading for Moulton (signposted). In 1¼ miles (2 km) cross stile on left (opposite a track and just before Stud Farm) and ⑥ head back to Pitsford along footpath following field edges (using large building with cupola as landmark). This means making for the NW corner of the first field, leaving by gate in W edge near

stone wall, and ⑦ keeping to the left edge of the next 2 fields until close to buildings, then following hedge towards rear gardens. Cross the stile ⑧ and re-enter the village.

➤ Collared doves are common.

➤ Summer visitors such as chiffchaffs, willow warblers and house martins are plentiful in this area.

➤ Tits and thrushes in the bushes, treecreepers in the trees, magpies and jays over the fields.

➤ Kestrels commonly prey on mice and voles around the car park.

➤ In spring and autumn, black, common and arctic terns pause here on passage in order to feed. Many gulls gather to roost at dusk in winter. Most are black-headed, but common, herring and black-backed also occur.

➤ Snipe, redshank, dunlin and other waders are seen on the exposed mud when the water is low, most often in autumn and winter.

➤ In autumn and winter the large gatherings of duck include goldeneye, goosander and wigeon. Coots are always present as are great crested and little grebes. Swans may include wintering Bewick's. Canada geese are resident. Other duck such as tufted, pochard and mallard are present for much of the year, but numbers fluctuate.

➤ In summer and at passage times, large concentrations of swifts and hirundines feed on flying insects.

➤ Grey herons regularly feed at the water's edge. Pied wagtails are common, but look out for grey wagtails too.

➤ Kingfishers are occasionally seen in undisturbed areas.

The old parkland trees are used by jackdaws and stock doves for nesting.

The ringing 'laugh' of the green woodpecker, and the drumming of the great spotted woodpecker are heard here, especially in spring.

Redwings, fieldfares and other thrushes feed on the berries in winter.

Tawny and little owls can be heard calling at dusk in the parkland and mature gardens. (See also between ② and ⑥.)

Great spotted woodpeckers often enter these gardens to feed at bird tables.

The roadside hedgerows provide cover for yellowhammers and dunnocks.

The quarry area has diverse flora and fauna, providing kestrels with good hunting opportunities. Hobbies may be seen in summer, especially towards dusk.

The rough vegetation attracts goldfinches and linnets in autumn.

There are goldcrests in the canopy of the belt of conifers on the S of the road.

Yellow wagtails and skylarks on the fields in summer; wrens near the walls.

In autumn and winter lapwings (many on passage) stop on the farmland.

Small numbers of partridge breed in the area; they are generally most easily seen in winter.

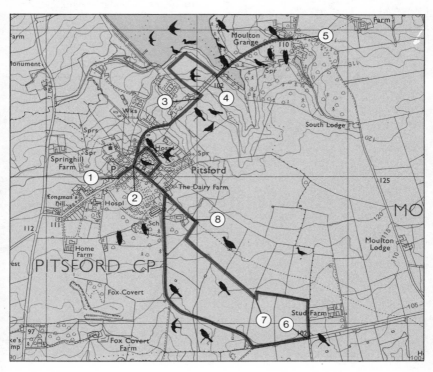

Long Mynd
*4½ miles (7 km) Landranger 137 424901
SO 49/59*

Exceptionally close views of raptors –
especially **buzzards** – searching for prey
are the highlight of this route.

Essentially an upland valley walk,
3 main habitats are visited: grassland,
covered with bracken in summer, where
wheatears and **stonechats** are typical;
farmland, with various broadleaved
trees attracting **summer visitors**; while
the heather-covered higher parts may
well produce **ring ouzels** and **red grouse**.

Time and season Most interesting in
summer.

Start From Little Stretton off the A49
take the minor road to Minton. Stay on
this road through the village and continue ½ mile (0.8 km). **Parking** on the
left verge immediately before the small
bridge and before the turning on the
right to the farm. Do not obstruct gate
to field. Alternatively park on the wide
verge of the access track on the right
to the farm.

① From the bridge walk S along the
road for 15 yards (14 m) and turn right
on to the farm track. Take the public
footpath from here: it basically runs
parallel to the stream right to the top
of the hollow, 2 miles (3 km) distant.
Pass farm buildings and house ② and
later Knolls plantation on the left. Continue following the path, which begins
to rise near the head of the hollow. Pass
over the small brook ③ and remain on
path until ④ it joins the road. Here take
the wide footpath on the right leading
to Packetstone Hill. ⑤ Turn right at the
junction with the broad footpath run-

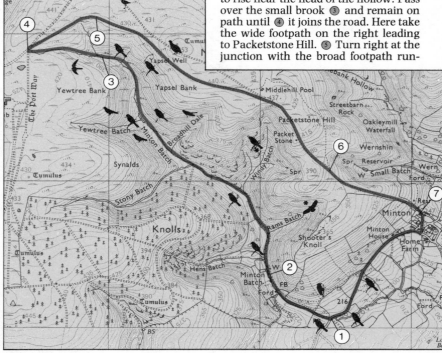

SHROPSHIRE

ning along the spine of the hill. Continue 1¼ miles (2 km) to ⑥ the junction with another path and carry straight on to Minton ⑦ – about ½ mile (0.8 km), ignoring the path to the right which follows the contour of the hill. Near end of path, go through field gate and bear right in centre of group of farm buildings, passing houses on the right. Join road and continue ½ mile (0.8 km) to ①.

Redstarts (summer) frequent these deciduous trees, and spotted flycatchers sally for insects from perches.

Green woodpeckers make their nests in holes in these trees; the bird is often heard calling a loud 'quen-quen-quen' before being seen. Also look for it searching out ants on the slopes of the hollow.

In autumn, mixed tit flocks, including blue, great, long-tailed and willow, feed along the overgrown hawthorn hedge. The birds call constantly when feeding.

Fine views of buzzards in search of prey in the small valley to the NE; stay still, and do not try to obtain closer views: the birds will merely glide away.

Goldcrests and coal tits inhabit Knolls plantation and may be seen feeding high up, passing from tree to tree.

Due to the rich insect population of the bracken and heather, meadow pipits are the most common birds of the hollow. Look for them flying a few feet above the vegetation and listen for the thin, squeaky 'tsiip-tsiip'.

Two or 3 cuckoos usually feed in the hollow in summer. They are normally seen in summer perching on hawthorn bushes halfway up the slope.

Several pairs of tree pipits hold territories in the valley; in spring watch for the vertical display flight with the 'parachuting' return to the top of bushes; a

good opportunity to separate the bird from the similar meadow pipit.

Magpies breed in the hollow. They feed on the abundance of carrion supplied by the dead sheep. The birds also eat eggs – especially meadow pipits'.

Grey wagtails frequent fast-flowing, rocky parts of the stream, feeding on insects near the water surface. The birds breed near some of the adjoining streams.

Jays nest in Knolls plantation and visit the slopes in search of food.

The stonechats are easily recognized by their call – the sound of 2 pebbles being knocked together. They often perch on the bracken or gorse.

In summer listen, and look for singing ring ouzels on rocks or bushes, particularly in the morning. They are usually seen from the bottom of the valley on the upper, heather-clad parts of the slopes. They are shy, and retire if approached.

Kestrels.

Curlews are vocal here in early spring, their 'bubbling' call being easily recognized and audible over considerable distances. Males display on the upper parts of the slopes.

Red grouse nest in the heather. The males often call from rocks on the top of slopes. When approached, they fly a few feet above the heather, then glide to alight after say 70 yards (65 m).

Whitethroats sing from the top of the hedgerow. The white chin is conspicuous, even at a distance, and is a help in locating the bird; another insect-feeder.

Yellowhammers also sing from the tops of the hedges, or from branches. The male's bright yellow face and chin are particularly conspicuous.

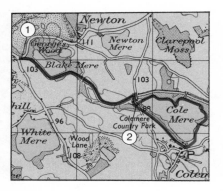

Male goosander, one of the easier duck to identify at long range. The green head, long red bill and black back are set off by considerable areas of white on the breast and flanks.

Shropshire Meres
5 miles (8 km) Landranger 126 407345

These are a series of natural, water-filled hollows, some having become in-filled to form peat bogs. The route visits Blake and Cole Meres, but The Mere, the largest, with its newly established heronry and easy public access, is also worth a visit. *Open water, reeds.*

All year great crested grebe, heron, Canada goose, tufted duck, pochard, kingfisher; **summer** reed warbler, yellow wagtail; **winter** wigeon, teal, goldeneye, goosander; **passage** black and common terns.

Start From Shrewsbury take the A528 NW towards The Mere; **parking** on the roadside along the SW edge of The Mere.

Walk SE along the A528 to ① the junction with the A495. Join the canal towpath here and follow it 1 mile (1.5 km), past Blake Mere, to ② a road bridge. Cross the canal via the bridge and walk around the perimeter of Cole Mere. Recross the canal by the same bridge and return along the towpath.

Earl's Hill
3 miles (5 km) Landranger 126 409048

This rocky hill, over 1,000 feet (305 m)

high and overlooking grassy or wooded slopes, is managed as a nature reserve by the Shropshire Conservation Trust. A 1-mile (1.5-km) nature trail guides visitors around the reserve, and there is a Conservation Centre, housed in a restored barn, which supplies trail guides and other information. *Cliffs, scree, woods, grassland; open Sat and Sun afternoons from Easter to end of Sept, and at other times by arrangement; free to members of any conservation trust, otherwise small fee.*

All year buzzard, green woodpecker, great and lesser spotted woodpecker; **summer** wood warbler, pied flycatcher, redstart.

Start Take the A488 SW from Shrewsbury to Pontesbury. **Parking** in the village, behind the Alexander and Duncan garage.

Walk S along a narrow lane behind the garage to the reserve entrance; follow the marked nature trail.

Belvide Reservoir
3½ miles (5.5 km)
Landranger 127 855107

This reservoir, lying close to the Shropshire Union Canal, attracts large num-

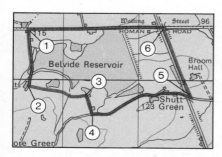

bers of wildfowl during the winter, while its natural banks provide food for waders. *Open water, farmland, woods.*

Summer yellow wagtail; **winter** wigeon, goldeneye, goosander; **passage** garganey, greenshank, common and green sandpipers, black tern; **all year** pochard, tufted duck, ruddy duck.

Start From Wolverhampton head N on the A449 and after 5 miles (8 km), at the roundabout, turn left on to the A5. **Parking** by the roadside in 3–4 miles.

① From the A5 a track runs S to the W edge of the reservoir. Follow the track past the reservoir and then ② turn left on to a footpath opposite 'The Hawkshutts'. After ½ mile (0.8 km) ③ turn right along a track to a minor road, where ④ turn left to the road and continue through Shutt Green to the Shropshire Union Canal. Cross and ⑤ turn left on to the tow path, which leads back to the A5. ⑥ Turn left on to the A5 and follow the N edge of the reservoir back to ①.

Coombes Valley
3½ miles (5.5 km)
Landranger 119 009534

Steep-sided Coombes Valley, with its fast-flowing stream, is ideal dipper territory, while the wooded slopes support a variety of breeding birds and mixed flocks of passerines in winter. Owned by

RSPB, managed jointly with the Staffs. Nature Conservation Trust. *Woods, river, heath, meadow; open 10–6 on Tues, Thurs, Sat and Sun from 1 April to 31 Aug and on Sat and Sun only from 1 Sept to 31 Dec. Closed from 1 Jan to 31 March; Information Centre and hides; free to members, otherwise fee; mud.*

Summer tree pipit, wood warbler, pied flycatcher, redstart; **all year** sparrowhawk, woodcock, long-eared owl, tawny owl, green woodpecker, great spotted woodpecker, lesser spotted woodpecker, grey wagtail, dipper, nuthatch.

Start From Leek take the A523 SE to Bradnop. 1 mile (1.5 km) after Bradnop turn right along the minor road directed to Apesford. Look out for the RSPB sign in about 1 mile (1.5 km); **car park** at the reserve.

Report to the Information Centre on arrival.

First flooded in 1952, Blithfield Reservoir now ranks as one of the most important in Britain for wildfowl, and as one of the best inland sites in Middle England for seeing a wide variety of birds. It covers 790 acres (320 ha) of the Blithe Valley and is crossed by the B5013 (Rugeley to Uttoxeter road), from which excellent views of the reservoir can be obtained.

Up to 3,000 duck are present in winter: wigeon, mallard, teal, shoveler, pochard, tufted duck, goldeneye and goosander are the most numerous. A special feature is 200 or more ruddy duck – a substantial proportion of the British population.

Cormorants now use the reservoir in some numbers, there is a big gull roost, while spring and autumn bring many migrating terns, waders and passerines. Ospreys occur every year on passage, and many other rarities.

Cannock Chase
*7 miles (11 km) Landranger 127 985156
SJ 81/91*

A route through the heart of this area of woodland and lowland heath, giving real opportunities of seeing the typical birds of those habitats, among them **whinchats, stonechats, grasshopper warblers, nightjars, redstarts, tits** and **owls. Woodcock** nest on the woodland floor. Most of the route is in a motorless zone. *From ⑫ to ⑭ is rough and badly gullied in parts. For this reason evening walkers are recommended to go as far as ⑧ and retrace.*

Time and season May and June for breeding species; evenings from 7 to 10.30 for woodcock roding over Sherbrook Valley together with nightjars and grasshopper warblers; any time of day during passage, Sept and April.

Start From the Brocton crossroads about 4 miles (6.5 km) SE of Stafford on the A34 continue S about ¼ mile (0.5 km) and turn left, following road signposted Hednesford and German Cemetery. In nearly 2 miles (3 km) turn left at the next sign to the Cemetery. **Parking** about 200 yards (180 m) down road by memorial and lodge.

① From parking continue down road until it joins a gravel track, and continue on this for ½ mile (0.8 km) where ② 2 tracks are visible; turn left to the marker post and then right on to the track marked 'Stepping Stones'. Carry on to ③ the Forestry Commission notice board, then continue to ④ where a track crosses. Carry straight on to where ⑤ the forestry on the right ends and the valley, with stream, opens out. Continue on track about another ⅓ mile (0.5 km) to ⑥ where a number of tracks converge; carry straight on following the 'Stepping Stones' sign. ⑦ Continue into the coppice; in another ⅔ mile (1 km) reach the Stepping Stones ⑧,

where turn left uphill into woodland. Continue along the main path, ignoring small paths joining left and right, winding through a more open area and reaching ⑨ the small car park at Coppice Hill. Continue along the track by the marker post to Camp Road. At Camp Road ⑩ turn left and at the second ramp bear left across an open grassy area to the top of the hill, where there is a glacial boulder mounted on a plinth and a trig. point ⑪. Go past these to the track and walk across to the top of the heathery bank for views across the Sherbrook Valley. Return to the track and continue to the left, past the motorless zone barrier, on the track curving across the heath. ⑫ Where the track forks, bear left across the heather slope to the brow of the hill and then down into the valley, joining the outward route at ④. Turn right to ①.

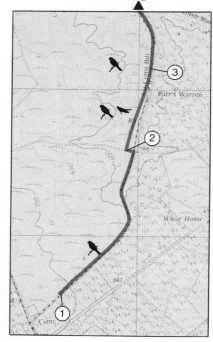

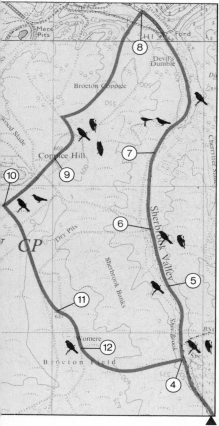

in the area of scattered trees around the notice board.

Another likely spot for the above species and also green woodpeckers.

The marshy area with prominent clumps of tussocky sedge attracts reed buntings, wrens and grasshopper warblers. The latter can be heard at dusk, often using small pines as song posts. Stonechats can often be seen perching boldly on bracken fronds, 'chacking' loudly and flying to feed in the marshy area.

The small alder spinney by the stream attracts warblers, and in autumn and winter tits, redpolls and siskins; another likely spot for green woodpeckers.

Nightjars and woodcock can occur from ④ onwards, but the 300 yards (270 m) from ⑦ before the start of Brocton Coppice is the best place to listen for nightjars in summer. They rarely start their churring song before 9.30 pm, but may be seen at dusk over the path. Woodcock, looking like large bats, with a low croaking note, also pass through this area on their roding flight – a display flight with slow wingbeats round a definite circuit, often several miles long. In October, jays are a frequent sight, carrying acorns out to the heathland for burying.

Small woodland species along the stream, including treecreepers, goldcrests and willow tits.

At the top of the rise, where there are a number of oaks up to 300 years old, look for tits, redstarts and green and great spotted woodpeckers; also a possibility of tawny owls.

Look among the tops of the thorn bushes to the left for a great grey shrike, which occurs fairly regularly from October to March. Fieldfares, redwings, blackbirds and occasionally ring ouzels frequent the bushes in autumn or winter.

A likely area for wheatears and meadow pipits on passage.

Look for robins, chaffinches, coal, great and blue tits and goldcrests in the pines and birches. The scattered birches and self-sown pines are a likely spot for tree pipits in summer.

In this open area watch for meadow pipits, whinchats and the cuckoo; the bracken slopes on the left of the track are also likely to produce these species over the next mile.

In summer tree pipits, willow warblers, yellowhammers and stonechats are likely

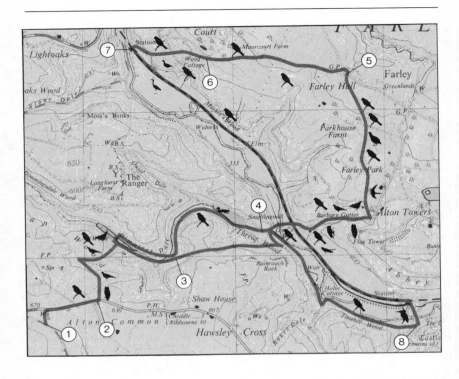

Mid-Churnet Valley

7 miles (11 km) Landranger 119 047426
SK O4

In contrast to the moorland of the upper Churnet Valley, and the flood meadows of the lower, the mid-Churnet is well wooded, with much mature timber besides small plantations. A fine range of mainly **woodland birds** can be seen. In recent years, efforts to clean the river have had excellent results. Fish numbers have increased and this has brought, for example, more kingfishers to the area.

Time and season All year; dawn and dusk choruses delightful in May and June.

Start From Cheadle take the B5032

towards Alton. In 2 miles (3 km) pass through Threapwood and in ¼ mile (0.5 km) take the lane to the right signposted Bradley and Great Gate (Greatgate on map). After about 300 yards (270 m) ample **parking** on verges.

① Enter field on left, cross marshy area, pass Cuckoo Cottage and turn right on to the road towards Alton. In 250 yards (230 m) ② pass through stone stile on left. From stile follow down through fields and woods to Dimmings Dale pools, where turn right and follow track about ¼ mile (0.5 km). (This was a private coach road on the Earl of Shrewsbury's estate, constructed during the early 1800s, when the large beeches were also planted.) At the old stone steps ③ leave the track (taking second path on right having left pools) and walk up wood into field. Keep stone wall on left, pass cottage on left and descend through woodland on path to road at Rambler's Retreat tea room ④. Cross road and take track opposite, going over Lord's Bridge, then cross bridge over disused railway. Continue on track, in ¼ mile (0.5 km) passing ancient chained oak (Druid.associations) and at lodge pass into field behind it. Continue across fields on track and in Farley ⑤ turn left down lane towards Oakamoor. Opposite Moor Court lower entrance ⑥ take footpath on left through fields about ⅓ mile (0.5 km) to the former Oakamoor station ⑦. Here follow disused railway line to Alton – about 1½ miles (2.5 km). At Alton old station go on to road and cross bridge. (The magnificent castle was designed by Pugin.) Turn right ⑧ along lane towards Oakamoor. In ¾ mile (1 km) reach the Rambler's Retreat. Continue along path past old smelting mill to ③ and follow the path which crosses the stream on the right, keeping the first 2 pools to the left. At top of second pool cross to foot of steep woodland path used on outward route. Retrace to ①.

Mistle thrushes, fieldfares and redwings flock here in autumn. A likely spot to see yellowhammers, nuthatches, little owl and turtle dove.

Jays in and around the woods; long-tailed, marsh and willow tits, plus goldcrests in this damp woodland; also willow warblers and chiffchaffs, blackcaps, garden warblers and treecreepers.

Whitethroats frequent the herbage in the vicinity of the bridge.

A likely stretch for whitethroats, redstarts and wood warblers. Listen and look for cuckoos. In the more open area to the left, watch for the tree pipit in song flight (summer). The mature trees hold green and great spotted woodpeckers.

The trees to the left hold pied flycatchers, redstarts and turtle doves; on the right, nuthatches; woodcock nest on the woodland floor and it is a likely spot for the dedicated to see the tawny owl at daybreak.

Kestrels and sparrowhawks fairly regular round most of the route.

Tree sparrows likely.

Another flocking place for mistle thrushes, fieldfares and redwings; Partridges occasionally seen.

Watch for finch flocks – goldfinches, linnets and redpolls. In summer, skylarks perform over the open areas.

Blackcaps and garden warblers.

Yellowhammers likely along this typical, old-fashioned English lane.

Scan these trees carefully for lesser whitethroats and spotted flycatchers. Look for finch flocks in the area to the left – greenfinches, bullfinches, linnets, redpolls and siskins. Swifts in summer.

Snipe, heron and pied wagtails in the marshy area; herons also to the right, near the river.

Listen, and search for the grasshopper warbler in the overgrown patches in the ½ mile (0.8 km) from Oakamoor Station. Another likely stretch of woodland for blackcaps and garden warblers.

Scan the river for grey wagtails – especially frequent round the weir.

The bridge is a suitable place to watch for kingfishers, which occur all along the river.

Tufted duck (irregular), mallard and little grebes on the pool.

Bramblings, feeding on the beech mast; redstarts again.

Charnwood Forest
*5 miles (8 km) Landranger 140 522098
SK 40/50 and SK 41/51*

Charnwood Forest's rocky outcrops, bracken-covered slopes and large expanses of woodland have a rich and varied bird population. All 3 **woodpeckers** breed; there is a fine variety of **warblers** and winter brings **wildfowl** to Cropston Reservoir. The route passes through Bradgate Park, birthplace of Lady Jane Grey, the 9-day Queen of England. The park, formerly the seat of the Grey family, is managed by a group of voluntary trustees through the Bradgate Park Estate Office in Leicester.

Time and season Interesting all year, but avoid in July and August, when the Park is most popular with visitors. An early start will often be rewarded. Spring is the peak period.

Start Leave Leicester on the B5327, passing through Anstey to Newton Linford. **Car park** on right by church.

① From car park go through gate into park and follow metalled road beside River Lin. ② Leaving the wooded hillside and entering an open area, there is a plaque on the right of the road; turn left to follow wide track through gate and uphill to Elder Plantation. At the top of the hill, where there is ③ a junction of paths, bear right, walking along the plantation edge. As 'Old John' comes into view the path forks ④; take the right-hand path and continue away from Elder Plantation keeping a group of scattered trees to the right. On joining the wide firebreak ⑤ turn left, then take first narrow path to right. Continue to where ⑥ the tracks converge and go straight on, ignoring the track leading away right. Continue through clumps of silver birch, leaving Sliding Stone Enclosure to the right, heading straight on down the hill to the gate in the wall. ⑦ Go through the gate and over the stile,

following the wide track downhill to the B5330. ⑧ Cross road and enter Swithland Wood through gap in wall; follow the track which keeps close to the boundary wall on the left. ⑨ Where paths converge by a gap in the boundary wall turn right and follow track past slate quarry waste to stone road, where ⑩ turn right and walk to bridge over stream. ⑪ Just before bridge, walk down steps and cross the small footbridge. Follow the well-worn track diagonally across the field, ⑫ crossing the stile and turning left on to the B5330; in about 175 yards (160 m) turn right into the car park. ⑬ Go through the gate and follow the metalled road, inspecting Cropston Reservoir. There are several vantage points from which one can see over or through the wall. ⑭ Just before the deer barn and lavatories turn left and walk down to the wall to inspect the bottom end of the reservoir. Retrace steps and continue along the road with open grassland on the left. At the end of the meadow ⑮ turn right and walk away from the road following the dry stone wall. Pause just before the gate at the top at the low piece of wall to examine the area to the left. ⑯ Go through the gate and turn left; continue, looking over the wall wherever possible. At the next gate ⑰ turn left and immediately right. Follow the path back to the metalled road and retrace to ①.

↙ Swallows, house martins and swifts.

↜ Moorhens nest along the river.

↘ Flocks of jackdaws nest in the holes in the old oaks; stock doves and woodpigeons can be found in their tops.

↘ Yellowhammers and reed buntings are the main birds of the bracken slopes, but linnets are also seen and whinchats sometimes breed.

◀ Nuthatches, tits and thrushes inhabit Elder Plantation. Nuthatches use mud to reduce the diameter of an old woodpecker nest hole to their own size requirement.

Meadow pipits in display flight here.

Jays, wary birds, like the quieter areas.

Fieldfares and redwings occur on these open fields in winter.

All 3 woodpeckers breed here; look for their holes and listen for the drumming of the great and lesser spotted. Wood warblers can be found in the area.

Wildfowl quite often haul out here to rest. Mallard are the most common, but in winter there are wigeon and goldeneye too. The great crested grebe is also present.

Skylarks perform their song flights over the bracken slopes.

The bottom end of the reservoir holds a variety of water birds. There is a gull roost and a regular early autumn gathering of lapwings and snipe. Other waders occur on passage.

There are frequent sightings of the little owl and green woodpecker in this area.

Partridges nest in this long grass.

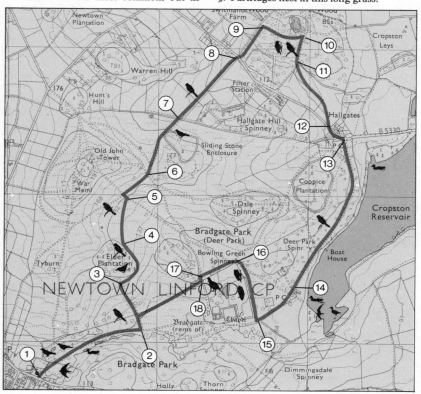

The Wash at Freiston Shore and Witham Mouth
4 miles (6.5 km) Landranger 131 398421

This is a really exceptional area – from the walker's and the birdwatcher's point of view, with the one caution that it only comes into its own at high tide. The low-water mark is up to 1 mile (1.5 km) from the outer sea wall, so the birds can spread out over a vast area, making observation difficult. At high tide, however, the concentrations are impressive, and some exciting rarities crop up. The marshes are generally undisturbed, except for aircraft overhead; an inhospitable, but often beautiful place. *Saltmarsh, sand and mudflats; take care not to be cut off by the tide.*

Spring gadwall, scaup, long-tailed duck, goldeneye, marsh harrier, avocet, black-tailed godwit, whimbrel, spotted redshank, greenshank, kittiwake, grey wagtail, wheatear with Montagu's harrier, osprey, hobby, purple sandpiper, little gull and black redstart as scarcities; **summer** little ringed plover, common sandpiper, Sandwich, common and little terns, turtle dove, hirundines, tree pipit, yellow wagtail, warblers, spotted flycatcher; **autumn** red-necked grebe, gannet, golden plover, little stint, ruff, green sandpiper, arctic skua, black tern, with occasional rarities including grey phalarope and long-tailed skua; **winter** red-throated diver, black-throated diver, little grebe, great crested grebe, pink-footed goose, brent goose,

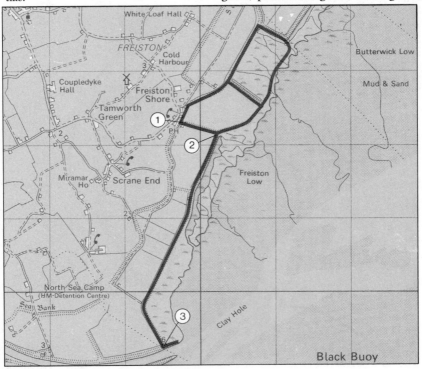

wildfowl, merlin, knot, snipe, bar-tailed godwit, curlew, redshank, turnstone, long-eared owl, meadow pipit, rock pipit, fieldfare, redwing, brambling, twite, red-poll, snow bunting, reed bunting.

Start From Boston follow unclassified roads via Fishtoft to Freiston Shore, where there is adequate **parking** in front of the old sea bank by The Plummer's public house, or the pub's **car park**.

① Turn right out of the pub car park, go through the turnstile and on to the sea wall. Inspect the reclaimed marsh to the left and right. Continue about 400 yards (350 m) out to the new sea bank ② and spend plenty of time watching the marsh directly ahead. Turn right and walk 2 miles (3 km) to the end of the sea wall at the mouth of the River Witham ③. Stop and inspect this area, which is the best in the locality. Retrace via ② to ①. *From The Plummer's it is also possible to walk N along sea walls to Butterwick Marshes, indeed to improvise a number of routes, using rights of way as marked on the map.*

Ropsley Rise Wood, Kesteven
½ *mile (O. 8 km) Landranger 130 972347*

An area of mixed coniferous and deciduous woodland. *Woods; keep strictly to the Forest Trail.*

Summer turtle dove, nightjar, garden warbler, blackcap, whitethroat, chiff-chaff, spotted flycatcher; **winter** siskin; **all year** long-eared owl, 3 woodpeckers, goldcrest, long-tailed tit, nuthatch, tree-creeper, redpoll.

Start From the B1176 turn left on to a minor road to Ropsley. After 1 mile (1.5 km) the road runs along the S edge of Ropsley Rise Wood; **parking** at the picnic site in the SE corner of the wood.

Follow the Forestry Commission's trail – directions on board.

Eyebrook Reservoir
5 miles (8 km) Landranger 141 847947

A 400-acre (160-ha) reservoir with natural banks, excellent for wildfowl in winter and waders in autumn, when low water levels expose mud areas. Goosanders are regular visitors – numbers may reach 200. *Open water, marsh, plantations.*

Winter Bewick's swan, gadwall, wigeon, pintail, goldeneye, goosander; **passage** black tern, greenshank, common, wood, green and curlew sand-pipers, ringed plover, dunlin, little stint, ruff; **all year** great crested and little grebes, heron, pochard, tufted duck.

Start From Corby take the A6003 N towards Caldecott. 1 mile (1.5 km) N of Rockingham, just before reaching Caldecott, turn left on to a minor road, passing through Great Easton towards Horn-inghold. In ⅔ mile (1 km) turn right, towards the reservoir, **parking** at side of road after ½ mile (0.8 km).

Follow the minor road along the edge of the reservoir for 1½ miles (2.5 km), turning right soon after the end of the reservoir, and following the road as it doubles back along the other side of the water. After 1 mile (1.5 km) the road turns away from the reservoir towards Stoke Dry. Return by same route.

> The Rutland Water Nature Reserve is a notable refuge for waterfowl and waders. It consists of part of the W end of the Rutland Water reservoir, enhanced by tree-planting and specially created lagoons and islands. One section of the reserve is open to the public from Good Friday to the end of Oct on Sat, Sun and Bank Holidays, 12–5; hides; entry charge. From Oakham take the A6003 S and turn off to Manton, taking the first left after the village.

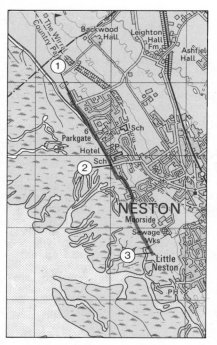

Gayton Sands, Dee Estuary
3 miles (5 km) Landranger 117
274789

In the Dee estuary, the receding tide leaves expanses of mudflats rich in invertebrates, providing a rich feeding ground for waders, whose numbers, in winter, may reach 140,000. Gayton Sands, indeed the whole estuary, is designated an SSSI and is owned by the RSPB. *Mudflats, saltmarsh.*

Summer sedge and reed warblers; **winter** cormorant roost, pintail, hen harrier, peregrine, merlin, water rail, grey plover, knot, bar-tailed godwit, brambling and twite; **all year** shelduck, oystercatcher, dunlin, redshank, skylark.

Start From Wallasey or Birkenhead follow the A551 S to the roundabout at Heswall, where take the A540 in the direction of Chester. After ½ mile (0.8 km) turn right on to the B5135 to Parkgate and Neston. Make for the estuary, where the road turns sharply left, with the Boathouse Restaurant on the right; trains to Neston. **Car park** just past the restaurant, from which the estuary can be viewed.

① Walk back to the B5135 and continue S for ½ mile (0.8 km). Where ② the road bends sharply to the left, continue straight on to join a footpath leading past houses and to the marshes. In just over ½ mile (0.8 km), ③, where the path turns left towards the town, turn and retrace to ①.

Delamere Forest
2–3 miles (3–5 km)
Landranger 117 552703

This remnant of a vast and ancient forest has been largely replanted by the Forestry Commission, and is now mostly coniferous; nonetheless, the species list is quite varied. *Forest.*

Summer tree pipit, blackcap, whitethroat, willow warbler, chiffchaff, wood warbler, redstart; **passage** siskin, crossbill; **all year** sparrowhawk, tawny owl, green woodpecker, great and lesser spotted woodpeckers, goldcrest, long-tailed tit, coal tit, redpoll.

Start From Chester take the A51 E for 3 miles (5 km) then fork left on to the A54 to Kelsall and fork left again, 2 miles (3 km) after Kelsall, on to the A556. After a further mile (1.5 km) turn left on to the B5152 at Delamere. Continue for 1½ miles (2.5 km) and then turn left to the railway station. In another ½ mile (0.8 km) is the Forest Office and a **car park**.

Follow any of the 4 waymarked Forest Walks shown by the Information Board.

Rostherne Mere
¾ mile (1 km) Landranger 109
743835

Rostherne Mere is a deep lowland lake of outstanding importance for wildfowl, designated a National Nature Reserve and owned by the Nature Conservancy Council. Large numbers of duck use the mere as a daytime roost, flying at dusk to night-time feeding grounds: up to 4,000 mallard and 2,500 teal have been recorded. In addition, up to 20,000 gulls (the majority black-headed and herring, but also including lesser black-backed, great black-backed and little) come here to roost. The reserve is not open to the public, but it can be viewed from the road in several places, and there is a hide (permits required – contact well in advance Mr D. A. Clarke, 13, Kingston Drive, Sale, M33 2FS) near Rostherne Church. *Open water, woods, scrub, farmland.*

All year great crested grebe, little grebe, cormorant, Canada goose, mallard, teal, pochard, tufted duck, sparrowhawk, moorhen, coot; **summer** reed warbler, yellow-wagtail; **winter** wigeon, pintail, shoveler, gadwall, goldeneye, goosander, ruddy duck, water rail; **passage** Bewick's swan, shelduck, kittiwake, black, common and arctic terns.

Start From Manchester take the A56 S to the M56 roundabout, where take the A556 (Chester) road. After 1 mile (1.5 km) turn left along Manor Lane to Rostherne. **Parking** in the village.

From the village walk back along Manor Lane to Rostherne Church and enter the churchyard, which gives good views over the mere and access to the hide. Return to the road and continue for 300 yards (270 m) to a footpath which gives further views across the mere. Return by the same route.

Bar-tailed godwit: a relatively large wader with long bill and legs; summer plumage is orange-brown. In flight, the slightly upturned bill, brownish upperparts and white V on the back are diagnostic.

The Goyt Valley
5¾ miles (9 km) Landranger 119 013756

The River Goyt, from its source down to the small village of Taxal, runs through a steep-sided valley of great variety. The river is dammed in two places, forming the Fernilee and Errwood Reservoirs, and the road from the A537 to the car park at the start of the walk is itself a good birdwatching route. The Goyt Valley is the first area of open country to operate a traffic-free system. *Open water, river, woods, moor, farmland.*

Summer common sandpiper, curlew, golden plover, whinchat, tree pipit, chiffchaff, wood warbler, wheatear, redstart, ring ouzel; **winter** stonechat, siskin; **all year** little grebe, great crested grebe, red grouse, woodcock, short-eared owl, kingfisher, green woodpecker, great and lesser spotted woodpeckers, grey wagtail, dipper, goldcrest, willow tit, coal tit, treecreeper, twite.

Start From Buxton take the A53 through Burbage and turn right on to the A54. After 1¾ miles (3 km) turn right on to the A537 and, in 250 yards (230 m), right again on to a minor road. After ½ mile (0.8 km) turn right at a T-junction and then bear left to follow the road down the Goyt Valley. The road runs along the W bank of Errwood Reservoir and at the N end, on the left of the road, there is a **car park** and picnic site.

From the car park cross the road and follow the footpath along the W bank of Fernilee Reservoir. At the N end of the reservoir, join the road which runs along the top of the dam, and cross to the other side of the valley. Continue down the valley, following the footpath which runs along the River Goyt. At Taxal cross the river via the bridge and follow the footpath on this side of the valley all the way back to the car park.

Dovedale is one of Derbyshire Peak District's most beautiful limestone valleys. Its wooded slopes are filled with birdsong in summer and the river has its share of dippers and grey wagtails. Much of the valley is owned by the National Trust, and access is by public footpaths. There is a car park at the bottom of the valley, near Thorpe, which is 2½ miles (4 km) NW of Ashbourne.

Attenborough Gravel Pits
2¼ miles (3.5 km)
Landranger 129 517344

These old gravel pits are owned by Batterley Aggregates (RMC group) and managed jointly with the Nottinghamshire Trust for Nature Conservation. Two hundred and seventeen species have been recorded on the reserve, with migration bringing such rarities as the spoonbill, little crake and bluethroat. *Open water, reedbeds, carr; trail guides from the Trust's caravan; keep to the marked paths at all times.*

Summer little ringed plover, common sandpiper, common tern, hirundines, yellow wagtail, grasshopper, sedge, reed and garden warblers, blackcap, whitethroat, lesser whitethroat, willow warbler, chiffchaff; **winter** water rail, green sandpiper, jack snipe, fieldfare, redwing, corn bunting; **passage** greenshank and other waders, black tern, common tern, rarities; **all year** little grebe, great crested grebe, teal, shoveler, pochard, tufted duck, snipe, reed bunting.

Start From Nottingham take the A6005 SW through Beeston and then turn left on to the minor road which passes through Attenborough. After the railway station, which is close to the reserve, follow the road around bends to The Strand **car park**.

From the car park a 12-post nature trail leads by a circular route round Duck Pond.

Clumber Park
1¼ or 2½ miles (2 or 4 km)
Landranger 120 625745

Clumber Park, one of the several great Midland estates in this area known collectively as the Dukeries, is owned by the National Trust and open to the public. The park was laid out by Capability Brown, with a long lake which attracts wildfowl in winter. The woodland areas support an interesting variety of breeding birds. *Open water, meadows, woods, heathland; trail leaflet available from the office in the stable block.*

Summer garden warbler, blackcap, willow warbler, chiffchaff, redstart; **winter** goldeneye, goosander, siskin; **all year** Canada goose, mallard, teal, shoveler, pochard, tufted duck, moorhen, coot, great and lesser spotted woodpeckers, goldcrest, nuthatch, treecreeper, redpoll, hawfinch.

Start From Worksop take the B6005 S for 1½ miles (2.5 km) and then turn left along minor road directed to Truman's Lodge. Continue through the Lodge and down Clumber Lane to the crossroads with Lime Tree Avenue. Continue straight on, past the cricket ground on the left to a junction. Bear right and follow the road around to the **car park**.

Follow the Heart of the Park walk in summer, through woods and parkland, or the shorter South Lawns walk in winter for good views of the lake and its wildfowl.

Martin's Pond
½ mile (0.8 km) Landranger 129 526402

Martin's Pond is an old pond, possibly of medieval origin, which was declared

Spoonbill, very occasionally seen on migration at Attenborough Gravel Pits; in the breeding season – April, May and June – adults develop a splendid crest.

a Local Nature Reserve as part of the 1976 European Wetlands Campaign. Only 3 miles (5 km) from Nottingham city centre, it contains a small wooded island, and the birds recorded there total 72 species. The reserve is owned by the City, and managed jointly with the Nottinghamshire Trust for Nature Conservation. It is open to the public. *Open water, reeds.*

Summer sedge, reed and garden warblers, blackcap, whitethroat, willow warbler, chiffchaff; **winter** spotted crake, woodcock; **passage** redshank, greenshank; **all year** little grebe, great crested grebe, water rail.

Start From Nottingham ringroad (A614) turn W at a roundabout on to the A609 (Ilkeston road). After ¾ mile (1 km) turn right in to Russell Avenue; **parking** in the Avenue.

Enter the reserve from the end of Russell Avenue and follow the circular footpath around the pond.

East Anglia and Region

By any standards, East Anglia is one of our best regions for birds. The variety of its habitats, especially wetlands, attracts breeding species which are rare or absent elsewhere. In spring and autumn, the jutting nature of the geography arrests birds which might pass unseen up and down other parts of the east coast. Many westward-bound Scandinavian and Siberian wildfowl, waders, thrushes and finches need go no further than East Anglia in winter.

There are highlights throughout the year. In winter, thousands of wildfowl visit the Ouse Washes (Hundred Foot Washes) and Grafham Water, while Walberswick and other marshes hold merlins, the hen harrier and short-eared owls. Spring birdsong fills the ancient woodlands such as Epping Forest, and even the modern pine plantations of the Brecks have their specialities – the crossbill for instance. The vast reedbeds of Broadland and the coast hold bearded tits and other classic species. In autumn, the famous north Norfolk coast, especially around Cley, is bound to have a sequence of scarce, rare and vagrant birds.

Most of the region is intensively farmed and this has the effect of excluding many bird species, as well as the public. Birds, birdwatchers and other visitors often end up in the same places. The conservation bodies have fortunately safeguarded many of these and rightly seek to show the birds to the people. The overall effect is that on a fine summer weekend, some popular spots may seem to have more birdwatchers than birds. If you prefer solitude, avoid the busy weekends, or visit early and late in the day.

North Sea gulls

Sawbridgeworth Marsh
1½ miles (2.5 km) Landranger 167 493156

Thirty acres (12 ha) of marshland with exceptionally rich plant and animal life, as well as wetland birds; designated an SSSI. Managed by the Herts. and Middx. Trust for Nature Conservation. *Marsh, meadows: entry only on application to the county trust.*

All year snipe; **summer** reed warbler, sedge warbler, reed bunting; **winter** water rail, jack snipe (occasional).

Start, about ½ mile (0.8 km) N of Sawbridgeworth Station on the unclassified road between Sawbridgeworth and Little Hallingbury; trains to Sawbridgeworth. Strictly limited **parking** at the reserve entrance.

Keep to established paths. It is possible to walk around the marsh and the willow plantation at the S end of the reserve, but care is needed in the marshy area. Many of the paths become overgrown in summer.

Broad Colney Lakes
1 mile (1.5 km) Landranger 166 176033

A rich and varied wetland habitat, close to London, formed by flooded, disused gravel pits alongside the River Colne. This is a valuable wildfowl refuge, and the surrounding woods and grassland offer a variety of other birds. *Open water, woods, grassland, scrub; open to the public.*

Summer great crested grebe, kingfisher, warblers; **autumn** tufted duck, pochard; **winter** wildfowl.

Start Leave St Albans S on the A6 and at the second roundabout take the third exit (the B556, signposted Radlett). In 1 mile turn R on to the B5378. Continue to reserve entrance on right,

S of London Colney; trains to St Albans Central and buses to London Colney. **Car park** at reserve entrance.

From car park follow the footpath over the bridge between the North and Small Lakes, both breeding areas for wildfowl, with reedbeds holding warblers in summer. Continue along the path, taking the first right fork, then the left, and walk along the NW shore of Long Lake, a flooded section of the River Colne formed during gravel extraction. Where the path joins the road at the end of the lake, turn right and continue towards the Green Dragon pub, then join the path again, crossing the Colne and then following the SE shore of Long Lake to picnic area. Return to car park along the road.

Cassiobury Park
1 mile (1.5 km) Landranger 166 092974

This reserve, originally mostly watercress beds, is now a varied freshwater habitat. *Open water, cress beds, woodland, marsh; mud. Free to any conservation trust member, otherwise small fee – contact county trust.*

Summer reed, sedge and grasshopper warblers; **winter** jack snipe, whinchat; **all year** water rail, snipe, woodcock, kingfisher, bearded tit, grey wagtail, corn bunting.

Start From the A411 N of Watford turn down Langley Way towards park and river; Watford Underground Station is less than ½ mile (0.8 km) away. **Parking** in side streets nearby.

Follow the track which is a continuation of Langley Way and in 200 yards (180 m) turn right to walk along the E bank of the River Gade. Follow the river and then its tributary to the N boundary of the reserve. The tributary forms a series of pools. Crossing is difficult, so return by the same route.

It is the snipe's specially shaped outer tail feathers, projected to vibrate in the airstream of a shallow dive, that produce the 'drumming' note of display flight.

Fingringhoe Wick
2 miles (3 km) Landranger 168 042195

This Essex Naturalists' Trust reserve on the Colne estuary provides a wide variety of habitats giving an interesting and varied day's birdwatching. Apart from the beach and saltmarsh adjacent to the estuary, there are extensive disused gravel workings which have left a lake and a number of ponds. There is also an area of woodland which, in summer, contains an unusually large number of nightingales. *Beach, saltmarsh, lake, fresh and brackish pools, scrub, woods; reserve open Tues–Sun, April–Sept, 9–7, Oct to March 9–4.30; shop, library.*

Summer shore-nesting birds, sand martins, nightingale; **passage** grey plover, brent goose, goldeneye, wheatear, whinchat; **winter** brent goose, waders, hen harrier, sparrowhawk, twite, siskin, fieldfare, red-breasted merganser.

Start From Colchester take the B1025 S in direction of West Mersea. In 2½ miles (4 km) fork left on to unclassified road, turn left at T-junction, then take first right signposted South Green. The road to the reserve runs E from this road: through main gate a drive leads to the **car park** and 'Interpretive Centre'.

The public Blue Nature Trail starts at the Interpretive Centre (where there is an observation tower) and leads through most of the reserve, with hides or seats at places of particular interest.

Blake's Wood
1 mile (1.5 km) Landranger 167 775064

This woodland reserve, just 3 miles (5 km) E of Chelmsford, is largely coppiced hornbeam and sweet chestnut, with some oak, birch and other trees. It has a rich plantlife, including orchids and some of the scarcer ferns, and many butterfly species, including speckled wood and purple hairstreak. The hornbeams attract hawfinches. *Coppiced woodland.*

Summer hawfinch, 3 woodpeckers, warblers, tits, treecreeper; **winter** siskin, redpoll.

Start From the A414 at Danbury turn N on to the minor road for Little Baddow; trains to Chelmsford and Hatfield Peverel. **Parking** at SE edge of reserve.

The footpath system around the wood is quite complex, but it can be adequately explored by following the public paths at will. For about a mile's walk (1.5 km), go clockwise or anticlockwise around the outermost paths, approaching the boundaries of the wood at various points but always staying inside, on the paths.

ESSEX

Epping Forest
5 miles (8 km) Landranger 177 398948
TQ 29/39 and TQ 49/59

For its closeness to London, Epping
Forest is a remarkably large wooded
area, extending over some 6,000 acres
(2,400 ha), of which some 4,000 acres
are woodland. It is noted for its wide
range of typical woodland species, but
actually sighting the birds can be a
challenge, probably because of the high
level of human disturbance. This route
aims to give a satisfying outing by passing through a range of forest habitats.
There is a fair chance of **treecreepers** and
**nuthatches; spotted flycatchers; marsh,
long-tailed** and **coal tits**, and it is a good
opportunity to test observation skills on
the elusive **hawfinch**. Some variety is
added in the form of open, cattle grazing
land. *Mud after rain.*

Time and season Human disturbance in
this popular recreation area is obviously
greatest during fine weekends in
summer. It really is worth rising early,
or getting home late, in order to have a
more peaceful and rewarding walk.
Mid-May to the end of June is the prime
period, but interesting all year.

Start Queen Elizabeth's Hunting Lodge,
on the A1069 about 1 mile (1.5 km)
SW of its junction with the A104
(former A11); Chingford bus terminus
and railway station are less than 1 mile
(1.5 km) from the Lodge. **Car park**
opposite the Lodge.

① From the car park take the path
on the E side of the Lodge, leading
across the cattle-grazed Chingford
Plain, and then past Connaught Water.
In about 1 mile (1.5 km), at Grimstone's
Oak (the large tree at the intersection
of several rides) ②, take the first green
ride on the left. At first this heads NW,
then almost due N for ¾ mile (1 km) to
Almshouse Plain (not marked on map) –
the first open space in the woods. ③

Take the left-hand path and in another
mile (1.5 km), at ④ Day's Farm, take
the footpath at top of hill marked No. 66
to Sewardstone Green. In about ¼ mile
(0.5 km) ⑤ bear left on to the footpath
marked No. 85, continuing across the
West Essex Golf Course to the main road,
where turn left and continue about 150
yards (140 m). Cross and ⑥ take the
by-road that runs due W along the edge
of the reservoir. At ⑦ the entrance to
Gilwell Park take the bridle-path on the
left and soon bear right towards Yardley
Hill. In about 450 yards (400 m) watch
carefully for a path on the left located
⑧ by a post on the main path. Follow
this path for about 1 mile (1.5 km) to
⑨ the obelisk. Turn left, follow the path
that runs between the edge of the golf
course and the housing estate, cross the
road and take the path leading to the
Lodge.

🐦 Canada geese, mallard and moorhens on
Connaught Water.

🐦 The mature deciduous woodland areas
all round the route are likely to hold treecreepers and nuthatches. The small,
brown treecreeper ascends tree trunks in
a series of jerky, mouselike movements,
then flies to the base of another tree trunk
to repeat the process. The nuthatch is
another active tree-climbing bird, easy to
identify by its plain grey upperparts and
a black stripe through the eye.

🐦 Finches are prominent in the woods all
around the walk. Small flocks of chaffinches and greenfinches are often re-
vealed in winter by neatly sliced hornbeam seeds on the ground. The shy and
elusive hawfinch could be seen; it flies at
tree-top level with rapid wing beats. Redpolls are widespread in winter and often
associate with siskins in silver birch. Bullfinches are regular.

🐦 In early summer, blackcaps, willow warblers and chiffchaffs are widely distributed; tree pipits occur in open areas.

In season, garden warblers and white-throats are usually found on Almshouse Plain (not marked on map), and there is a possibility of hearing a nightingale.

Marsh, coal and long-tailed tits are resident in the woodland all round the walk.

Look for turtle doves and yellowhammers in the blackthorn along the road.

Spotted flycatchers usually breed in the Gilwell Park area, and may be seen along this bridle-path.

Red-legged partridges may be seen on farmland adjoining Yardley Hill.

This woodland holds the three regular woodpecker species.

In Nov and Dec redwings and fieldfares are often present in large numbers on the golf course. On winter evenings, thousands of gulls roost on the reservoirs – fine views from the Pole Hill obelisk.

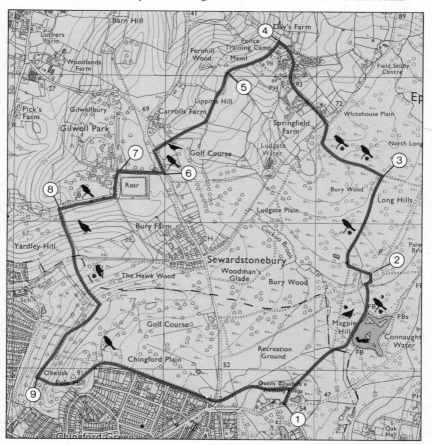

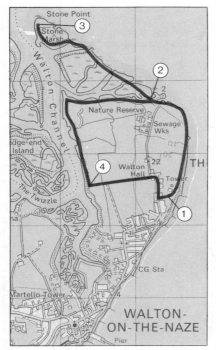

The brent, a small goose, has pronounced barring and a white neck patch.

Walton-on-the-Naze
5½ miles (9 km) Landranger 169 264235

This is one of many excellent sites on the Essex coast, especially active during winter and migration. The key features are the tidal flats and saltings, the Red Crag cliffs of the naze overlooking Hamford Water and the Essex Naturalists' Trust reserve of grassland, thickets and pools. Nearby Horsey Island supports a flock of feral greylag geese. *Grassland, tidal water, marsh.*

Summer redshank, common and little terns; **autumn** grey plover, godwits, whimbrel, greenshank and other waders, migrant passerines; **winter** brent goose, red-breasted merganser, goldeneye, curlew, grey plover, bar-tailed godwit, purple sandpiper, twite; **all year** shelduck.

Start Drive N through Walton-on-the-Naze. **Car park** on the cliff tops.

① From car park follow the cliff path N. The bushes here often harbour migrant passerines. ② Continue along the coast, crossing the various dykes. This can only be done at low tide, so check that there is time to make the return crossing before the water rises too high. Continue to ③, Stone Point. At the right season, wildfowl and skuas may be seen out to sea, twite and snow buntings on the shore. Return to the mainland, recrossing the dykes at the same points. At ② follow the sea wall W,

Abberton Reservoir near Colchester, covering more than 1,000 acres (400 ha), is one of Britain's best for birdwatching. Its closeness to the coast makes it an excellent wildfowl site, and also for waders and passage migrants. Access to the perimeter of the reservoir is limited to permit holders, but there is a great deal to be seen from the surrounding roads. The nearby river may also be worth visiting, particularly when flooded. From Colchester take the B1026 S; it leads across the reservoir, with good views on both sides. Further on, the minor road leading back N to Layer Breton recrosses the water.

then S, along the Walton Channel, which separates the Naze from Horsey Island. ④ Turn E, back towards ①.

Grafham Water
4 or 10 miles (6.5 or 16 km)
Landranger 153 162665

The N and NW shores of this, one of the largest man-made lakes in England, are managed by the Beds and Hunts Naturalists' Trust. The reserve includes two ancient woods, but the main attraction is the reservoir itself, whose 1,500 acres (607 ha) may, in winter, hold thousands of wildfowl. *Woods, open water.*

Summer shelduck, little ringed plover; **passage** waders, terns, occasional osprey; **winter** large gull roost, goldeneye and many other wildfowl; **all year** great crested and little grebe.

Start At Buckden on the A1 turn W on to the B661; trains to St Neots and Huntingdon, and hourly buses between these stop at Buckden, 1 mile (1.5 km) from reservoir. Two **car parks** along this road adjacent to the reservoir, Plummer first, Mander second.

From Plummer Car Park walk west along the road to the Mander Car Park – fine views of E part of reservoir from Plummer Car Park. At Mander CP consult information display/map. Follow path shown along S edge of reserve (on W side of wood). Retrace after 1½ miles (2.5 km). (Access to the reserve is not allowed, but on Sundays non-members may use the hide for a small charge, Oct–March.) The 10-mile (16-km) plus circumnavigation of the reservoir offers more exercise than additional birdwatching. Continue along the path to the road W of the reservoir. Walk N along this and return to the reservoir by the footpath skirting the N edge of the reserve. This joins a road, passing Hill Farm. Bear right at all junctions, following the edge of the reservoir back to Plummer CP.

Bewick's swan: seen at Grafham on a few occasions each winter.

Wicken Sedge Fen
2 miles (3 km) Landranger 154
565705

One of the last remnants of the fenland which once covered much of East Anglia, Wicken Fen is an SSSI carefully managed to preserve the habitat. Wildfowl are the attraction in winter, largely due to the 10-acre (4-ha) mere excavated in 1955 and visible only from the look-out tower. The National Trust's William Thorpe Building has an information display. *Sedge and reedbeds; marsh, alder buckthorn scrub, open water, mud; entry fee.*

Spring lapwing, redshank, snipe, long-eared owl, great and lesser spotted woodpeckers, warblers, nightingale; **summer** turtle dove, cuckoo, warblers; **autumn** wildfowl, hobby, waders, hirundines roosting, large starling roost; **winter** bittern, wildfowl, hen harrier, owls, great grey shrike.

Start Seventeen miles (27 km) N of Cambridge on the A10, turn right on to the A1123 towards Wicken. On entering the village a large sign to Wicken Fen indicates a right turning along Lode Lane; **car park** on left. Buy permit and trail guide from the William Thorpe building.

The route forms a rough square round the outer edge of the fen. Follow the path without turning on to any of the Droves which lead into the Fen.

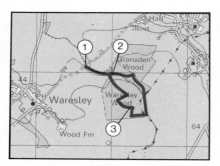

Waresley Wood
1½ miles (2.5 km) Landranger 153 260550

Waresley Wood is a relic of the ancient woodland which once covered most of East Anglia. It is mainly hazel coppice with oak and other standards and has been managed this way for centuries. In April, oxlips flower in profusion and other plantlife is very varied, including several species of orchid. As well as abundant birdlife, fallow deer and badgers occur here. *Coppiced woods; free to any conservation trust member, otherwise small fee – contact county trust; closed for shooting some Saturdays in winter.*

Summer three woodpecker species, willow tit, long-tailed tit, treecreeper, blackcap, garden warbler, willow warbler, chiffchaff.

Start From Gamlingay drive N on the B1040 to Waresley and continue ¾ mile (1 km) as far as the concrete drive on the right (leading to a sewage works). **Parking** on the verge.

① Walk down the concrete drive to the wood entrance and bear left with the paths, roughly following the course of Waresley Dean Brook until ② the path meets the central Howard Ride. Turn left along Robin Path, which bears right into South Path and right again into Aspen Way. From here turn ③ left on to Mear Ride and right on to Middle Way. This leads back on to Howard Ride. Turn left and follow it back to the entrance.

The Ouse or Hundred Foot Washes
4 or 6 miles (6.5 or 9.5 km)
Landranger 143 471862

The parallel channels of the Old and New Bedford Rivers, constructed in the 17th C., drain much of the Fens, making extensive cultivation possible. But between the two rivers, in the area known as the Ouse Washes, extensive flooding still occurs. This is of great value for birdlife and much of this internationally important wildfowl site is owned by the RSPB, Cambient and the Wildfowl Trust. Ideal conditions occur for a wide range of species when flooding is incomplete. Winter flocks of duck may reach 40,000 in number, and up to 2,500 Bewick's swans have been recorded. Conditions in summer have enabled the ruff and black-tailed godwit to re-establish themselves as breeding birds in Britain. *Flooded water meadows.*

Spring waders, snipe, black tern; **summer** black-tailed godwit, black tern, yellow wagtail; **winter** Bewick's and whooper swans, pintail, wigeon, teal, pochard, tufted duck, shoveler, goldeneye, goosander, golden plover, ruff, hen harrier, thrushes; **all year** waders, snipe, short-eared owl.

Start From Chatteris take the B1098 to Horseway; on the 90° bend just after the village, having crossed the Forty Foot Drain, turn right on to the minor road and continue via Manea to Welches Dam (signposted from Manea). **Car park** and visitor centre (open only at weekends) at Welches Dam.

Walk NE from the car park as far as the six hides overlooking the Washes. Retrace steps to start. For an extra 2 miles (3 km), walk SW from car park to further two hides. Retrace to start.

Minsmere
2 or 6 miles (3 or 10 km)
Landranger 156 478677

Late arrivals at the RSPB's famous Minsmere reserve may find that the day's allocation of permits to non-members has already been sold. Moreover, the RSPB are increasingly concerned about disturbance to some of the species: there are tens of thousands of visitors each year. Users of the public right of way that runs through the adjacent Dunwich Heath National Trust property, and along the seaward boundary of the reserve, therefore do the birds a service as well as enjoying a fine seaside walk together with second-to-none views of the artificially created pools known as 'the Scrape'. Here, a number of small islands offer a variety of habitats for nesting species, and carefully controlled salinity and depth of water provide ideal conditions for a variety of exciting and rare birds, including, of course, the avocets. (Their name comes from the French *avocat*, meaning barrister – a reference to the pied plumage.)

In spite of the distinctive, upcurved bill, avocets can quite effectively disguise their identity by burying the bill in plumage. However, no other wader has narrow, black chevrons on the back. The bill serves for a specialized feeding method: it is swept from side to side in the surface layers of water, capturing small invertebrates.

Spring spoonbill, spotted redshank, black-tailed godwit, bar-tailed godwit, ruff; **summer** purple heron, marsh harrier, osprey, avocet, common, little and Sandwich terns; **autumn** spotted redshank, little stint, curlew sandpiper, black- and bar-tailed godwits, ruff, black tern, wryneck; **winter** red-throated diver, scoter, eider, hen and marsh harriers; **all year** bittern, kingfisher.

Start In Westleton, 5 miles (8 km) NE of Saxmundham, follow signs to Dunwich. In 1¾ miles (3 km) turn right at signs for Dunwich Heath and Minsmere. Continue to NT entrance hut (small fee) and then to **car park**, where tarmac road ends. *Please respect all notices; on weekends and some weekdays there is an RSPB information hut on the beach about 550 yards (500 m) from car park.*

Follow the obvious path downhill, pausing to enjoy the bird's-eye view of Dunwich Heath (worth a scan – plenty of stonechats) and beyond the conspicuous bank the vast expanse of Minsmere's marshland and reedbeds, the latter stretching out of sight inland. On the beach, head S (in the direction of Sizewell nuclear power station). Concentrate on the sea birds until reaching the Minsmere boundary; from there, check all pools and islands. Continue to the bushes, opposite the concrete sluice, which provide cover for migrant warblers and thrushes. For the shorter walk, retrace to the conspicuous public hide and use this for further inspection; return to car park. For the longer walk, continue from the sluice as far as Sizewell – mainly sea birds, especially terns in summer. Retrace to car park.

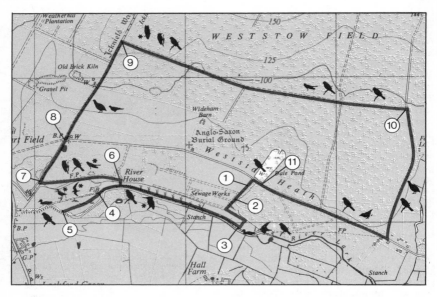

West Stow

5 miles (8 km) Landranger 144 796714
TL 77 and TL 87

Breckland, the location of this route, was once a vast, open expanse of heath, grass and blown sand. Fragments of this habitat still exist, but are often private or used for military training. To get a true picture of the Brecks today, a walker in search of birds should see not only heath but forestry, farm and wetland. This walk takes in each of these, and several **typical Breckland species** are to be seen.

Time and season Spring perhaps best because human disturbance is slight, but interesting all year.

Start From the A1101 between Icklingham and Lackford take the unclassified road leading to West Stow. In ¾ mile (1 km) turn right into West Stow Country Park. **Car park** and lavatories at park entrance.

① From car park make towards the reconstructed Anglo-Saxon village ②, and continue with path as it turns slightly downhill towards the woodland edge – 50 yards (45 m) on. Turn left along the outside of the trees and continue about 200 yards (180 m); turn right into obvious way through trees and ③ arrive at riverside. The gravel pits seen ahead and left are worth investigation, but to continue the walk turn right and follow the river downstream for about ¼ mile (0.5 km) to where ④ a lake with islands opens out on the right. Follow the bank between lake and river for another 300 yards (270 m) to ⑤, where river runs into a shallow pool. Retrace steps for about 400 yards (350 m) and leave the riverside up the track to the left. In about 150 yards (140 m) ⑥ turn left on to the broad track over heath, passing a thicket of silver birch to the right. In about 350 yards (320 m) fork right towards a gate. ⑦ Through gate turn right and in 350 yards ⑧ cross road and continue straight ahead along track. In about ½ mile (0.8 km) the track enters forest; ¾ mile (1 km) on, ⑨ turn right along ride no. 207. Continue about 1¼ miles (2 km) to the edge of the forest and ⑩ turn right. Continue past Forest Lodge to road. Turn right and follow verge, passing Dale Pond ⑪ in about ½ mile (0.8 km), and carrying on to park entrance.

A good opportunity to compare the song of several warbler species, including garden warbler and blackcap.

The River Lark supports mute swan, mallard, tufted duck and, Breckland's special duck, the gadwall. Across the river the old gravel pits hold the same species, plus shelduck in summer and pochard, goldeneye and sometimes goosander in winter. Sand martins fly very close.

Where the river runs through the trees sedge warblers, whitethroats and other warblers are common; spotted flycatchers hunt from the bare branches. In winter, siskins and redpolls feed in the alders. Kingfishers all year.

The lake holds gadwall and Canada geese. In winter wildfowl numbers increase and diving duck such as pochard and golden-eye arrive, with occasional goosanders. Great crested grebes nest on the island fringes, coots are numerous and there is a chance of terns and common sand-pipers in spring.

Where the river runs between walls and into the pool there is a chance of grey wagtail.

The heath has several typical Breckland species. Great and lesser spotted wood-peckers feed in the pines and birch, and the green woodpecker comes down to feed in the open. The mistle thrush is conspicuous, as elsewhere in the Brecks, and the tree pipit performs its 'parachute' display flight; the bird is one of the hosts of the cuckoo. (At dusk there is a chance of a woodcock passing on its territorial 'roding' flight.)

The dry fields of Breckland suit the red-legged partridge, and the native grey partridge also occurs. Pheasants are common, and there is a chance of the elusive, introduced golden pheasant – look for it especially where fields border conifer plantations. Stock and turtle doves are common here.

The plantation tends to be rather uni-form, but it will reward patient bird-watching, especially in summer. Ride edges, particularly where native trees have been planted, are worth inspecting for tits and woodpeckers, and the rides themselves for golden pheasant. Use your ears to pick up calls of anxious birds, which may be mobbing an owl, possibly even the scarce long-eared owl, which favours Breckland pines. Crossbills may be given away by their calls.

This area of younger trees breaks the uniformity of the plantation – which means more birds. The nightjar favours this habitat – to hear, and perhaps glimpse it, means visiting between dusk and dawn, when woodcock may also be seen roding.

This part of the plantation is native Scots pine; coal tits, goldcrests and chaffinches are common, with the outside chance of a sparrowhawk.

Red-legged partridges, linnets and other birds of open ground.

The mixture of pine and broadleaved trees along the roadside attracts several tit species, nuthatch and treecreeper. Finches are notable; there is a chance of a crossbill, and of the elusive hawfinch.

Dale Pond is actually a stand of reed with willow and alder. Reed warblers nest and long-tailed and marsh tits visit.

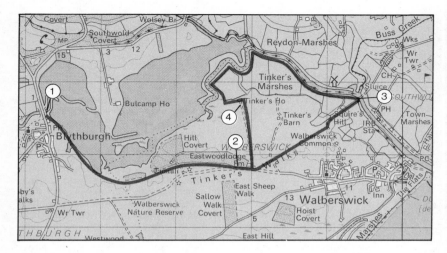

Blyth Estuary
4 or 8 miles (6.5 or 13 km)
Landranger 156 452751

The River Blyth enters the sea just below Southwold, and the tidal part was originally contained within banks and flanked by water meadows. In the 1920s a 2- to 4-mile (3- to 6.5-km) stretch broke its banks. The flooded area has never since been reclaimed, and remains a first-class waterfowl and wader habitat, notably for gadwall, black-tailed godwit and spotted redshank. *Open water, mudflats, marsh, heath.*

Spring grey plover, black-tailed godwit, bar-tailed godwit, whimbrel; **summer** shelduck, redshank, common tern; **autumn** grey plover, spotted redshank, greenshank, whimbrel; **winter** wigeon, shelduck, spotted redshank.

Start Blythburgh, 10 miles (16 km) N of Saxmundham on the A12; trains to Saxmundham and 3 buses daily to Blythburgh. **Parking** with care to avoid obstruction in Blythburgh.

In the foreground, the little gull – graceful, delicate, obviously smaller than other gulls. Behind, a black tern looks for insects. The birds are typical of several routes in this section, often occurring together on pools or estuaries.

① Follow the right of way beside the White Hart to the disused railway track. Follow this along the S side of the estuary and return from ② by the same route. For the longer walk, follow the railway as far as ③, the bridge over the Blyth, but do not cross. Take the footpath leading left along the river for almost 2 miles (3 km) before ④ turning back towards the railway track and retracing to the start.

Holme and Thornham harbour
3 miles (5 km) Landranger 132 698439

The coast line at the NE corner of the Wash is strategically positioned for the arrival of migrants, and the two adjacent reserves here offer a wide variety of species. Extreme rarities like the collared flycatcher, nutcracker, red-rumped swallow and Pallas's and Bonelli's warblers have occurred. Wrynecks, hoopoes and ospreys occur almost annually. The area has some interesting plantlife, too, notably orchids. *Shore, dunes, conifers, open water, marsh; permits to both reserves (open 10–5) may be bought from The Firs or Holme Bird Observatory.*

Spring godwits and other waders, terns, marsh harrier; **summer** little tern, grasshopper warbler, dunlin; **autumn** bartailed godwit, grey plover, whimbrel, knot, spotted redshank, greenshank, migrant passerines; **winter** knot, bartailed godwit, sanderling, brent goose, great grey shrike, hen harrier, short-eared owl, snow bunting, shore lark, twite; **all year** shelduck, oystercatcher, ringed plover, bearded tit.

Start From the A149 in Holme village take the side road furthest W; turn second left on to side track leading to *The Firs*; buses to Holme from King's Lynn. **Public car park** on left, 700 yards (650 m) after turning, or at *The Firs* for permit holders.

From car park join the footpath running along the N boundary of the 2 reserves (partly waymarked with yellow arrows). In 1½ miles (2.5 km) the path joins the sea wall; return by the same route or along the beach. Alternatively, follow the sea wall to Thornham harbour, and take the harbour road back to Thornham village. *From there it is best to take a bus back to Holme as much of the A149 is unpaved and it is a busy road to walk along.*

The unmistakable hoopoe: when perching, its tail looks exceptionally long – unlike in flight. The jerky flight action helps make the white barring on the upper wing a visual baffle – perhaps to confuse predators.

Roydon Common
4 miles (6.5 km) Landranger 132 681230

North Norfolk has several important heathlands, of which Roydon is one of the finest. *Dry and wet heath.*

Summer curlew, nightjar, stonechat, nightingale, grasshopper warbler; **winter** merlin, hen harrier, great grey shrike.

Start From junction of A149 and A148 turn E in direction of Fakenham. In 300 yards (270 m), turn right on to minor road for Grimston; continue about 1 mile (1.5 km) to where public footpath leads off on right. **Parking** on Common adjacent to footpath.

Follow the footpath S across the Common to an unmade road. Turn right on to this and continue to the village of Pott Row. Take the first left in the village, then turn left on to the Grimston–King's Lynn road and return to the start.

SUFFOLK

Walberswick
3 miles (5 km) Landranger 156 501745
TM57

This walk touches the edge of one of Britain's finest coastal National Nature Reserves, and gives excellent opportunities for seeing both a variety of **ducks, waders, seashore** and **reedbed birds** and an exceptional range of **birds of prey**. Mud.

Time and season Excellent throughout the year, but winter is the most exciting period. Afternoon and evening are the best times to see raptors.

Start Drive E through Walberswick village on the B1387 and turn right at the sharp bend towards the end of the village. Immediately bear left on to the tortuous concrete track to reach the beach **car park**.

① From the car park, skirt the beach huts to reach the sea-wall by the shingle bank ②, about 50 yards (45 m) ahead. Scan the sea for divers, grebes and ducks. Turn right and walk S along the beach. Keep an eye out for birds on both the sea to your left and the brackish pools, mud and weed-grown shingle to your right. After about 1¼ miles (2 km) reach ③, looking out on the right for the two low banks a few yards apart. Follow the second bank, which immediately doubles back sharply. Walk on about ½ mile (0.8 km) to the derelict brick wind-pump ④, checking the pools and reedbeds on either side as you go. The rising land halfway along and to the left of this stretch is part of Dingle Hills, where bushes may hold migrant and wintering passerines. At the pump itself, enjoy the distant view over the reedbeds to the left, and spend some time watching for birds of prey. Continue, bearing right along the track at the bottom of the wall, heading NE. Follow this for a little over ¼ mile (0.5 km), then cross the dyke to the left via the footbridge at ⑤.

After a further 400 yards (350 m) or so, take another footbridge to the right ⑥ and walk the few yards back to the sea wall. *The walk can be extended S along the beach from ③. The attractive village of Dunwich is about 2½ miles (4 km) away, with good sea, beach and marsh birdwatching en route. Also, from the high ground near Westwood Lodge, reached via the no through road running S off the B1387 2 miles (3 km) W of Walberswick, there are particularly fine views of raptors over the marshes.*

Red-throated divers, grebes and sea-duck (including the occasional eider and velvet scoter) on the sea in winter. Views are often distant and hampered by overcast conditions: a telescope will prove useful.

Greenfinches, linnets, yellowhammers and reed buntings search for seeds here. In winter look out also for the tight, restless flocks of twites, linnet-like, but tawnier, constantly uttering their distinctive nasal chirps and twitters.

The pools of the Corporation Marshes are good for oystercatcher, ringed plover, grey plover, dunlin and redshank in winter. Among the ducks our largest, the sheldduck, and smallest, the teal, are regular here.

Most species of gulls, including kittiwake and the odd glaucous, off the coast in winter.

Shore lark and snow bunting on the flats behind the sea-bank in winter. The latter is striking, with flashes of white; the lark is more subdued, but the yellow and black head pattern is like that of the skylark, likely to be seen close by. The shore lark and snow bunting are among the most exciting winter visitors to Britain, elusive, but worth looking for.

In winter, pools in the reeds are preferred by shy birds such as water rail, snipe and, when hunger makes it desperate, the bittern.

A wide vista such as this gives the best chances of seeing birds of prey. Kestrels and sparrowhawks hunt the heath and arable slopes to the right, and the latter often cross the reeds to the distant pines. One or two merlins sometimes hunt the bushes and the reeds to your left. This is also one of the best places in East Anglia to see a rough-legged buzzard. An occasional wintering marsh harrier may be seen, but the most dependable raptor is the hen harrier. Towards dusk, these come floating over to roost in the reeds, often hunting the great crowds of roosting starlings, a memorable sight in themselves.

The hen harrier, a winter highlight of Walberswick, beats the air lazily or glides with its wings slightly raised in its low-level hunting flight over reedbeds. It feeds on small ground-living animals and birds on the wing.

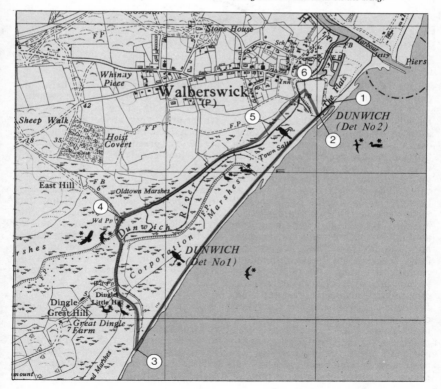

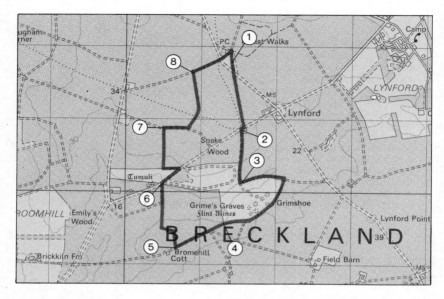

Thetford Forest
6 miles (9.5 km) Landranger 144 814918

Largely planted from 1922–37, the forest is 90% coniferous – mostly Corsican and Scots pine – and contains all the typical bird species for this habitat, with the 50–60-year felling rotation giving added variety. The area includes the prehistoric flint mines known as Grime's Graves, together with an SSSI which provides a heathland site for breeding curlews. Roe and muntjac deer also inhabit the forest and it is a rewarding area for butterflies, flowers and fungi. Breckland, or Brecks, is the name given to the great area of heath and forestry in this part of East Anglia. It was originally mainly heath, grass and sand; the conifer plantations are a modern development. Another Breckland route is on pages 166–7. *Coniferous forest, heath; keep to the forest rides; areas are sometimes closed for management purposes, with warning signs displayed – but there is no shortage of alternative routes.*

Summer nightjar, cuckoo, whitethroat, grasshopper warbler, redstart, wheatear, tree pipit, stone curlew, curlew; **winter** great grey shrike, fieldfare, redwing, redpoll, brambling; **all year** great spotted and green woodpecker, crossbill, siskin, long-eared owl, kestrel, sparrowhawk.

Start Take the A134 (Mundford road) from Thetford and, after passing the turning to Brandon on the left, look out for the Forestry Commission picnic site on the right, where there is **parking**. This picnic site is closed from mid-Oct to Easter. Emily's Wood picnic site on the A1065 Newmarket to Swaffham road is open all year.

① From the picnic site walk back along the entrance drive, crossing the main road, and continue along the forest ride to the Brandon road ②. Turn right on to this and walk a few yards to the next ride on the left, marked as the entrance to Grime's Graves. Follow this to the

Male bearded tit: this much illustrated but charming pose, a reed grasped in each foot, is very characteristic of the bird. It flies extremely fast, very close to the tops of the reeds, and plunges abruptly back into cover.

Titchwell Marsh
2½ *miles (4 km) Landranger 132*
749437

This reserve is part of the north Norfolk coastal plain, which until 350 years ago was natural sand dunes and saltmarsh. Since then, man has reclaimed much of it for farming and tourism. However, some sections have escaped modification, or reverted to their original state. In part, Titchwell is one of the latter. In addition, skilful wetland management by the RSPB has created an interesting range of semi-natural habitats and an impressive list of birds. *Freshwater reedbeds freshwater marsh, brackish marsh, dunes, seashore, tidal creek, sea; free entry; leaflet available; information centre; hides open during daylight hours all year except for the Tern (sunken) Hide, which is open April–July inclusive.*

All year little grebe, cormorant, bittern, shelduck, redshank, ringed plover, oystercatcher, bearded tit; **summer** marsh harrier, common, little and Sandwich terns; **winter** brent goose, wigeon, teal, goldeneye, red-breasted merganser, scoter, eider, hen harrier, short-eared owl, snow bunting; **autumn** ruff, spotted redshank, greenshank, little stint, dunlin, curlew sandpiper, bar-tailed godwit, grey plover, sanderling, turnstone, avocet, skuas.

Start In Titchwell on the A149 head W in the direction of Thornham, turning right into the RSPB **car park** in about 500 yards (450 m).

From the car park visit the Centre, if open. Then head N along the sea wall, visiting the 2 hides on the way. Reaching the far end of the wall, turn right along the foreshore and visit the sunken hide, which in summer gives ground-level, close-up views of nesting little and common terns. This is an ideal, exciting way to view the birds – and probably unique in Britain.

fenced entrance ③ where, unless visiting the flint mines, turn left and follow the fence which surrounds the DOE's SSSI. The area is sheep-grazed to maintain the habitat. At the SW corner of this area ④ the fence bends sharply to the right and has no path alongside while the ride continues straight ahead. Follow this ride and at the second crossroads ⑤ turn right on to a more overgrown path. This again joins the Brandon road ⑥. Turn right on to the road, walking along the W boundary of a small piece of Ministry of Defence land. Turn left at the first opportunity and then right after about 200 yards (180 m). At the next T-junction ⑦ turn right, walking alongside Snake Wood which contains Scots pine and mixed broad-leaved trees, then take the next ride to the left, crossing clear areas felled in 1981 and 1982. At the next T-junction ⑧ turn right back to ①.

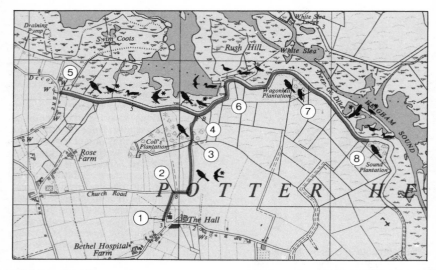

Hickling Broad
4½ *miles (7 km) Landranger 134 419199*
TG 42

It is said, with some truth, that access to the Broads is better by boat than on foot; however, this walk does give a fair chance of seeing typical Broadland birds in pleasant surroundings and from a dry path. The wall south of the Broad looks out over reedbeds, pools, one arm of the Broad itself and Heigham Sound. Small woods and bushy areas add variety. *Long vegetation, soaking in wet weather.*

Time and season The path is a popular one, so for solitude, do the walk at off-peak periods. Spring and summer are best for the birds. Avoid the heat of the day for finest song.

Start Potter Heigham church, on the NE side of the village, which lies between Ormesby and Stalham on the A149. **Parking** near the church.

① Walk down the road to the west of the church for about 150 yards (140 m)

to ② where the road bends left. Follow the public footpath to the right; it bears left after about 100 yards (90 m) – a broad track between crops. In about 350 yards (320 m) the track turns right to ③, a notice board with information on the Hickling Broad National Nature Reserve. Cross the stile and walk through the wood of oak and birch for about 200 yards (180 m), then cross a footbridge over a narrow dyke to the wall ④, where turn left and walk along the wall for just over ½ mile (0.8 km) to ⑤, another stile. From here retrace steps to ④ and continue straight ahead along the wall, walking E. In about 100 yards (90 m) one bay of the Broad is visible and shortly after that ⑥, there is an excavated pool at Rush Hill. Because of the reedbeds, tall people are at an advantage here. Follow the path as it bears right alongside Heigham Sound. After about 130 yards (120 m), ⑦ pass Wagonhill Plantation on the right, viewing it from the wall. Continue for about ¼ mile (0.5 km) to ⑧ Sound Plantation, also easily viewed. Return by same route via the footbridge at ④ to Potter Heigham church. *This route is best for birds, but a circular route S from Sound Plantation, then W and N to the church is also possible on public footpaths.*

The crops either side of the path may hold yellow wagtails and reed buntings. The oak trees provide song posts for yellow-hammers and other birds. Kestrels hunt this open country.

Plenty of small birds in this damp, oak woodland, particularly tits (including long-tailed) and willow warblers. As with all woods, patiently overlooking a clearing or pathside or drinking pool pays dividends.

Sedge and reed warblers sing from the reed stems. Cuckoos seek out their nests in this area, and young cuckoos can sometimes be seen out of the nest in July, still demanding food from their fosterers. Bearded tits whirr low over the reeds and drop quickly out of sight. Once seen, recognizing the bird is easy: no other European species has anything like its combination of shape or plumage. The 'beard' is actually a pair of moustachial tufts, which hang loose and are responsible for the many changes of expression.

Insects are plentiful over reedbeds and swifts, swallows and both species of martin regularly hunt them here.

The bushes along the track and invading the reedbeds contain numbers of warblers, including the grasshopper warbler; finches, especially redpolls and reed buntings; also turtle doves. Look out for moorhens in the overgrown channels.

This inlet will test your gull identification, as immature birds in all plumages occur here of great and lesser black-backed, herring and common gulls. The floating structures on which they perch are part of a water-quality experiment. Also seen here are great crested grebes, feral greylag geese and coots. Common terns hover

and plunge for fish, and there is a good chance of a little tern, rare inland, something of a Hickling speciality.

This pool at Rush Hill is particularly favoured by waders. Redshank are usually present and spring and autumn bring sandpipers and others, with rarities in most years. Even if there are few waders about in summer, Canada geese, common terns, black-headed and non-breeding large gulls are to be seen, or you may surprise a heron fishing in one of the nearby smaller pools. The hides visible from here are not accessible from the wall; property of the Norfolk Naturalists' Trust, which owns the reserve, they may be visited with a permit.

This small plantation, with many oaks, is a pleasant contrast with the reeds and holds marsh tits and woodpeckers. The edges, often the best part of a wood for birds, are easily viewed from the wall.

The wide view NE over Heigham Sound may reveal a hunting marsh harrier, cruising low over the reedbeds and channels. Here, as elsewhere along the wall, there is a chance in spring of hearing the bittern's 'booming' call (this species is fast declining on the Broads) or even glimpsing the bird flying between feeding area and nest. In flight it looks something like an owl, with rounded wings, bent noticeably downwards when reaching the bottom of their stroke. The long bill and trailing legs are also conspicuous in flight, in the same way as a heron's. In contrast to the booming song, the flight call is harsh. The bird's 'frozen' alarm posture is one of the most painted sights of birdlife: head and neck are stretched straight upright so that the vertical markings on the neck act as camouflage.

Check the edges of Sound Plantation for warblers, tits, spotted flycatchers and finches. Redshank, snipe and teal are often present in the pools on either side of the wall.

NORFOLK

Ranworth Broad
1 mile (1.5 km) Landranger 134 356148

This broad has poor-quality water but is surrounded by large areas of rich fenland, and harbours large numbers of wildfowl, including Bewick's swan in winter. There is also the Broadland Conservation Centre, with exhibits illustrating Broadland's interest, and its problems. *Open water, fen, carr; open April–Oct Tues–Fri and Sun 10.30–5.30, Sat 2–5.30; Wed pm party bookings only; free to any conservation trust member, otherwise small fee – contact county trust.*

Summer common tern, reed and sedge warblers, reed bunting; **winter** wigeon, teal, shoveler, gadwall, goldeneye, pochard, Bewick's swan, feral greylag geese.

Start Ranworth, 10 miles (16 km) NE of Norwich, just off the B1140; 5 buses a day on weekdays to and from Norwich. **Car park** in village opposite the Granary on Ranworth public staithe (lavatories nearby).

From car park walk towards the church, passing to right of it; take path on right opposite the church. Follow this through Ranworth marshes to the Conservation Centre. The centre's upstairs gallery gives panoramic views of the marsh and broad. Retrace to start. Ranworth church is worth a visit – fine painted rood screen.

Strumpshaw Fen (Marsh)
2½ miles (4 km) Landranger 134 338070

This RSPB reserve is adjacent to the polluted River Yare, to which the area was originally connected by water courses. Now it is isolated from the river, and this has resulted in the return of many wetland bird and plant species. The reserve is also noted for its Chinese water deer and noctule bats. *Fen, reed, marsh, woods, open water; open all year*

Curlew, right, and whimbrel, left, are separated when standing mainly by size and bill length; the whimbrel's eye markings are a distinguishing feature, but not particularly easy to make out. In flight, a whimbrel's wings beat more rapidly.

every day except Tues and Fri; charge to non-members.

Summer wildfowl, water rail, marsh harrier, bearded tit, grasshopper warbler, Cetti's warbler; **autumn** common and green sandpipers, greenshank; **winter** grebes, bean goose, hen harrier, bearded tit, redwing, fieldfare; **all year** great crested grebe, redshank, woodpeckers.

Start In Blofield, E of Norwich on the A47, take the minor road to Brundall, where turn left at T-junction and continue under railway bridge. Bear right and right again to reserve entrance; trains to Buckenham, less than 1 mile (1.5 km) away. **Car park** on the reserve, or for the winter route (Dec–Feb) near Buckenham Station.

From reserve car park walk directly towards river, turn left and follow river bank to the drive which leads towards the railway station, turning left on to the road. Continue back to car park and take a second path leading upriver for ½ mile (0.8 km). From December until the end of February, walk from the car park near the station downriver past the mill to a hide overlooking the haunt of the bean geese.

Breydon Water
7 miles (11 km) Landranger 134
522075

Just W of Great Yarmouth, the Rivers
Waveney and Yare flow into a large area
of tidal mudflats bounded by marshland
either side. This attracts moderate numbers of waders and wildfowl, and a
variety of species during migration.
Mudflats, open water.

Spring curlew, whimbrel, spotted redshank, bar-tailed godwit, black-tailed
godwit, ruff, terns; **summer** shelduck,
redshank; **autumn** curlew, whimbrel,
greenshank, spotted redshank, bar-
tailed godwit, black-tailed godwit, ruff,
grey plover, marsh harrier, short-eared
owl; **winter** shelduck, wigeon, pintail,
shoveler, scaup, goldeneye, brent goose,
Bewick's swan, knot, grey plover, hen
harrier, short-eared owl, twite, snow
bunting, Lapland bunting.

Start Great Yarmouth; frequent buses
and trains. **Car park** near the Two Bears
pub.

① From pub cross Southtown Bridge
and take the first right. Trace roads
through to riverside, taking path to
bank. Continue to ② broken bridge and
③ follow rough road. Continue about
3 miles (5 km) to ④ a stile. Retrace to
①, or continue along bank for optional
visit to Burgh Castle, impressive remains
of a Roman fort.

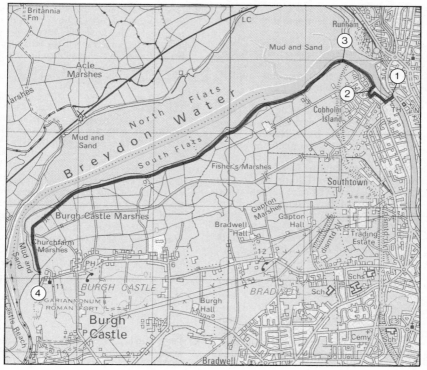

Cley next the Sea
3 miles (5 km) Landranger 133 054441
TG04

This is perhaps the most famous bird-walk in Britain. The land it skirts belongs to the Norfolk Naturalists' Trust and access to their hides within the marsh requires a permit. However, a marvellous variety of birds can be seen from the public hides provided by the Trust, and from surrounding paths and roads. **Waders, wildfowl** and other water birds are numerous; the scarce and the rare turn up regularly – so much so that to single out highlights would be meaningless.

Time and season Excellent at all seasons; may be positively crowded on fine weekends, particularly during migration.

Start Drive E through Cley village on the coastal A149, shortly stopping at **car park** (NNT) on right. The information centre here is worth a visit and supplies permits for the reserve itself.

① Cross the road and walk E, looking out over the marsh and taking advantage of the public hides on both sides of the road to view the pools. In about 400 yards (350 m) ② turn N, towards the sea, at the famous East Bank. Continue nearly ½ mile (0.8 km) to the end of the wall, where ③ turn left and walk along the top of the shingle sea-bank for ¾ mile (1 km) to ④ the Coastguard lookout. Turn S along the made-up road to Cley, ¾ mile (1 km) away. On reaching ⑤ the A149 turn left for the car park, ½ mile (0.8 km) on, mindful of the traffic. *About 200 yards (180 m) along the road from ② is the migration watch point of the Norfolk Ornithologists' Association at Walsey Hills. Another extension is to continue from ④ along the beach to Blakeney Point, for views over the harbour – terns in summer and migrants in the bushes, especially in autumn; 7 miles (11 km) there and back.*

Most surface-feeding duck species can be seen from the public hides, including gadwall and, in spring, garganey.

The roadside pools hold waders all the year round; avocets are the stars in summer, but spring and autumn passages bring wood and curlew sandpipers, spotted redshank, little and Temminck's stints, ruff and many more.

Look out for gulls and terns here in summer; common terns and black-headed gulls are easy to spot, but there may be little gulls (small size and buoyant flight) and black terns (picking insects from the water surface while in flight).

Breeding reed and sedge warblers much in evidence; the first tend to stay in the reeds, but should be visible with patience; sedge warblers often sing in the bush tops here – a mixture of many different notes, – with some harsh churring and scolding sounds and much mimicry of other birds.

The conifer plantation and the bushes often hold warblers, goldcrests and other small birds, especially on migration; no entry, but easily visible from the N side of the road.

East Bank gives fine views over the reed-beds to the left and the grazing marsh to the right. In spring and early summer, listen for the peculiar 'booming' of the bittern; later in the year, hope for one of the infrequent flying views of it.

Metallic 'pinging' calls mean bearded tits. Look for them flying over the reedbeds or clambering among the stems – still days are best. More reed and sedge warblers; also reed buntings.

Large numbers of swallows, martins and swifts often gather over the reedbeds to feed in summer.

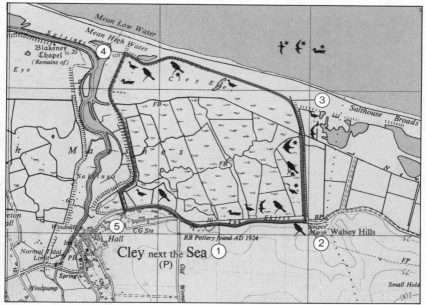

The marsh, known locally as Arnold's Marsh, is an excellent place for waders. Ringed plover, turnstone, common sandpiper, redshank, dunlin and others are regular; best in spring and autumn, when rarities turn up frequently.

Also a fine spot for terns – common, little and especially Sandwich. The last are much whiter birds than common terns (and are larger, too); the head and bill are more substantial and the tail is shorter. The distinctive shaggy 'cap' is a feature of breeding plumage and whitens quite early on in the breeding season. The bird dives from greater heights, and plunges deeper than other British terns.

From autumn to spring, look out to sea for divers, particularly red-throated; gannets, sea-duck, auks and gulls (including the regular glaucous) may be seen too. Autumn brings arctic and a few great skuas, also the chance of rarer, migrating seabirds. Fulmars may be seen year-round: note their powers of flight.

The pools visible S from the sea wall hold many waders, including both species of godwit, avocet, whimbrel and spotted redshank. Spring and autumn are the best times.

Snow buntings, the occasional Lapland bunting and shore lark, plus many other small, seed-eating birds, use the lee of the sea-bank and the marsh edges in winter.

Feral greylag and Canada geese are resident. Brent geese, wigeon and occasionally wild grey geese graze this marsh in winter, when golden plover, lapwings, larks and thrushes are numerous. The pool to the S often has diving ducks at the same season.

Check the damp areas to the E and W for migrant waders and yellow wagtails in summer.

Northern England

Sheep far outnumber the human population over most of this region; it is a big, empty landscape where some of our most spectacular and rare birds occur. The sea bird cliffs of Yorkshire, the offshore islands and sweeping bays of Northumberland, the uplands of the Pennines and the Lakeland fells are only the best known of its outstanding bird localities.

Increasing numbers of peregrines, as well as England's only golden eagles, breed in the Lake District. Curlews, golden plover and dunlin are memorable summer features of the uplands; guillemots, razorbills, puffins, terns, eiders and the only mainland gannet colony in Britain are the highlights of the coast.

The small woodlands and hedgerows which chequer the landscape attract large populations of songbirds, while the vast coniferous forests have thriving populations of crossbills and siskins.

In autumn there are many days when south-bound migrants make the east coast from Holy Island to Spurn Point (Head) a national focal point for birdwatching. Winter brings huge numbers of fieldfares and redwings from Scandinavia, whooper swans from Iceland, barnacle geese from Spitzbergen to the Solway Firth and pale-bellied brent geese from Svalbard to Holy Island.

Merlin

Ribble Estuary
3 or 1½ miles (5 or 2.5 km)
Landranger 108 338186 and
102 370200 SD 21/31 and SD 32/33

This roadside causeway gives every opportunity of seeing **duck**, flocks of **waders** and a variety of **sea birds** along the Southport foreshore and over the Marshside and Crossens Marshes. To the N is the Ribble National Nature Reserve, where huge numbers of geese, duck and waders occur from mid-autumn to spring. For some the highlight is the wintering flock of **Bewick's swans** numbering some times more than 200 birds.

Pink-footed geese fly to and from their feeding grounds at dawn and dusk except at full moon, when they may continue feeding by night. A very vocal goose.

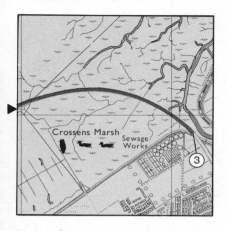

Time and season Outstanding in winter for the visiting wildfowl; best within 2 hours of high tide, when birds are forced off the estuary areas to feed or roost in concentrated numbers on the Marshside and Crossens Marshes.

Start Take the coastal road running N from the centre of Southport, or join the same road at the roundabout on the A565 (Preston–Southport road) and drive S. **Car park** (fee) nearly ¾ mile (1 km) NE of the pier; alternatively leave the car close to the sand-winning plant or along Marshside Road at 352205.

① From the car park turn right and walk NE on the path running beside the foreshore road. In a little over 1½ miles (2.5 km), at the sand-winning plant ②, continue along path to ③, the sewage works complex at the end of Crossens Marsh. Retrace to ①. *For a shorter walk, park near ② and walk ②–③–②.*

Before leaving the car park, scan the marine lake, particularly in winter when it can hold cormorants, goldeneye and a variety of gulls. After strong W winds species such as the Manx shearwater, Leach's petrel and kittiwake may show up. The snow bunting is not infrequent.

The marshes are host at different seasons to a range of species. Herons are resident. Duck present in winter include wigeon and pintail. Waders include huge numbers of oystercatchers, dunlin, knot, grey plover, bar-tailed godwits, snipe, sanderling, curlew and redshank. These are supplemented in spring by black-tailed godwits, ruff, common sandpipers, ringed plovers and often whimbrel.

In winter large numbers of pink-footed geese (and occasionally other geese species too) feed inland of Southport. They fly out to roost overnight on the estuary and the sight of their skeins (flight formations) winging their way towards the muddy expanses at dusk is unforgettable.

In winter, a hen harrier quartering the marsh is a frequent sight. Kestrels and merlins are regular visitors; peregrines regularly cause havoc among the wader flocks.

Look for short-eared owls over the marsh in winter. Particularly after high tides, when the water covers the ground vegetation of the estuary, a bird (or birds) is likely to be flushed out. It may then start hunting over Crossens Marsh.

The flock of Bewick's swans on Crossens Marsh is now famous.

One of the most enjoyable sights of Crossens in spring is the shelduck displaying in the fields or out on the estuary. Pursuit flights, together with much bobbing and neck-stretching, make this attractive bird even more interesting to observe than usual.

Besides being a haven for water birds and waders, the Ribble marshes attract passerines, particularly during the autumn and spring migrations. Watch for wheatears, whinchats, wagtails and warblers. During summer, regular nesting species are skylarks, meadow pipits, reed buntings and linnets.

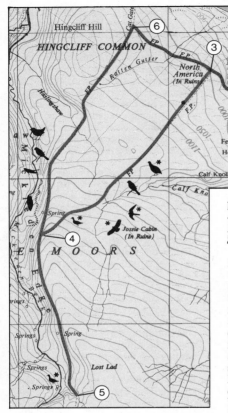

Langsett Moors
$4\frac{1}{2}$ miles (7 km)
Landranger 110 215997
SK 29

Moorland requires patient examination, and several visits may be needed to see all the specialities of this route – among them **golden plover** and (in winter) range of raptors including **hen harrier** and very occasionally **peregrine**. Frequent scanning with the binoculars (not forgetting to look back) pays dividends and adds to the enjoyment of the scenery. The area covered is within the Peak District National Park, easily accessible from the cities of S and W Yorkshire. *Well-used but exposed moorland path – dress appropriately with correct footwear; please keep to the footpaths; mud.*

Time and season Spring offers most bird activity, but no time of year is dull; best left to the hardier individual in deep winter.

Start In Langsett on the A616 take the road running S signposted 'Derwentdale and The Shrines'. Pass Langsett Reservoir and go through Upper Midhope. **Parking** in rather over 100 yards (90 m) on open area adjacent to road.

① From parking area go through bar-

Male red grouse; the bird utters a strident 'go-back' call when flushed from heather moorland. Rapid wing beats alternate with long glides, often in a rolling motion. Groups may fly low at great speed over moor.

rier and straight down towards the reservoir, passing through mixed woodland on the right and left. Bear left and ② go through the gate, rounding the S edge of the reservoir. Continue on this track with open moor to the left and conifer woodland on the right. In rather under ½ mile (0.8 km) the fenced edge of the woodland suddenly turns right. Immediately opposite this point ③ a path (sometimes obscured by bracken in summer) strikes off to the left. Follow it up the slight rise; after about 50 yards (45 m) it is better defined and marked by cairns. Continue on path across the moor and in about 1 mile (1.5 km), at ④ the junction with the well-defined path running N–S, bear left and continue S on this path about another mile (1.5 km) after which ⑤ retrace to ④ and continue straight ahead. In about 1¼ miles (2 km), at the junction with a path running off to the right ⑥, turn right (reservoir and woodland in sight), and follow this path, passing through ruins of North America Farm; retrace from ③ to car.

Before leaving the parking area check the surrounding fields in winter for flocks of fieldfares, bramblings or greenfinches. In spring the air is likely to be alive with the bubbling of curlews and 'drumming' of snipe.

Passing through the woodland, listen and watch for coal tits and goldcrests; also the possibility of hearing the 'tchek' of a great spotted woodpecker, or in spring the sound of it drumming on a trunk.

Tree pipits in song flight.

Once on the open moor, be alert for the often loud 'go-back, go-back' calls of the red grouse; these familiar birds of open moorland can fly in parties at terrific speeds, following the ground contours at low level. The dark tail is particularly conspicuous at take-off. With luck, you may see the twite, the upland equivalent of the linnet.

Raptors can be seen anywhere on these uplands. Kestrels and sparrowhawks are regular; merlins and hen harriers quite possible and peregrines occasional. (There are mountain hares up here, too; brown coat in summer, sometimes completely white in winter.)

In spring and early summer listen for the liquid calls of golden plover. The slow display flight performed over the bird's territory is conspicuous. They are slightly more numerous on the higher than on the lower ground. The birds' winter quarters are at lower levels.

The extension from ④ to ⑤ gives more opportunities of seeing all the moorland birds mentioned and may increase the chances of seeing golden plover.

Short-eared owls occasionally breed on this moorland. Their moth-like display flight, performed by day in spring, is well worth seeing. In winter they depart from higher ground.

Cuckoo calls ring round this valley in spring; there are numerous meadow pipits to be parasitized.

Dippers can still be seen along the Mickelden Beck (stream), although they are not so regular as they were. Also watch for ring ouzels – similar to blackbirds but with a white gorget or neck patch. Its call is a harsh 'tac tac tac'. Spend some time looking out over the bracken for whinchats.

After returning to the car, drive through Upper Midhope and park by the reservoir. Scan it for duck, especially in winter, when a gull roost also forms there. Look carefully for the individual, all-white gulls – glaucous gulls – uncommon winter visitors. In spring and summer listen and watch for the piping calls and rapid flight of common sandpipers, which breed on the reservoir edges.

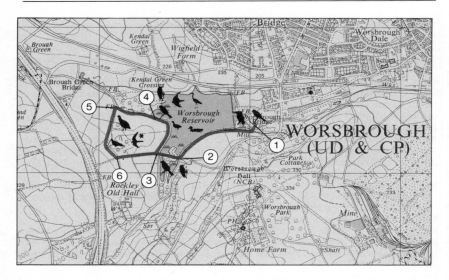

Worsbrough Mill Country Park
3 miles (5 km) Landranger 110 350033
SE 20/30

The focal point of this route is the reservoir, but the woodland, some of it damp, together with the adjacent farmland offer the fascination of a wide range of habitats with a remarkable range of birds concentrated in a small area. There is a fair chance of seeing the **lesser spotted woodpecker** and **water rail**. *The Mill Museum (convenient shelter if it rains) offers information about the area; mud after rain.*

Time and season Relatively low-lying, the reservoir rarely freezes over, and keeps its ducks in winter. Spring and autumn are considerably enlivened by birds on passage.

Start The Park is 2 miles (3 km) S of the centre of Barnsley on the A61. **Car park** well signposted immediately adjacent to the main road.

① Take the exit path at the W corner of the car park. Ignore the road leading right marked 'Mill Museum' and go through the gate forking left with the path. In about 50 yards (45 m) bear right over the bridge and up the steps on to the bank of the reservoir. Continue to the far end, rejoin the footpath and turn right. In 20 yards (18 m) ② turn right and then in 100 yards (90 m) ③ turn right again along the surfaced track running round the margin of the reservoir. Soon after the track curves left, stop at the hide ④. Continue along the track until ⑤, a footbridge with a path leading off left; follow this – it circles some woodland and a meadow, then joins ⑥ a farm track. Turn left and follow track to ③: retrace to car park.

As soon as you leave the car park look to the right over the River Dove. Kingfishers, which breed nearby, can often be seen along this stretch.

The mature trees and other vegetation in the vicinity hold a variety of commoner species, including great tits, blue tits, wrens, goldfinches and blackbirds. Spotted flycatchers will often be seen in the trees close to the Mill in summer.

Herons are common around the reservoir. Great crested grebes, little grebes, mallard, tufted duck, coots and moorhens all breed on the reservoir. In winter pochard are usually present; tufted duck and goldeneye are less common here.

Great spotted woodpeckers usually breed in this area together with willow warblers and blackcaps. The willow tit, which favours damp woodland, is quite easily seen – locate it by the nasal call. Do not worry about confusing it with the very similar marsh tit, which is not at all regular in the area.

The hide gives a fine view of the muddy spit where the migrating waders stop to feed. Lapwings, little ringed plovers, snipe, greenshank and common sandpipers are regularly recorded.

In September, the swallow roost is a spectacle. From early in the evening, the birds start congregating to feed over the water, their numbers building up into the hundreds; they then roost in the reedbeds close to the hide.

Another speciality is the water rail; in winter especially a patient vigil looking out through the channel cut in the reeds will produce excellent views of this shy skulker of the waterside vegetation.

The hide is also likely to give a glimpse of a reed warbler, a skulker best located by its song. However, it does emerge to sing from a reed stem occasionally, and may also be seen working along the edge of the reedbed, or in characteristic bouncing flight over the reed tops.

The lesser spotted woodpecker has bred in this area in recent years. One year it made its nest hole in an old tree beyond the reedbed opposite the hide, which gave excellent views of this tiny, highly attractive bird. It is worth looking closely to see if it has nested in another tree nearby.

In autumn and winter look for a covey of grey partridge flying over the fields behind the reservoir or, in summer, an individual pair; they are resident.

Kestrels around the reservoir.

In addition to the commoner passerines, woodpigeons are present in the spinneys and are frequently seen feeding in the fields.

The lesser spotted woodpecker is tiny – almost sparrow-sized. There are several points to distinguish it from the great spotted, the most obvious, in flight, being the lack of white shoulder patches and vivid red splash of the under-tail coverts. Its drumming, less loud than the great spotted woodpecker's, but of longer duration, may be heard in spring.

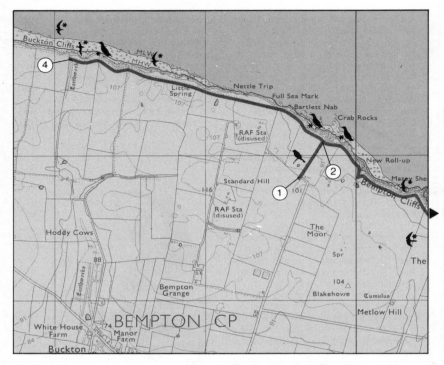

Bempton Cliffs
$3\frac{1}{2}$ miles (5.5 km)
Landranger 101 200737 TA 26/27

An opportunity to view at close quarters the largest sea bird colony in England, as well as the only mainland nest site for **gannets** in the British Isles.

The chalk cliffs, in places 400 feet (120 m) high, are topped by a layer of boulder-clay, and there are 2 layers of chalk of which the upper, being more flinty and weathering more easily, provides plenty of nest sites.

The area is an RSPB reserve.

Close to the E end of the walk is the N end of the huge earthwork Danes' Dyke; believed to be pre-Bronze Age, its origins are uncertain. *Mud after rain.*

Time and season Outstanding in spring and summer; autumn can be interesting, too.

Start From Bridlington take the B1255 signposted Flamborough. In 2 miles (3 km), entering the village of Marton, take the minor road on the left signposted Bempton. Go straight over the main road in Bempton following sign to RSPB reserve. In 1 mile (1.5 km) is the RSPB **car park**.

① From the car park follow the track past RSPB display area and in $\frac{1}{4}$ mile (0.5 km) join cliff-top path, where ② turn right. Follow the footpath 1 mile (1.5 km) to its junction with Danes' Dyke. Retrace to ② and continue straight ahead on the footpath for a

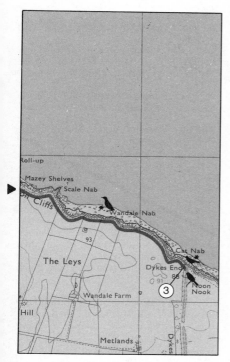

is a memorable feature of the cliffs in the breeding season.

The comical-looking puffin is one of the most striking and colourful birds to be seen along the cliffs. They lay their single eggs in cracks and holes along the entire length of the cliffs.

Another hole-nesting species often found at sea bird colonies is the jackdaw. The smallest of the crow family, it feeds and nests near the tops of the cliffs.

A variety of small passerines take advantage of the food and shelter provided by the trees of Danes' Dyke, particularly in the autumn. Tree sparrows occur here and even on the cliffs.

Kestrels regularly hover over the fields behind the cliff-top.

Britain's only mainland gannet colony is on this section of the cliff. They are one of the biggest of our sea birds and can be seen plunge-diving for fish out at sea. They may drop from more than 100 feet (30 m), holding their wings right back before entry.

The large gull species also nest here; herring and great black-backed can be seen drifting along on rising air currents by the cliffs.

Fulmars are masters at using rising air currents, and can rise from sea level to the top of the cliff in seconds without a wing beat. Take time watching them: their range of aerobatics is truly remarkable: it is almost as if they are performing especially for the spectator.

Cormorants are often seen flying by, particularly in spring and autumn; small numbers of shags breed low down on the cliffs.

The cliffs are excellent vantage points for watching migrant terns in autumn being harried by the predatory arctic skuas.

further ¾ mile (1 km) to the point ④ where a well-defined footpath joins from the left. Return to ②, where turn right and follow track alongside hedge to car park. *From ③ a detour can be made by turning S along Danes' Dyke; return at will.*

The hedgerow is a likely place for yellowhammers and corn buntings. Whitethroats and other migrant warblers can be found here in spring and autumn.

Large numbers of guillemots and razorbills breed on the high cliffs and can be seen flying back and forth with food for their young during summer months.

Thousands of pairs of kittiwakes, the most numerous of Britain's sea birds, breed on the cliffs; their continuous noisy clamour

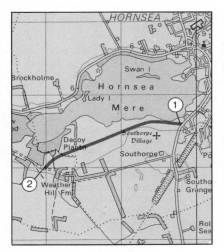

Hornsea Mere
2½ miles (4 km) Landranger 107 197466

A large, freshwater lake owned by the RSPB holding a typical variety of wild-fowl and waders; less than 1 mile (1.5 km) from the sea, it also attracts many unusual species on migration. *Open water, reeds, woods, farmland.*

Summer cormorant, garganey, little gull, reed warbler, yellow wagtail; **autumn** waders, black tern, migrant warblers, whinchat, wheatear; **winter** teal, wigeon, pochard, tufted duck, goldeneye, goosander; **all year** great crested grebe, heron, water rail, corn bunting.

Start Travelling S through Hornsea on the B1242, turn right before the railway bridge on to a minor road (to Great Hatfield). **Parking** at Kirkholme Point.

① Follow the footpath W for 1¼ miles (2 km) and ② return by same route.

Water rail, easy to identify – no water bird of similar size has a beak the same length.

Blacktoft Sand
4 miles (6.5 km) Landranger 106 843232

This large, tidal reedbed, situated at the confluence of the rivers Trent and Humber, is an RSPB nature reserve. A number of lagoons have been created, and there are hides; interesting all times of the year. *Reedbed, saltmarsh, open water.*

Summer shoveler, marsh harrier, little ringed plover, grasshopper, sedge and reed warblers; **winter** pink-footed goose, teal, hen harrier, merlin; **passage** little stint, spotted redshank, greenshank, sandpipers; **all year** shelduck, gadwall, water rail, redshank, short-eared owl, bearded tit, reed bunting.

Start From Goole take the A161 E along the river and after 2 miles (3 km) turn left in Swinefleet on to a minor road to Ousefleet. Continue past Ousefleet. RSPB **car park** in ½ mile (0.8 km).

There is a hide immediately opposite the car park. Walk to this and then follow the track behind the sea wall, walking E for one mile before returning and walking W for 1 mile (1.5 km). Return to car park.

Bolton Abbey Woods
4½ *miles (7 km) Landranger 104*
075553

The wooded valley of the River Wharfe just N of Bolton Abbey is a rich bird-watching area, particularly in summer. *Woods, river.*

Summer common sandpiper, pied fly-catcher, redstart; **all year** sparrowhawk, kestrel, woodcock, kingfisher, grey wag-tail, dipper.

Start From Ilkley take the A65 NW for 2 miles (3 km). Then turn right on to the B6160, which joins the A59 after 2 miles (3 km). Turn left on to the A59 but in 200 yards (180 m) turn right, back on to the B6160 to Bolton Abbey. **Car park** 1 mile (1.5 km) after Bolton Abbey, on the right.

From the car park walk to the river and ① follow the path which leads NW alongside the river. After 2 miles (3 km) the path reaches ② a road bridge; cross the river here and return along the other bank. After 1½ miles (2.5 km) the path joins a road ③. Follow it for only 200 yards (180 m) and then ④ return to the path which leads to ⑤ another bridge, opposite the car park. Cross the bridge and return to the car park.

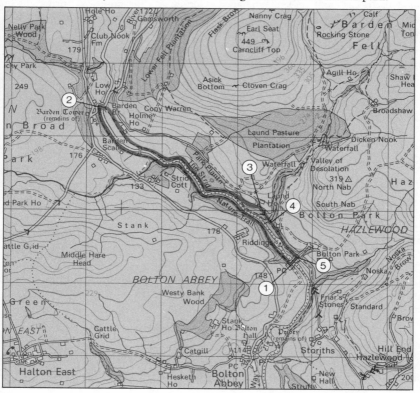

Ainsdale Sands
6 miles (9.5 km) Landranger 108
292084

A National Nature Reserve owned by the Nature Conservancy Council and managed to preserve the sand-dune system, which consists of a range of habitats from sandy beach to plantation. *Beach, dunes, slacks (wet hollows); do not wander from the paths.*

Summer cuckoo, blackcap, chiffchaff, willow warbler, whitethroat; **winter** scoter, sparrowhawk, turnstone, sanderling, bar-tailed godwit, woodcock, siskin, willow tit; **passage** black-tailed godwit (occasional), green sandpiper, greenshank, arctic skua, terns, auks, whinchat; **all year** shelduck, kestrel, partridge, long-eared owl (occasional), tawny owl, little grebe, snipe, coot, moorhen, great spotted woodpecker, skylark, goldcrest, coal tit, treecreeper, yellowhammer, reed bunting, redpoll.

Start Freshfield railway station in Formby. **Car park** at the station.

Paths on the reserve are marked by white-topped posts. ① From the station follow the road N alongside the railway line. Continue ⅔ mile (1 km) then ② cross the line and follow the footpath, known as the Fisherman's Path, out to the dunes. At the dunes ③ turn right on

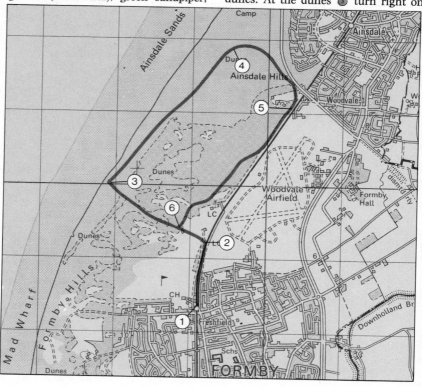

to the Dune Path North, which runs N through the NNR and continues to the Local Nature Reserve. From the LNR boundary the route continues N for ⅔ mile (1 km) and ④ veers right, returning to the NNR along the Pinfold Path. Follow this path to the railway line, where ⑤ turn right and follow the Woodland Path, which runs SW back to the Fisherman's Path, where ⑥ turn left, recross the railway line and retrace to the car park.

Morecambe Bay
6 miles (9.5 km) Landranger 97
467666

Morecambe Bay is the premier estuary for waders in Britain, attracting more than 200,000 at peak times every winter, together with large numbers of wildfowl. The vast estuarine sand- and mudflats provide food for the waders at low tide, and as the tide rises the birds gradually move inshore, clustering in spectacular flocks as space becomes restricted. The RSPB owns about 6,000 acres on the E of the bay, N of Morecambe, but by no means all of it is protected against development threats. *Sand- and mudflats, saltmarsh, sea; information hut at Hest Bank open on spring tide weekends, March; dangerous channels and quicksands and extremely rapid incoming tide on the foreshore.*

All year shelduck, oystercatcher, ringed plover, dunlin, redshank, curlew; **winter** divers, great crested grebe, pink-footed goose, wigeon, pintail, scaup, eider, scoter, goldeneye, red-breasted merganser, peregrine, merlin, turnstone, knot, sanderling, purple sandpiper, golden plover, grey plover, bar-tailed godwit; **passage** curlew sandpiper, ruff, black-tailed godwit, greenshank.

Start From Morecambe follow the A5105 NE along the bay to Hest Bank, where there is a **public car park.**

From Hest Bank follow the shoreline to the stone jetty at Morecambe, which is a good vantage point for sea-watching. Return by same route.

Leighton Moss
1¼ miles (2 km) Landranger 97
478751

Leighton Moss, although a comparatively small RSPB reserve, is one of the largest reedbeds in N England and the only nesting place of the bittern and bearded tit in this part of the country. Before the 1914–18 War, the land was reclaimed by drainage, but it has since reverted to marshland, providing a rich habitat for birds at all seasons. *Reed-marsh, meres, scrub; visitor centre and shop; open 10–5 April–March, Sat, Sun, Wed and also Thurs, April–Sept; entry fee, children half price.*

All year bittern, teal, gadwall, shoveler, pochard, tufted duck, sparrowhawk, water rail, woodcock, barn owl, bearded tit, reed bunting; **summer** garganey, grasshopper, sedge and reed warblers, lesser whitethroat; **passage** occasional marsh harrier and osprey, ruff, spotted redshank, greenshank and other passage waders, black tern, swallow and wagtail roost; **winter** wigeon, pintail, goldeneye, redpoll.

Start From Junction 35 on the M6 join the A6 heading N towards Kendal. After 3 miles (5 km) turn left on to a minor road to Yealand Redmayne. Turn right in the village and after ½ mile (0.8 km) bear left to Silverdale. The RSPB **car park** is on the left after 1 mile (1.5 km). Report to Warden at visitor centre on arrival.

A bridleway runs along the causeway between Leighton Moss and Storrs Moss. Follow this for ⅔ mile (1 km) and return by the same route. There is a public hide on the causeway.

Whitestone Cliff
*3 miles (5 km) Landranger 100 515830
SE58 or Outdoor Leisure Map, North York
Moors, W Sheet.*

Some fine, natural tree cover has developed on the steep slopes of the W escarpment of the North York Moors and this walk is largely devoted to its impressive range of woodland species, from the tiny goldcrest of the coniferous plantations to the spectacular redstart of the hardwoods. Part of the route follows the Cleveland Way long-distance path and there are splendid views of Gormire Lake. *Mud after rain.*

Time and season Best in spring and summer, but worthwhile at other times.

Start From Thirsk take the A170 signposted Scarborough and in 6 miles (9.5 km) slow down at the top of the 1 in 4 Sutton Bank. **Car park** on left (the first one) just beyond road to Cold Kirby.

① From car park walk back to top of Bank and cross road on to well-defined track with conifer wood on right and escarpment on left. In about 550 yards (500 m) ② take track downhill to left, where white arrow on path marks nature trail. Follow track down towards Gormire Lake. At signpost D of the nature trail, ignore the arrow pointing right and take the main track straight downhill to the lake shore, where ③ turn right on track following edge of lake. Continue with obvious main track for 550 yards (500 m) to T-junction and Garbutt Wood nature reserve sign, where ④ turn left for short detour to old cottage, going through white gate on green track marked Public Bridleway and continuing 100 yards (90 m) for a close look at ⑤ wet area in field on left. Retrace to ④ and continue directly uphill with Whitestone Scar visible ahead. Follow the steep, well-defined track to the top of the escarpment where ⑥ it joins the Cleveland Way. Turn right and

follow the track along the escarpment edge for 1 mile (1.5 km) to the car park.

🗡 Linnets and yellowhammers frequent the hawthorn scrub at the top of the escarpment. The latter hold the head back and open the bill wide when singing.

🗡 Coal tits favour the coniferous woodland on the right of the track.

🗡 Descending the track to the lake gives views in spring of willow warblers and chiffchaffs singing in the tops of the trees below.

🗡 Tree pipits rise, and parachute down on to isolated trees here in their song flight.

🗡 Look for wrens flitting about in the dense under-storey on the lower slopes.

🗡 Open glades are usually the best places to look for warblers. Here, look especially for blackcaps and garden warblers.

🗡 Redstarts occur in fair numbers where the oaks predominate.

🪶 The lake does not support large wildfowl populations, but coots, moorhens and mallard occur.

🗡 Sedge warblers in the reeds at the end of the lake in spring and summer; reed buntings all year.

🗡 Relatively immature mixed woodland such as this supports large numbers of common birds such as blackbirds, robins and chaffinches.

🗡 Swallows nest in the outbuildings of the dilapidated cottage and there are blackcaps in the orchard.

🗡 The small, reed-covered pool in the field has sedge warblers, yellow wagtails and moorhens, while the trees and hedgerows nearby contain a wide range of species, including redstarts.

- Where the more mature trees occur half-way up the slope, listen (in spring and early summer) for wood warblers.

- Migrating wheatears use the escarpment for stopovers during spring; they're less evident in autumn because then the migration is staggered.

- Large numbers of swallows and swifts hunt the flying insects along the escarpment on spring and autumn passage.

- Upcurrents of air along the escarpment edge give kestrels effortless lift while hunting for small mammals in the vegetation at the top of the cliff.

- Spotted flycatchers sit in the small copses along the track, frequently sallying forth to catch flies.

- Woodpigeons and occasionally stock doves over the tree tops below.

Male redstart in full breeding plumage: the russet tail is constantly quivered and sets off the blue-grey upperparts to great effect. By the time birds are ready to leave for Africa in October the grey fades to brown.

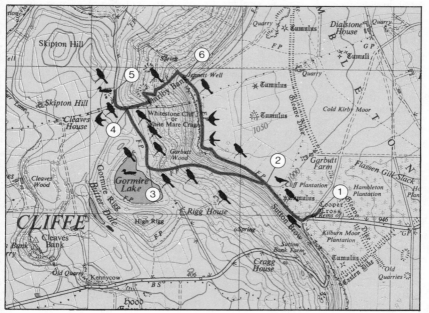

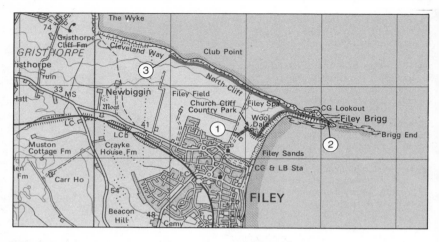

Filey Brigg
4 miles (6.5 km) Landranger 101 117813

A rocky promontory in the North Sea providing an excellent vantage point for watching sea bird passage; at low tide the area is a feeding ground for waders. *Open water, rocks, sand flats.*

Summer common, arctic, Sandwich and little terns, wheatear; **autumn** red-throated diver, Manx shearwater, scoter, skuas, migrant warblers, fly-catchers, chats, thrushes and finches; **winter** scoter, turnstone, knot, sanderling, snow bunting; **all year** fulmar, gannet, cormorant, oystercatcher, dunlin, redshank.

Start At the roundabout on the A1039 in Filey follow the signs to the caravan park and Church Cliff Country Park and a large 'pay and display' **car park.**

① From the car park follow the path leading down the cliff to the sailing club. If low tide, walk along the beach to Filey Brigg. At high tide, follow the cliff-top path. From Filey Brigg ② follow the cliff path W for about 1 mile (1.5 km) to ③ and retrace to ①.

Ingleborough
8 miles (13 km) Landranger 98 701731

A walk through the open moorland of the Yorkshire Dales National Park, via the summit of Ingleborough, at 2,372 feet (723 m) the second highest peak in England. Besides a view indicator, the summit plateau has primitive hut circles and remains of Iron Age walls. *Moor; do not attempt in poor visibility.*

Summer golden plover, curlew, whinchat, wheatear, ring ouzel; **winter** hen harrier, peregrine; **all year** red grouse, meadow pipit.

Start From Lancaster take the A683 and A687 NE for 16 miles (25.5 km) to the outskirts of Ingleton where the road meets the A65 at a staggered cross-roads, where take the B6255 into Ingleton. **Parking** in the town.

Continue along the B6255 for 3½ miles (5.5 km). Beyond a small wood (the only wood along this road), a bridleway leads up Ingleborough. Follow it to the summit and then take the bridleway SW directly back to Ingleton.

Sparrowhawk in pursuit of blackbird: the smallish head, shortish but broad wings, their ends rounded, and a long, squared-off tail identify this predator.

Wykeham (formerly Broxa) Forest
1¾ or 3 miles (3 or 5 km)
Landranger 101 965945

Reasty Hill picnic site gives views over this area of forest and farmland, and is a starting point for several Forestry Commission walks. For the energetic, a 16-mile (25.5-km) route gives beautiful views over the Derwent Valley and Vale of Pickering. But for birdwatchers, the Silpho Forest Walks of 1¾ miles (3 km) with a 1¼-mile (2-km) extension should yield a good variety of woodland species. Although the woods are mainly coniferous, created by modern forestry, they do 'nurse' some broadleaved trees. *Woods; leaflets are available from the National Park Information Centre, Pickering Railway Station.*

Summer turtle dove, nightjar, garden warbler, blackcap, whitethroat, chiffchaff, spotted flycatcher; **winter** siskin; **all year** sparrowhawk, long-eared owl, green woodpecker, great and lesser spotted woodpeckers, goldcrest, long-tailed tit, coal tit, treecreeper, redpoll, jay.

Start From Scarborough take the A171 to Scalby and then turn left (N) on to a minor road leading to Harwood Dale. After 1 mile (1.5 km) bear left, and left again after a further ½ mile (0.8 km) along an unsigned road to Coomboots. After Coomboots turn first right and continue for 2¼ miles (3.5 km) to the Forestry Commission's Reasty Hill picnic site and **car park**, which is immediately before a steep downhill drop in the road.

Follow directions for the Silpho Forest Walks given on the Forestry Commission's information board.

Goldcrest on juniper: agile as a tit (and about half the weight), restless and often difficult to locate in foliage.

Ullswater SE Shore

5½ miles (9 km) Landranger 90 423197 NY 41 and Outdoor Leisure Map, The English Lakes, E Sheet.

The route gives excellent opportunities of seeing typical Lake District woodland and upland species, as well as following the shore of one of the best known lakes with fine views of Helvellyn and the surrounding mountains. The predominant woodland is birch, with some mature oak and the occasional stretch of juniper, the formerly widespread species of conifer favoured by several bird species, but notably goldcrests and here also wrens. One short fell stretch has *mud after rain*.

Time and season Best in spring and summer – several of the most interesting species are summer visitors.

Start From the M6 at Penrith take the A66 signposted Keswick. At the first roundabout take the A592 to Waterfoot, then the B5320 to Pooley Bridge, where fork right on to the minor road signposted Howtown and Sandwick. After 4 miles (6.5 km) the road ascends in a series of sharp bends; take the first, unmarked right-hand fork. In 1 mile (1.5 km) turn sharp right on to road signposted Sandwick. **Parking** on broad verge opposite houses at Sandwick.

① From Sandwick follow the well-defined track marked Patterdale, keep-

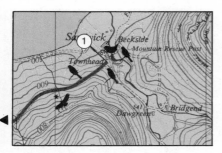

ing the dry stone wall on the right, and keeping right immediately after passing a stone barn. After crossing the stream by the wooden footbridge, ascend the short bank, again with the wall on the right. On turning right at the corner of the wall, keep to the right-hand track. From the bottom of the hill continue with the single, well-defined stony track close to the shore and for about $\frac{3}{4}$ mile (1 km) through mature birch and oak woodland. On leaving the woodland ② follow the track round the N side of Silver Crag. In a further $\frac{3}{4}$ mile (1 km), just where the trees end on the right, ③ turn sharp left uphill on the well-defined track by the small group of larch trees. Follow the track gently uphill to just below the summit of Silver Crag (on left) before descending quite steeply through juniper and hawthorn to ② the junction with the main track, where turn right and follow track back to ①.

Dippers and grey wagtails are particularly attracted to the fast-flowing hill streams.

Pied wagtails find food easily on the short turf by the path.

The mature oaks and alders on the right of the track are excellent for chaffinches and redpolls.

Buzzards are regularly seen soaring over the open fell sides.

Meadow pipits find plentiful choices of nest sites in the tussocky grass clear of bracken.

Dippers sometimes build a nest behind the waterfall on the hillside to the left.

Broken crags with generous vegetation cover attract ring ouzels.

Where the path passes through open fell side above the lake, watch out for buzzards, kestrels and peregrines.

Common sandpipers feed along the lake's stony shore; also watch for tufted duck and red-breasted merganser.

Where the birch woodland begins, redstarts are often perched prominently.

The juniper scrub provides excellent cover and nest sites for small birds such as goldcrests and wrens.

Where the older and more decayed birch trees occur, great spotted and green woodpeckers may be seen. Also a likely area for spotted flycatchers.

Ravens occur on the crags high above the path and can usually be heard calling before they are seen.

Coal tits, great tits and blue tits are common in this woodland; willow warblers and chiffchaffs (spring, summer).

Black-headed and herring gulls roost on the lake.

Jackdaws, which are hole-nesters, are sometimes very common where the older trees occur; they may also use crevices among rocks for nesting.

Wheatears are attracted to the sheep-grazed grass on the hillside and nest under the scattered boulders.

Whinchats also occur on the open hillsides, often perching prominently.

CUMBRIA

St Bees Head
$6\frac{1}{2}$ miles (10.5 km)
Landranger 89 961118

The red sandstone cliffs of this RSPB reserve harbour more than 5,000 breeding birds, the largest sea bird colony on the W coast of England and the only mainland breeding site in England of the black guillemot. The reserve is mainly of interest during the summer, although unusual species may occur on passage. *Cliffs, gorse, grassland.*

Summer fulmar, shag, kestrel, herring gull, kittiwake, razorbill, guillemot, black guillemot, puffin, rock pipit, stonechat, raven.

Start Leave Whitehaven S on the B5345. After about 4 miles (6.5 km), at a staggered crossroads where the B-road turns left, carry straight on along a minor road to a T-junction and turn right. Continue $\frac{1}{3}$ mile (0.5 km) to end of road; trains to St Bees, $\frac{1}{2}$ mile (0.8 km) from ①.

① From the car park follow the cliff path around South Head, St Bees Head to reach ② the lighthouse at North Head after about $2\frac{1}{2}$ miles (4 km). Continue $\frac{3}{4}$ mile (1 km) and ③ turn right, away from the cliffs, along the path which in $\frac{1}{4}$ mile (0.5 km) joins ④ a track. Continue another $\frac{1}{4}$ mile (0.5 km) to the staggered crossroads and carry straight on. In $\frac{1}{2}$ mile (0.8 km) the track turns ⑤ sharp left, but a footpath carries straight on. Follow this to St Bees Head. At the cliffs turn left back to ①.

Adult black guillemot in summer plumage; winter plumage is not nearly so distinctive. Breeding displays include water dances.

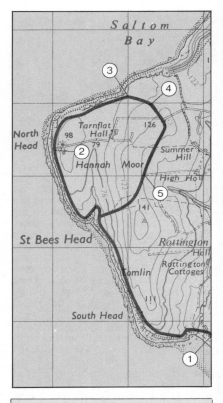

Siddick Pond is an interesting stretch of water supporting a variety of birds throughout the year in industrialized surroundings. It is only $\frac{1}{2}$ mile (0.8 km) from the sea. Reasonable views of it may be had from the A596, 1 mile (1.5 km) N of Workington.

The village of Ravenglass is a fine vantage point for viewing the nature reserve on Drigg Dunes at the mouth of the Rivers Irt, Mite and Esk. The reserve has a large colony of breeding black-headed gulls, also wildfowl and waders. Ravenglass is close to the A595, 16 miles (24 km) S of Whitehaven.

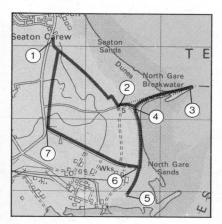

Tees Mouth
4½ miles (7 km) Landranger 93 525291

This route gives fine views NE to North Sea and E and S across the estuary of the River Tees. Wildfowl and waders are numerous all year, and particularly in autumn and winter. *Tidal estuary.*

Autumn little stint, curlew sandpiper, ruff, greenshank, wood sandpiper, bar-tailed godwit, whimbrel; **winter** shelduck, wigeon, teal, pintail, shoveler, pochard, scaup, long-tailed duck, goldeneye, golden plover, grey plover, knot, sanderling, ruff, bar-tailed godwit; **all year** wildfowl, waders.

Start Leave Hartlepool S on the A178 to Seaton Carew; trains to Seaton Carew station, 1 mile (1.5 km) from the start of the walk. **Parking** in Seaton Carew.

① Take the footpath which leads SE from the A178 on the S edge of Seaton Carew, soon ignoring the right-hand fork. Continue nearly ¾ mile (1 km), through left and right turns, to the private road, where ② turn left and make for the breakwater. Continue to ③ the end of the breakwater, retrace

to ④ and turn left to walk along the sea wall. In about ¾ mile (1 km) ⑤ turn back having viewed Seal Sands SSW across the water. In ¼ mile (0.5 km) ⑥ turn left along private road. Follow this nearly 1 mile (1.5 km) back to the A178, where ⑦ turn right on to the footpath running N, close to the road. Follow this back to ①.

Witton-le-Wear
1¼ miles (2 km) Landranger 92 162315

Durham County Conservation Trust's programme of tree-planting and provision of nest boxes has encouraged a variety of woodland birds, including the tawny owl and stock dove, to breed on this 80-acre (32-ha) reserve. Lakes and pools, relics of gravel extraction, attract a variety of water birds, and the sewage works, overlooked by Oak Tree Hide, are a feeding ground for waders. *Woods, grassland, scrub, open water; free entry to members of any county conservation trust; non-members should ask permission from the Warden (038888) 559.*

Summer oystercatcher, little ringed plover, common sandpiper, curlew, sand martin, tree pipit, grasshopper, sedge, garden and willow warblers, whitethroat; **autumn** greenshank, green sandpiper; **winter** wigeon, shoveler, pochard, goldeneye, goosander; **all year** little grebe, heron, greylag goose, teal, snipe, stock dove, tawny owl, kingfisher, grey wagtail, dipper, tree sparrow.

Start From Tow Law take the A68 to Witton-le-Wear, turning left into the village along minor road. Continue through the village, across the level crossing and then for a further ¼ mile (0.5 km) to a signposted one-bar white gate. Turn right through gateway. **Parking** near the farmhouse and laboratory, along the road.

There is a circular nature trail around the reserve; follow the guide posts.

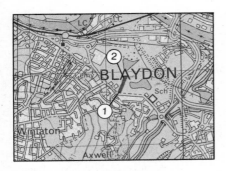

Shibdon Pond Nature Reserve
1 mile (1.5 km) Landranger 88
192627

The pond, a nature reserve managed by the Durham County Conservation Trust, lies on the outskirts of Newcastle upon Tyne. Despite the urban surroundings, it has an interesting variety of birds with several species of warbler breeding and an occasional whooper swan in winter. *Open water, reedbeds, marsh, scrub; the reserve is open to the public, but visitors must keep to the route given below.*

Summer water rail, swift, swallow, house martin, yellow wagtail, grasshopper warbler, sedge warbler, whitethroat; **winter** teal, shoveler, pochard, tufted duck, goldeneye; **all year** heron, coot, moorhen.

Start From Newcastle upon Tyne take the A6125 and the A692 towards Blaydon. Leave the A692 and take the A69 at the junction directed to Blaydon; take the A694 and at the second roundabout take the second exit, the B6317. Continue ½ mile (0.8 km) to the public swimming baths, on the right. **Parking** at the baths.

A public footpath starts ① close to the swimming baths, and leads to ② the start of the circular nature trail. Follow the numbered guide posts (1–8).

Adult arctic skua (pale phase) mobs a common tern. Juveniles lack the long, projecting tail feathers. Besides harassing birds to make them release food, skuas take eggs, young and adults of several species. Watch for the remarkable burst of speed arctic skuas make when a victim is sighted – the wings practically meet under the body.

Trimdon Grange Quarry, a disused magnesian limestone quarry managed as a nature reserve by Durham County Conservation Trust, is overlooked by hawthorn scrub and ash woodland which support a large number of resident birds with additional winter visitors. The quarry lies 9 miles (14.5 km) W of Hartlepool, to the W of the back road between Trimdon and Trimdon Grange. It is not open to the general public, but access is free to members of any county conservation trust.

Hamsterley Forest, 10 miles (16 km) W of Bishop Auckland, contains a number of interesting forest walks. The Forestry Commission's Information Centre gives details and contains a display describing wildlife in the forest. From Hamsterley village approach Bedburn and turn left near the bridge to reach the centre.

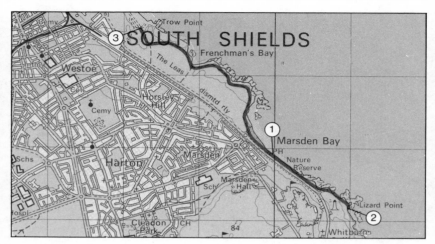

Marsden Rock
5 miles (8 km) Landranger 88 397653

An easy and pleasant walk along the cliffs looking out across the North Sea. The main attraction in summer is Marsden Rock, an isolated stack cut off from the main cliff providing a nesting site for kittiwakes and fulmars as well as an important breeding site for cormorants. *Sea, cliffs, grassland; keep strictly to the paths – the cliffs can be dangerous.*

Summer fulmar, cormorant, shag, kittiwake; **autumn** skuas, terns; **winter** divers, scoter.

Start Approach South Shields on the A183 coastal road from Whitburn. After passing the lighthouse on the right, in ¼ mile (0.5 km) there is a small **car park** at the Marsden Grotto public house immediately adjacent to Marsden Rock, or a larger one a little further along the road.

① From either car park, follow the path near the cliff edge SE to ② the lighthouse. Return to car park and follow the cliff path N to ③ Trow Point. Return to car park.

Chopwell Wood
½ to 2 miles (0.8 to 3 km)
Landranger 88 136598

Originally old Crown woodland, but now about 80% coniferous forest. The Forestry Commission picnic site provides a starting point for 3 waymarked walks. *Forest.*

Summer willow warbler, chiffchaff, wood warbler; **all year** sparrowhawk, kestrel, long-eared, little and tawny owls, green and great spotted woodpeckers, goldcrest, long-tailed, willow and coal tits, treecreeper, siskin.

Start From Newcastle upon Tyne take the A694 via Blaydon to Rowlands Gill. Turn right along a minor road through the forest, which is signposted from the A694. The picnic site with **parking** is ½ mile (0.8 km) from the main road.

Follow one of the 3 waymarked walks from the picnic site.

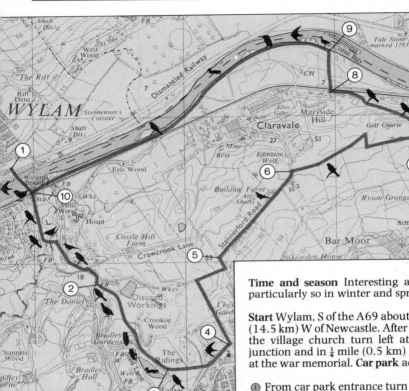

Tyne Valley
5 miles (8 km)
Landranger 88 117646 NZ 06/16

The route meanders through some of the typical farmland and small-scale woodland of the S slope of the main Tyne valley, and finally along the river itself. This wide range of habitats, and birds using the valley as a migratory flight line, means a fine cross-section of species from **common garden birds** to wintering **goldeneye** and **goosander**. Although the walk starts in Northumberland, all but ½ mile (0.8 km) lies in Tyne & Wear.

Time and season Interesting all year, particularly so in winter and spring.

Start Wylam, S of the A69 about 9 miles (14.5 km) W of Newcastle. After passing the village church turn left at the T-junction and in ¼ mile (0.5 km) fork left at the war memorial. **Car park** adjacent.

① From car park entrance turn left and follow the footpath over Wylam Bridge; follow the road straight ahead for ⅓ mile (0.5 km) to the main Y-junction, where take the right-hand fork marked Sled Lane. In 150 yards (140 m) ② turn left on to the public footpath marked 'Crawcrook ½ mile'. After crossing the small footbridge walk straight to the crest of the small mound, then follow hedge line around 2 sides of the field, crossing wooden stile in far corner. There bear left on to track around field to house, where cross the wall by the stone stile. Take the narrow path on high ground to the left through woodland. In ¼ mile (0.5 km) ③ turn left over stile and follow track through field for 200 yards (180 m). Cross another stile, make short descent to main road and turn left. In 200 yards (180 m) turn left past filling station on to public footpath ④ and follow it downhill for 400 yards (350 m) to access road to gravel pit. Turn right and in 200 yards (180 m) left on to main road. In 100 yards (90 m) ⑤ turn right on to road signposted Clara Vale. After ½ mile (0.8 km) ⑥ take path on right (marked Public Footpath), entering golf course. Keep hedge on right for 100 yards (90 m), then keep straight on into field with hedge now on left. At end of field cross stile into golf course practice ground. Keep hedge on left and follow around lower edge of practice ground for about ⅓ mile (0.5 km) to ⑦ T-junction with main track near green corrugated building. Turn left on to this track and follow initially across course, then gently downhill through woodland to railway crossing ⑧. Take care crossing the line and continue straight ahead across golf course, following line of small trees to river bank and ⑨ junction with well-defined metalled track, where turn left. Continue along river bank for 1½ miles (2.5 km) to Wylam Station and ⑩ turn right through station yard, over bridge and back to ①.

A pair of dippers often nest under the bridge and can be seen on rocks in the river; swifts, swallows, house and sand martins (summer) in larger numbers.

Grey wagtails regularly feed where the burn (stream) comes close to the road.

Mistle thrushes and treecreepers in mature trees; nuthatches uncommon.

Woodpigeons and stock doves are regular where the road goes under the tree canopy; willow warblers in summer.

The hedgerows are favourite yellow-hammer song posts; the rough grass at the base of the hedge is ideal for partridges.

Tawny and little owls nest in the old trees with natural holes; great spotted woodpeckers excavate their own.

The shallow pond, though suffering from human disturbance, does attract little grebes.

A small, rough patch of ground such as that beyond the stile is a likely place to hear and see a grasshopper warbler.

A sand martin colony is visible in the face of the quarry across the field to the left of the path; birds present April–Sept.

Collared doves frequent the farm buildings, eating the animal feed grain.

Corn buntings sing from the top of the hedge: a strange, jangling song.

The seed heads of the thistles in the field below the path attract goldfinches late in the year.

Dense, low woodland with a plentiful food supply: a place for long-tailed tits in winter.

When the rocky island is exposed at low tide common sandpipers use it as a feeding place (summer) and along the bank.

A good view to the small sand martin colony in the river's N bank.

Occasional kingfishers over the river or perching on overhanging branches.

Goosanders breed on this stretch and are joined by others in winter; goldeneyes also winter here; occasional cormorants. Shelduck from the W coast are often seen flying through the valley in late summer on their way to moult in Heligoland.

The trees along the river bank are a fine year-round habitat, with warblers in great variety in summer, and tits and finches, including siskins, during winter.

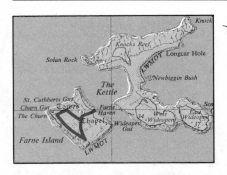

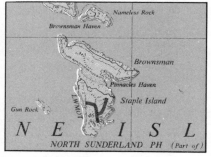

Roseate tern; flight outline shows the exceptional length of the tail streamers.

The Farne Islands
½ *mile (0.8 km) on each island*
Landranger 75 218358 and 237375

There are a total of 30 Farne Islands 2 to 5 miles (3 to 8 km) off the Northumberland coast; wild and beautiful, they support large populations of breeding sea birds. The National Trust are the owners, and keep 2 of the islands, Farne Island (also called Inner Farne) and Staple Island, open to the public. Outside breeding season, sea watching can be rewarding; migration brings rarities. *Sea, cliffs, grassland, beach; both islands are open daily from 10–6, April to end September, except from 15th May to the end of July, when Inner Farne is open from 2–5 and Staple Island from 10.30–1.30; landing fee in addition to cost of boat trip.*

Summer Sandwich, common, arctic and roseate terns, lesser black-backed gull,

razorbill, guillemot, puffin; **winter** divers, common scoter, turnstone, purple sandpiper; **passage** divers, shearwaters, scoter, turnstone, whimbrel, skuas, terns, Scandinavian thrushes and other passerines; **all year** fulmar, cormorant, shag, eider, oystercatcher, ringed plover, herring gull, kittiwake, rock pipit.

Start Take the A1 S from Berwick upon Tweed for 12 miles (19 km) to Belford. Immediately after Belford turn left on to the B1342 to Bamburgh, where take the B1340 to Seahouses, from where there are daily boat trips to the islands. These are, however, subject to weather conditions and visitors are advised to contact the National Trust Information Centre, 16 Main Street, Seahouses – 0665 720424 – for information.

On Inner Farne follow the path from the landing point at St Cuthbert's Gut past 2 ancient stone chapels (one dedicated to St Cuthbert, the other now used as an information centre by the National Trust). Continue out towards the modern lighthouse, from where follow the path to the W corner of the island. Retrace to the landing point.

At Staple Island there are 2 landing points and a footpath runs from one to the other via Kittiwake Gulley and the ruined lighthouse.

Dunstanburgh to Cullernose Point
3½ *miles (5.5 km) Landranger 75 243223*

Near the start of this walk, magnificent Dunstanburgh Castle stands dramatically on cliffs which provide nest sites for a range of sea birds. At the far end, the cliffs beyond Cullernose Point have the unusual feature of a colony of cliff-nesting house martins. In autumn the interest is mainly sea birds on passage. *Sea, cliffs, rocky shore.*

Summer fulmar, kittiwake, guillemot, shag, house martin; **autumn** gannet, skuas, terns.

Start From Embleton on the B1339 take the minor road SE towards Craster. After ¼ mile (0.5 km) turn left on to the road to Dunstan Steads Farm. **Parking** on verge at Dunstan Steads Farm.

① Follow the footpath S through the sand dunes on the seaward side of the golf course to Castle Point. ② Continue past the castle entrance and follow the coastal path almost a mile to Craster. Walk through village, skirting the harbour, rejoin the coastal path and carry on about ½ mile (0.8 km) to ③ Cullernose Point. Return by the same route.

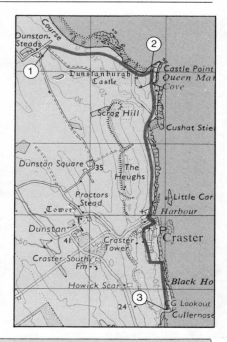

Arnold Reserve, belonging to the Northumberland Wildlife Trust, lies on the Great Whin Sill, the rock system running from the Pennines to the Northumberland coast (and part of which carries Hadrian's Wall). The reserve's diverse woodland and scrub habitats support a small breeding bird population, but there are many migrant visitors, including such rarities as the wryneck, icterine and barred warblers, red-breasted flycatcher and bluethroat. The reserve (which has an information display) is at Craster, 6 miles (9.5 km) NE of Alnwick. Keep to footpaths.

Cresswell Pond, a mining subsidence pond only 150 yards (140 m) from the sea, is an ideal wildfowl, wader and tern habitat. It also attracts migrants, with a number of rarities. The pond is on private land just N of Cresswell, which is 4 miles (6.5 km) N of Ashington; the nearby footpaths and the coast road give excellent views.

Grindon Lough, a 230-acre (94-ha) reserve of the Northumberland Wildlife Trust, comprises grassland and a natural lake of 20–30 acres (8–12 ha). There is a varied population of breeding birds and an interesting selection of wildfowl in winter and during migration. Geese include bean, greylag and pink-footed, and both whooper and Bewick's swans visit. There is no public access to the lake, but excellent views are to be had from the minor road between Grindon Hill and Morwood. Grindon Hill is 3 miles (5 km) N of Haydon Bridge.

Budle Bay and Spindlestone
6 miles (9.5 km) Landranger 75 184349
NU 13/23

A first-class stretch of coast for sea ducks: **eiders** are plentiful all year, joined in winter by **common scoters, long-tailed ducks** and also **divers** and **grebes.** Budle Bay, whose mudflats provide rich feeding, and whose sand bars give seclusion, has particularly large numbers of wildfowl and waders in winter. Away from the coast, there is a rich mixture of species from **grey wagtails** and **grasshopper warblers** to **sparrowhawks.** *The beach section should not be attempted at high tide – use suggested alternatives; mud after rain.*

Time and season All year, but outstanding in winter.

Start Close to Bamburgh Castle on the B1340 (Seahouses to Bamburgh road). **Car park** below the castle.

① On leaving the car park turn left and walk to the first corner. Cross the road and ② follow track through playing field below castle. At far end of playing field, as track passes through castle wall, keep left following fence line. Where track emerges on to road in 150 yards (140 m) keep right and immediately beyond cottage ③ enter sand dunes by main track. At this point a stream flows on to the beach; cross and follow the obvious track N through the dunes; alternatively, walk along the beach. In ½ mile (0.8 km) reach the lighthouse and continue following shoreline for a further ¾ mile (1 km) to Budle Point either along beach (or, at high tide, along edge of golf course). Continue along the shore of the bay and in ¾ mile (1 km) ④ turn left, following the track uphill to the road, where turn right. Follow track on right side of road for 800 yards (700 m) and ⑤ turn left at Waren House. (The one which the map marks further on is a *second* Waren

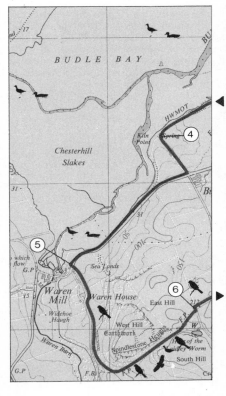

House.) Follow narrow road for ¼ mile (0.5 km) and turn left through gate on to track marked 'Drawklin Hill ½ mile'. Follow track below high crag for ½ mile (0.8 km), passing through 2 gates, the second into a caravan park. Keep to the right, along the hedge, leaving the park ⑥ through a hunting gate on to the road. Turn left, then right at the corner and follow road ¼ mile (0.5 km) to T-junction, where turn left and in 30 yards (27 m) right on to track marked 'Galliheugh Bank ¾ mile'. Keep to the left of the hedge and follow track downhill to small wood; walk along its right-hand side. At end of gorse, cross field to stile near corner of field; turn left

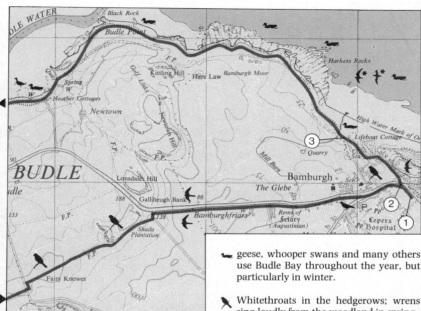

and then immediately right on to main road; return to Bamburgh Castle.

- Fulmars on and around Castle Rock.

- Pied wagtails pick around on the mown grass of the playing field.

- Eiders bathe and drink in the fresh water of the stream running across the beach.

- Terns, auks, gannets, eiders and kittiwakes feeding and on passage through spring, summer and autumn.

- Wintering long-tailed ducks, scoters, eiders, divers and grebes.

- Red-breasted mergansers at entrance to the bay in winter.

- Bar-tailed godwits, grey plovers, redshank, dunlin, shelduck, wigeon, greylag geese, whooper swans and many others use Budle Bay throughout the year, but particularly in winter.

- Whitethroats in the hedgerows; wrens sing loudly from the woodland in spring.

- Willow warblers favour the secondary woodland along the edge of the path, where sparrowhawks may also occasionally be seen hunting.

- Lapwings feed in these rough fields and are joined late in the day by night-feeding curlews.

- The distinctive reeling call of grasshopper warblers can be heard from thick cover in this area, mainly in the early morning and late evening.

- Yellowhammers on these hedgerows.

- Spotted flycatchers nest in the dead tree stumps. Linnets like the thick cover provided by the gorse.

- Kestrels quarter the fields either side.

- Rooks in the trees on the village green.

Scotland

The mountains and moorlands of Scotland are a
challenge to the energetic, and a fit setting for the
birds. Visitors – and they arrive from all over Europe
just for the birds – naturally wish to see golden
eagles, divers, greenshank and ptarmigan in
appropriately wild and spectacular surroundings.
Lower key, but just as rewarding experiences for the
patient, are the specialities of the pine woods –
capercaillie, crested tits and crossbills. Many of the
woods retain a flavour of the primeval forests;
certainly, the birdwatching is more varied and
interesting where mature trees are mixed with recent
plantation.

The northern and western islands, with their
teeming sea bird populations, come into their own
during the breeding season, and some are of special
interest for rare migrants in spring or autumn. Those
prepared to venture out in winter on to bleak
mudflats or black estuaries are compensated by truly
vast flocks of geese, waders and duck.

Getting out the map and exploring at will is the
right approach for Scotland, but not entirely
straightforward. With no public rights of way in the
English (or Welsh) sense, walkers may generally
wander the moors and mountains. But there *is* such
a thing as trespass in Scotland, and it is prudent to
seek the landowner's permission to walk and watch
birds, especially in the August to mid-October
stalking season.

Golden eagle nest

Balcary and Loch Mackie
3 miles (5 km) Landranger 84 821495
NX 85

A rich combination of thin woodland, sea, mudflats, cliffs, rocky ledges, rough grassland and bracken, exposed rocky hillside, conifer plantation, loch with willow scrub and wetland. Among a correspondingly wide range of species, specialities of the area include willow tits, pink-footed geese, black guillemots, divers and sea duck. There are some splendid long views to the Isle of Man and the hills of the Lake District. *Mud after rain and parts trampled by cattle; a narrow, rough path in places.*

Time and season All year, but April–late July best for breeding sea birds, waders and summer visitors. Winter brings divers and scoters, flighting geese and hunting predators.

Start From Dalbeattie take the A711 S to Auchencairn. On passing the village sign and going over a small hump-backed bridge, turn immediately left on to minor road marked Balcary. After passing entrance to Balcary Hotel continue to an officially marked **parking** area on the right.

① From parking follow the road straight ahead, keeping ahead where road turns left, and following the sign marked Balcary Heughs. Cross stile to enter pasture ②, keeping to the field edge closest to the bay. Cross stile into wood and continue, passing useful gap ③ for viewing Auchencairn Bay. Continue with path as it leaves the wood for open cliff-top, where for nearly ½ mile (0.8 km) between ④ and ⑤ it frequently runs close to the edge. Note that the cliffs are dangerous: it is advisable to stay on the landward side of the fence. From ⑤, opposite Lot's Wife, the rocky outcrop, continue through grasses and bracken as the cliffs decrease in height until some of the ruin of the disused

Barytes Mine can be seen. ⑥ Take the path to the shore and continue about 1½ miles (2.5 km) to ⑦ the ruined cottage and several timber dwellings. Follow the path as it leaves the shore, along the burn (stream) which leads to Loch Mackie, crossing 2 stiles and going through gate to track ⑧ at the loch. Turn right and follow the track ½ mile (0.8 km) to ⑨ Airds Cottage. Continue another ½ mile (0.8 km) to the road. Turn right to ①.

Pied wagtails feed around the cattle in this pasture; goldfinches may be seen feeding on the seed heads of thistles and other plants. There are rather distant views N over Auchencairn Bay of waders and gulls, the former most likely to be curlew and oystercatchers.

Many small woodland birds occur between ② and ③, but notably the willow tit (all year) and willow and garden warblers (summer). Spotted flycatchers (summer), wrens and bullfinches are common.

In winter pause at the gap in the trees giving an open view over the bay. Depending on the state of the tide, waders will be spread apart on the mud or more concentrated along the high-water line. In winter, great crested grebes, common scoters and divers may well be sheltering here. Pink-footed geese could be seen flighting to and from feeding places.

Look for breeding sea birds over the whole stretch from ④ to ⑤. Carefully search the innermost parts of the bays and low, exposed rocks for black guillemots – there are only 1 or 2 pairs. The bird is much smaller than the guillemot, all black except for highly conspicuous white patches on the upper wing, and striking red legs. In winter their plumage changes completely, with the upperparts grey and the underparts white.

The most common gull is the kittiwake, with its completely black wing tips; but there are quite large numbers of herring gulls. Razorbills, guillemots and fulmars should also be seen.

The lower cliffs, shelves of rock or areas of shingle are favoured by turnstones on passage.

Out to sea will be gannets (nearest gannetry, Ailsa Craig), which may be seen diving for fish, and in late summer to early autumn, arctic skuas. Sometimes these can be spotted harrying gulls and terns with the object of making them disgorge their last meal.

Look for whinchats and wheatears in the rough grassland and bracket between ⑤ and ⑦. The wheatear is easy to identify by its conspicuously white rump as it flies away to re-settle, often on a rock or stone dyke. Both birds like to perch on prominent look-outs.

From ④ through to ⑦, rock pipits in-

habit the higher cliffs, or feed on the rocks on shore. On your approach, they usually try to sneak round a corner out of sight; but they are extremely curious birds, and, if you wait, will come back to have a look.

Take time to stand on the track and look for coal tits and goldcrests in the conifers across the burn.

Pause by the willow scrub and wait for sedge warblers and reed buntings.

Teal and mallard on the loch.

Another likely spot for wheatears.

The rough, boggy grazing from the loch to Airds Cottage is ideal breeding ground for curlew and snipe. Sparrowhawks may be seen hunting from the conifer plantations; buzzards; hen harrier, peregrine and merlin (winter) over open ground.

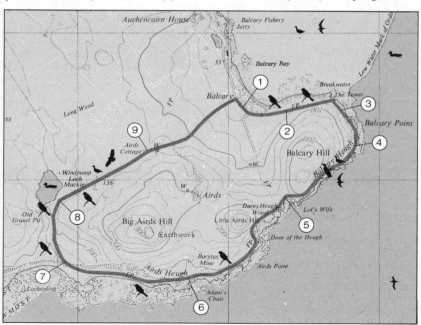

Glentrool Forest
¼, 2½ or 4½ miles (0.5, 4 or 7 km)
Landranger 77 373786

Glentrool Forest, part of the Galloway Forest Park, contains a variety of young and old plantations plus some ancient oak woodland. The Water of Trool runs through the glen via Loch Trool. *Forest, open water, river, moor.*

Summer common sandpiper, tree pipit, grasshopper warbler, pied flycatcher, whinchat, redstart, ring ouzel; **winter** peregrine; **all year** sparrowhawk, buzzard, hen harrier, black grouse, woodcock, · short-eared owl, grey wagtail, dipper, stonechat, willow tit, crossbill, raven.

Start From Newton Stewart take the A714. After 8¼ miles (14 km) turn right to Glentrool Village; immediately after the village turn right again. After ⅔ mile (1 km), take the second road on the right. **Parking** at Caldons Campsite.

From the campsite follow one of the 3 waymarked walks.

Southerness Point
1 mile (1.5 km) Landranger 84 977543

A fine vantage point for sea-watching on the Solway Firth. *Open water, marsh.*

Winter red-throated diver, great crested grebe, barnacle goose, wigeon, pintail, scaup, scoter, velvet scoter, red-breasted merganser, turnstone, purple sandpiper, knot, bar-tailed godwit; **all year** oystercatcher, dunlin, redshank.

Start From Dumfries take the A710 S to New Abbey and then to Kirkbean. One mile (1.5 km) after Kirkbean turn left on to a minor road to Southerness Point. **Parking** at end of road.

Walk along the coast W for ½ mile (0.8 km) and return to start.

After the dive: having plunged feet first for a fish (and often getting completely immersed in the process), an osprey flaps off, carrying the victim head first. Then it climbs to about 50 feet (15 m) to dry itself off with a terrific shake.

Inverliever Forest
2¼ miles (3.5 km) Landranger 55 998178

A largely coniferous forest of mature trees overlooking Loch Awe. The Forestry Commission have devised a number of walks through the forest. Full details from the Forest Office at Dalavich. *Forest, loch.*

Summer tree pipit, pied flycatcher, redstart; **winter** whooper swan, golden eagle, peregrine; **all year** hen harrier, buzzard, kestrel, woodcock, great spotted woodpecker, crested tit, siskin, redpoll.

Start From Oban take the A85 E to Taynuilt and then turn right along the B845 to Kilchrenan; ¼ mile (0.5 km) after Kilchrenan turn right on to the minor road towards Ford. Forestry Commission **car park** giving splendid views of Loch Awe.

Follow the green waymarked Waterfall Walk from the car park.

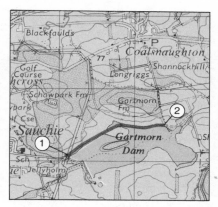

Scottish crossbill feeding: the crossed bill is extremely efficient for extracting seeds from cones, but the precise method used is not fully understood. Certainly, a twisting motion is involved.

Falls of Clyde
4 miles (6.5 km) Landranger 71 882425

Immediately S of New Lanark the River Clyde runs through a deep, wooded gorge with a series of beautiful waterfalls. The Scottish Wildlife Trust manages most of the surrounding land; facilities include riverside walks and an information centre. *River, woods.*

Summer turtle dove, garden warbler, blackcap, willow warbler, chiffchaff, pied flycatcher, redstart; **winter** fieldfare, redwing, brambling; **all year** stock dove, kingfisher, green woodpecker, great spotted woodpecker, grey wagtail, goldcrest, long-tailed tit, willow tit, coal tit, treecreeper, siskin, redpoll.

Start Leave Lanark SE on the A73 but after only ¼ mile (0.5 km) turn right on to a minor road to New Lanark. **Parking** in New Lanark.

A walk, open to the public, follows the E bank of the River Clyde.

Gartmorn Dam
3½ miles (5.5 km) Landranger 58 911942

A 200-acre (80-ha) reservoir, much wooded on the N side. *Open water, woods, arable farmland; hide, information centre.*

Summer dunlin, redshank, common sandpiper, garden and willow warbler, pied flycatcher; **winter** greylag goose, whooper swan, goldeneye, goosander, buzzard; **passage** greenshank; **all year** great crested grebe, heron, teal, wigeon, pochard, tufted duck, snipe.

Start From Alloa, 7 miles (11 km) E of Stirling, take the A908 N towards Tillicoultry. After ⅔ mile (1 km) the B908 branches off to the left; continue on the A908 for ¼ mile (0.5 km) after this and then turn right on to a minor road. After ½ mile (0.8 km) the road bends sharply to the left but an access road continues straight on. Follow the access road for another ½ mile (0.8 km) to a **car park**.

① From the car park walk along the access road on to the dam. Follow the S shore of the dam to the Lade Bridge. ② Cross via the wooden bridge and gain access via footpath to the N shore of the dam. Follow the N shore and continue back to the car park.

Lunderston Bay

2½ miles (4 km) Landranger 63 216738
NS 27 and Part of NS 17

This walk starts from a popular leisure
centre, but the route itself is rarely busy.
The path passes close to the shore,
giving fine views of **waders, wildfowl**
and **sea birds**, including **arctic terns**.
There is a well-established heronry in
the woods at the path's end. *Beach generally level, with a firm base.*

Time and season All year, but best concentrations of waders and ducks in late
summer and early winter.

Start The Lunderston Bay Camp Site,
adjacent to the A78, Greenock to Largs
road; regular buses from these 2 towns.
Car park at the camp site.

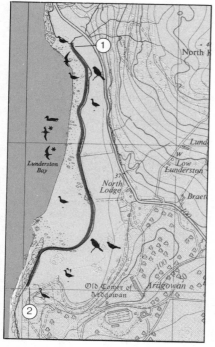

① From the car park follow the track
running almost due S between the shore
and adjacent farmland. Continue rather
over 2 miles (3 km) to ② the woods
of the Ardgowan Estate. Do not proceed
any further – there is no right of way.
Return by the same route.

Before leaving the car park, look towards
the mouth of the stream at the N end of
the site for dunlin and turnstones, which
are often seen feeding in the area, especially in winter.

Several species of gull congregate here,
taking advantage of the scraps of bread
left by visitors. There are substantial
numbers of black-headed, herring and
lesser black-backed gulls, together with
oystercatchers.

In late summer goldfinches may be seen
feeding on the heads of these healthy
stands of thistles.

The wader feeding sites along the Clyde
estuary are covered at high tide, when
the birds use these fields for roosting. Look
for curlew, redshank, oystercatchers and
lapwings.

Several species of duck breed on the
Clyde, and this bay is frequented by eider,
shelduck and red-breasted mergansers all
year round. Goldeneye, wigeon and mallard join them from September. Further
offshore, gannets may be seen diving for
fish. Common and arctic terns, from the
breeding colonies further down the Clyde,
also feed here.

Where the shore becomes a mixture of
rocky outcrop and sand, pause to look for
ringed plovers, redshank, oystercatchers
and curlew. Other waders may be seen
on passage.

Chaffinches and greenfinches forage in
these fields, especially after the harvest
when there is grain left on the ground.
Stonechats and whinchats perch along

the fence line. There are both carrion and hooded crows, the latter identified by the grey rather than black body.

The shelter afforded by the trees makes this a favourite roosting place for lap-wings and curlew. Note how variable curlew can appear. When sleeping, they often plant the downcurved bill well out of sight in the back plumage. Resting, the head is hunched well down on to the body, giving the impression of practically no neck. Alert, the bird straightens out, revealing quite a long, elegant neck and a sedate, upright posture.

This marks the spot of the heronry in the Ardgowan Estate woods; birds are seen passing overhead regularly.

Top, centre and bottom right, arctic terns; above, common terns; notoriously difficult to separate, especially in flight. However, the arctic's primaries all appear translucent against light; on the common, only the inner four.

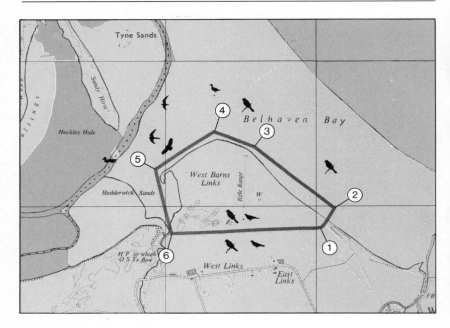

Tyne Estuary
2 miles (3 km)
Landranger 67 652788
NT 67

This estuary, to which there is access through the John Muir Country Park, is an important wintering place for duck and waders and a staging point for migrating waders. The habitats are mainly sand-dunes, saltmarsh and mudflats. *Note that the 1 : 25,000 sheet does not show that West Barns Links is now a conifer plantation; that there is an access road to the car park; the position of the sand-dune running NW–SE in Belhaven Bay and the Hedderwick Burn footbridge.*

Time and season The walk comes into its own in autumn and winter when most wader and duck species will be seen. Best concentrations of waders at high tide.

The ringed plover often has a hunched, demure look. It lays its eggs in a simple scrape, typically in shingle; although the fine camouflage is excellent protection against plundering gulls, all too often humans crush the eggs unawares.

Start Going E on the A1 just W of Dunbar fork on to the A1087 (signpost for John Muir Country Park). In ½ mile (0.8 km) turn left (Country Park signposted again) and continue to Linkfield **Car Park**.

① Leave the car park by its N end, passing the wooden Information Shelter. Keeping the conifer plantation to the left, follow the path towards the sea for about 100 yards (90 m). At the edge of the dunes and saltmarsh ② turn left and follow the saltmarsh edge. Carry on, keeping the dunes and plantation on the left. At the clump of seabuckthorn scrub ③ the estuary is visible, flanked by trees on the far side. Keep straight on. In about 200 yards (180 m) at the point ④ overlooking the estuary, turn left along the shore, following the high-tide mark and keeping the estuary on the right. Keep off the mudflats as they are covered quickly by the incoming tide. Where ⑤ the wooden bridge over the Hedderwick Burn (stream) becomes visible below some conifers, make for the bridge. ⑥ To the left of the bridge is a Park information board; follow the path on the right of it. Keep the plantation on the left and the fields to the right. Continue to car park.

Full breeding plumage, above, of the grey plover is almost completely black underparts; however, the black 'armpits', remaining all year, and easily seen in flight, are the failsafe field mark. The bird has a highly distinctive, three-part call, 'pee-ou-ee'.

🐦 Skylarks, meadow pipits and pied wagtails are seen on the saltmarsh.

🐦 Linnets and skylarks can usually be seen on this stony area of saltmarsh. With luck, you could see shore larks, which turn up annually here from November to February.

🐦 At high tide, considerable numbers of waders roost here, and the range of species is impressive: oystercatchers, redshank, ringed plover, grey plover, bar-tailed godwits and knot can usually be seen. If the tide is low, the birds are spread out, feeding on the estuary. On autumn passage, whimbrel, little stint, ruff and curlew sandpiper may be seen.

🐦 There are plenty of gulls on the estuary – the most common being herring, lesser and great black-backed and black-headed.

Little gulls, though less common, turn up each year. Sandwich, arctic and common terns can be seen in autumn.

🐦 Kestrels and sparrowhawks are regular on the estuary; peregrines and merlins can occur.

🐦 Mallard, wigeon and sometimes teal are seen. Eider and shelduck occur, also red-breasted merganser and goosander. Herons feed here. There are mute swans, and from October to April there may be whooper swans. The pale-bellied brent goose appears in hard winters.

🐦 Flocks of coal and long-tailed tits in the conifer plantation, together with chaffinches. Woodpigeons usually present.

🐦 Mistle thrushes feed on the fields. Crows, rooks and jackdaws will also be seen.

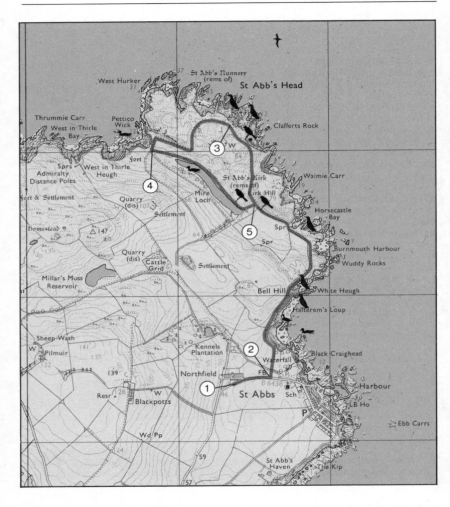

St Abb's Head

3½ miles (5.5 km) Landranger 67 913673
NT 86/96

This is a nationally important site for **cliff-nesting seabirds**, and the route gives spectacular views of colonies of guillemots, razorbills, kittiwakes and shags. Modest numbers of other seabird species breed here, as do land birds associated with the coast such as rock pipits and wheatears. A freshwater loch supports small numbers of common water birds and in winter may hold wintering duck. The area is a nature reserve owned by the National Trust for

Scotland and managed in collaboration with the Scottish Wildlife Trust in co-operation with the neighbouring farmer. *Do not cross private farmland; please keep disturbance to a minimum at all times; mud after rain. Ranger service.*

Time and season By late July most of the breeding sea birds have left the colonies – so early summer (May and June) is when the reserve is at its best.

Start ⅓ mile (0.5 km) W of St Abbs is the reserve **car park** at Northfield Farm.

① Follow the path from the bottom of the car park alongside the B6438 about 300 yards (270 m) and ② turn left on to the waymarked path and continue along the cliffs rather over 1 mile (1.5 km) to ③ the lighthouse. From here follow the metalled road to its lowest point at Pettico Wick ④, where turn left and follow the E bank of the Mire Loch to rejoin the path at ⑤. Turn right and retrace to ①.

🦆 As coastal views open out from the path, scan the water for duck – there are frequently eider here – and auks.

🦅 At all seasons except high summer the rocky coast provides food for waders such as oystercatchers, redshank, turnstones and purple sandpipers. These last are especially hard to see, but patient searching with binoculars usually pays off.

🐦 The S face of the White Heugh supports nearly 3,000 auks. The majority are guillemots, which nest shoulder to shoulder on the wider ledges, but from the path razorbills are also to be seen. These look blacker on the back, and usually nest singly in nooks and crannies.

🐦 Look across to the N face of the White Heugh to see the spectacular kittiwake colony. Several hundred birds have attached their grassy nests to the sheer cliff and during the breeding season their call of 'kittiwa-ake' fills the bay. There are also scattered herring gull nests on the rocks near sea level.

🐦 Another kittiwake colony, but at a lower level. As numbers have increased this century, so the kittiwakes have started to nest lower and lower on the cliffs.

🐦 Wheatears nest in the rabbit burrows on the slope of Kirk Hill.

🐦 Rock pipits nest in most of the bays along the coast, and they frequently feed on the grassy cliff-top along with the smaller, paler meadow pipits.

🐦 In the mouth of the bay just S of the lighthouse is a classic seabird cliff. It shows the way herring gulls, kittiwakes, guillemots, razorbills and shags each select a different type of nest site.

✝ In summer there is a constant stream of gannets from the Bass Rock passing offshore; in spring and autumn these may be joined by other seabirds such as skuas and shearwaters.

🐦 The biggest gatherings of auks nest N of the lighthouse. There are also a number of fulmars here and careful searching of the cliffs may produce puffins, which nest here in very small numbers.

🦆 Another likely bay for seeing eider during autumn, winter and spring. There is no mistaking the adult drake because it is the one duck that looks white above and black below. You may see them diving in breaking waves to feed from the bottom.

🦆 Moorhens, coots, little grebes and mallard nest here, but other duck, including goldeneye and teal, are winter visitors.

🐦 The vegetation around the loch supports a few breeding land birds, including sedge warblers and reed buntings, and it is in this area that spring and autumn passerine migrants may congregate.

Largo Bay
Up to ¾ mile (1 km)
Landranger 59 422026

A sheltered bay on the N coast of the Firth of Forth, holding a variety of waders, wildfowl and sea birds throughout most of the year, but mainly noted for the large variety of diving duck present in winter. *Sea, sandy beach.*

Summer Sandwich tern, razorbill, puffin; **winter** red-throated diver, eider, scoter, long-tailed duck, tufted duck, pochard, scaup, goldeneye, grey plover, bar-tailed godwit, knot, sanderling; **passage** arctic and great skuas, black tern, little gull; **all year** oystercatcher.

Start From Kirkcaldy take the A915 NE to Windygates and continue past Leven to Lower Largo. **Parking** in Lower Largo.

From the SE corner of the town walk along the front and continue around the bay. Return by same route.

Montrose Basin
2½ miles (4 km) Landranger 54 663584

The River South Esk flows out to the North Sea at Montrose, and the tidal estuary formed behind the town is a site of national importance for waders and wildfowl, managed by the Scottish Wildlife Trust. Winter birds include more than 3,500 wigeon and 1,500 pink-footed geese, the latter roosting on the basin at night. The area can be viewed from the road on all sides. *Mudflats, saltmarsh, reedbeds.*

Winter pink-footed and greylag goose, wigeon, pintail, goldeneye, knot, bar-tailed godwit, golden plover, turnstone; **passage** ruff, whimbrel, black-tailed godwit; **all year** shelduck, eider, heron, dunlin, redshank, oystercatcher.

Start From Montrose take the A935 W

for 3 miles (5 km), then turn left on to a minor road to Bridge of Dun; **parking** S of the bridge.

Take note of the map and information board at the parking area. Go down the steps by the bridge and follow the footpath along the river until it joins the sea wall looking out to the mudflats. Continue to Old Montrose; return either by the same route or along the road via Barnhead.

Rannoch Forest
1 to 5½ miles (1.5 to 8 km)
Landranger 42 616572

An area of natural Scots pine and birch woods on the banks of Loch Rannoch. *Forest, loch.*

Summer common sandpiper, willow warbler, pied flycatcher, whinchat; **all year** goosander, buzzard, golden eagle, black grouse, capercaillie, great spotted woodpecker, grey wagtail, Scottish crossbill, jay, raven.

Start From Aberfeldy take the B846 to Kinloch Rannoch. In Kinloch Rannoch turn left on to a bridge over the River Tummel. After the bridge turn right, and right again after ½ mile (0.8 km). Follow this minor road along the S shore of Loch Rannoch for 2½ miles (4 km) to another river bridge. On the left, immediately after the bridge, is a Forestry Commission picnic site and **car park**.

Follow one of the waymarked Forestry Commission walks starting from the picnic site.

The cock capercaillie's display is inimitable – and intimidating. The body and neck swell; the tail fans; at intervals he may leap up to 3 feet (1 m) into the air, wings flapping. Aggressive birds will threaten intruders of any size, even moving cars. These antics are accompanied by extraordinary noises, including a final 'pop' – like a cork being drawn from a bottle, and a wheeze. The perching bird is a hen.

Culbin Bar and Forest
11 miles (17.5 km)
Landranger 27 998611

An area of some variety on the S side of the Moray Firth, where Forestry Commission plantations of Corsican and Scots pine are planted on what was the largest sand dune system in the UK, extending to some 3,600 acres (1,460 ha) and created largely by the action of a storm in the 1690s. Sand dunes still survive to the W. *Forest, dunes, salt-marsh, shingle.*

Summer Sandwich, common, arctic and little terns; **winter** whooper swan, wigeon, pintail, goldeneye; **passage** arctic skua; **all year** gannet, shelduck, tufted duck, eider, scoter, red-breasted merganser, capercaillie, dunlin, redshank, curlew, goldcrest, long-tailed tit, crested tit, coal tit, treecreeper, siskin, crossbill.

Start Leave Nairn on the A96 towards Forres. After 6½ miles (10.5 km) turn left on to a minor road leading immediately over a railway bridge and then across a bridge over the Muckle Burn. Turn right to Dyke and after Dyke turn left towards Muirtown and Kintessack, but turn left again, just before entering Muirtown. After 200 yards (180 m), turn left at T-junction and then after ⅓ mile right to Cloddymoss; **parking** at Cloddymoss.

① Continue NW along the road, following it 2 miles (3 km) to the coast and ② return by the same route. The forest rides can be explored at will, but beware of getting confused by the considerable number of alternatives.

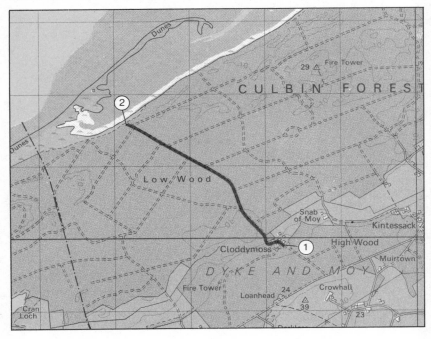

Forest of Deer
1 or 3 miles (1.5 or 5 km)
Landranger 30 956513

This is a small forest area in the NE corner of Grampian, containing larch and spruce trees plus old beech woods. It is managed by the Forestry Commission and the starting point is maintained as a picnic site with additional facilities. Nearby Deer Abbey is the site of a former Cistercian monastery founded by Comyn, Earl of Buchan in 1219. The village of Old Deer, also nearby, was the site of an even older monastery, a centre of Celtic Christianity. It was founded by St Drostan in the 7th C., and here it was that monks created the most prized literary relic of the Celtic Church, the *Book of Deer*: the text is a Latin version of parts of the New Testament, but the marginalia, in Gaelic, are the earliest known

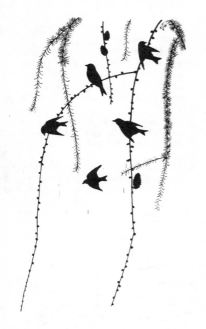

examples of Scottish Gaelic writing. *Woods.*

Summer tree pipit, willow warbler, wood warbler, pied flycatcher, redstart; **winter** brambling; **all year** buzzard, kestrel, great spotted woodpecker, goldcrest, long-tailed tit, crested tit, coal tit, treecreeper, siskin, redpoll, crossbill, jay.

Start From Peterhead take the A950 W, crossing the A92 at Mintlaw and continuing past Deer Abbey; in 1½ miles (2.5 km) turn right along a minor road towards Adziel and Strichen. After 1½ miles (2.5 km) **parking** at the Forestry Commission's White Cow Wood picnic site.

From the picnic site follow one of the 2 waymarked walks through the forest. The red walk is 1 mile (1.5 km) long and the yellow walk 3 miles (5 km).

Fowlsheugh
Up to 3 miles (5 km)
Landranger 45 880798

The RSPB reserve at Fowlsheugh comprises grass-topped cliffs providing nesting sites for large numbers of sea birds. These cliffs can be dangerous, so great care should be taken. *Sea, cliffs.*

Summer fulmar, shag, eider, herring gull, kittiwake, razorbill, guillemot, puffin.

Start From Stonehaven take the A92 S for 3¼ miles (5.5 km), then turn left on to a minor road signposted Crawton, which ends in ½ mile (0.8 km) in a small **car park**.

Walk N from the car park along the cliff path for up to 1½ miles (2.5 km). Return by same route.

A typical view of siskins feeding, here on larch. The principal summer diet is seeds taken from spruce cones. Alder is an important winter food source.

Loch Garten
2½ miles (4 km) Landranger 36 981183
NH 81/91

Following a path through the heart of Abernethy Forest, an internationally important tract of ancient Scots pine woodland, large sections of this walk run along the NW shores of Loch Garten and Loch Mallachie. As a result of its continuous existence for the past 8,000 years, the forest supports a rich dependent flora and fauna. All the local Speyside breeding birds, including **capercaillie**, **crested tit** and **Scottish crossbill**, can be seen here. The last is the only bird species unique to Britain. In spring and autumn, the lochs attract good numbers of roosting wildfowl – up to 1,000 **greylag geese** in autumn – but the Garten area is best known for **ospreys**, which in the early 1950s started to breed here after an absence from the British Isles of almost 40 years.

Time and season Excellent all year, although spring to early autumn is best and May and June are especially outstanding, with the ospreys returning to their eyries, breeding and rearing their young, and all the resident and visiting species in full song.

Start Off the A9 or A95 heading S to Aviemore. From April to August, the routes from the main roads to the hide are signposted. At all other times, follow the minor road, signposted Loch Garten, that runs SE off the B970 between Boat of Garten and Nethy Bridge. There is roadside parking only – use one of the frequent pull-off places.

① From the hide entrance, walk back about ½ mile (0.8 km) along the road just driven on, at first skirting the NE shore of Loch Garten then through mature woodland, and at ② turn left along the forest track. Follow the track S and in about 300 yards (270 m), at ③, bear left, walking past Loch Garten to Loch Mallachie. At ④, bear right, ignoring all the tracks leading off to the left, and head back N to join the original track. Retrace steps for about 200 yards (180 m) then turn right to the prominent sandy bay by Loch Garten ⑤. From here follow the path along the loch shore to rejoin the minor road ⑥ leading back to the hide entrance. *Outside the period April to August, when the osprey hide is closed, start the walk from the parking areas to the N end of Loch Garten.*

Within the semi-mature Scots pine woodland, interspersed with birch trees, goldcrests, coal tits and chaffinches are common, willow warblers flit about restlessly, and long-tailed tits are occasional.

Among those birds breeding in the canopy of the pine trees and in the juniper understorey are willow warblers, wrens, redstarts, spotted flycatchers, coal, crested and occasionally great tits. Scottish crossbills, the male crimson, the female yellow-green, may be seen extracting seeds from pine cones. In the daytime, a tawny owl, roosting in a tree, may be located by following up the noise made by smaller birds mobbing it. Woodcock regularly rode over this area in the evenings.

This is a fine locality for great spotted woodpeckers, and for siskins, their circular display flight a feature in spring.

The dense young pine on the right of the path holds substantial numbers of breeding willow warblers, robins and goldcrests, while the varied mature pine woodland on the left is the habitat for small numbers of siskins, Scottish crossbills, treecreepers, crested tits, coal tits and, depending on the severity of the previous winter, wrens.

Within this large expanse of mature Scots pine woodland mistle thrushes, goldcrests, spotted flycatchers, coal and crested tits, woodpigeons, tree pipits and the occasional siskin and crossbill all nest;

winter roost of 60 to 180 carrion crows.

In the Scots pine woods set back from the loch, hole-nesting redstarts and spotted flycatchers occur, along with treecreepers, Scottish crossbills and siskins. Kestrels hunt the area, and the loch edge is a feeding ground for herons, curlews and redshank. Common sandpipers may be seen flying low over the water.

The heather moorland and open young Scots pine woodland are habitats for tree and meadow pipits, willow warblers and, outside the breeding season, is a likely area for small flocks containing coal and crested tits.

Breeding in the mature and semi-mature pine woodland along the N shore of the loch are spotted flycatchers, crested tits, siskins, crossbills, pied and occasional grey wagtails, common sandpipers and tawny owls. A buzzard, sparrowhawk or peregrine may occasionally be seen overflying the area. In winter, look for redwings, fieldfares and bramblings. To see capercaillie, an early morning drive round the minor roads is advised: the birds will be taking in grit from the sides of the roads and tracks to aid digestion.

On the loch in spring there is a roost of some 3,000 black-headed gulls, along with goldeneye, teal, tufted duck, redbreasted mergansers and goosanders. There may be an occasional little grebe; passage greenshank, redshank and oystercatchers visit the area. Osprey regularly over-fly the loch and sometimes fish there. In autumn there are roosting whooper swans, great black-backed gulls and up to 1,000 greylag geese, many more of which pass over in Nov–Dec.

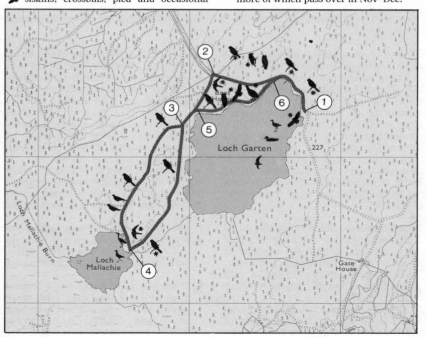

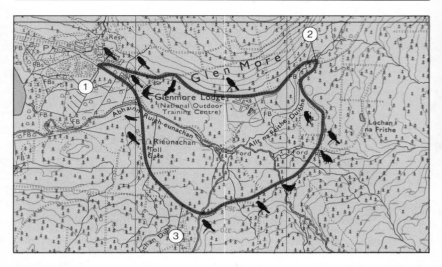

Glen More
3 miles (5 km) Landranger 36 978098
NH 80/90

All the regular pinewood species are likely to be seen on this route, including the local specialities, **crested tits, Scottish crossbills** and **capercaillie**. The woodland itself is varied, with some areas of the old Scots pine forest. Several streams with their origins in the surrounding mountains provide the right habitat for dippers and grey wagtails. *Path conditions good in all weathers (follows course of Forestry Commission River Trail); additional points of interest covered in booklet available from Information Centre.*

Time and season Best variety of resident and breeding birds during spring and early summer, though the resident tit flocks are an attractive feature all year. In years when there is a substantial crop of pine cones, crossbills may be resident.

Start Take the minor road from Aviemore to Cairn Gorm and stop at the Forestry Commission Information Centre opposite the Glen More Camp Site; **parking** in front of the Information Centre.

① Take the track to the right of the Information Centre, heading E, and keeping above the main road. Continue with track past Reindeer House and on to the made-up road heading to Glenmore Lodge. (The route is waymarked light blue.) Just past Glenmore Lodge the road becomes a forest track; carry on along this for about ¼ mile (0.5 km) past the fenced plantation on the right. At ② follow the River Trail Pointer, heading off to the right. Follow the waymarks to the main Coylumbridge road, where ③ turn right and continue back to ①.

🐦 Check the stream by the car park for grey wagtails, which nest and feed along the small streams in the area and are particularly frequent where the water flows fast.

🐦 After passing Reindeer House, the mature Scots pine woodland on the left of the path is a likely area in which to see feeding Scottish crossbills. The best way to locate them is by listening for falling cones: the birds feed on the seeds within the cones, which they can extract by means of their powerful crossed bills. Also look for the remains of the cones on the ground: the birds make a thorough job of extraction.

Coal tits and chaffinches are also here. Redstarts are most easily found while they are singing in May and June. Mistle thrushes breed.

The dense, scrubby woodland on the right is ideal for willow warblers and robins, which breed here in fair numbers. Towards the end of the breeding season, in August, is the time to look for dense tit flocks and family parties of siskins. In the birch wood areas, listen for redpolls.

Just after passing the Norwegian Hostel, a fine view opens out to the S; check for a soaring buzzard and/or sparrowhawk. A similar check can be made just after Glenmore Lodge. Although golden eagles are extremely scarce in the immediate vicinity, a wandering bird may be seen over the mountains to the S.

The dense conifer stands in this area provide ideal nesting and feeding sites for goldcrests.

In early spring and summer, great spotted woodpeckers can be heard drumming out their territory – a signal to other males not to encroach on a specific 'patch'.

The 'Christmas tree' forest of Norway and sitka spruce provides the branch nest sites with dense cover favoured by woodpigeons and goldcrests. Look for coal tits and Scottish crossbills all along this path. Stripped cones on the path indicate red squirrels as well as crossbills.

An early morning walk through this quieter apart of the forest may reveal capercaillie and roe deer.

Check the streams as they are crossed for dippers and grey wagtails.

In places, the older Scots pine forest is visible among more recently planted conifers, and these are likely areas for nesting wrens, treecreepers and spotted flycatchers. The latter often nest in holes made by heavy snowfall tearing branches from trees. One of the Spey valley specialities, the crested tit, may also be found here. Outside the breeding season you may see this bird almost anywhere along the route, but from April to June it will be restricted to the older forest areas, containing dead tree nest sites. Look for siskins again here, too, the males in the small breeding flocks uttering a sweet, twittering song, usually accompanied by a bat-like display flight. Along this section of the route also look for the typical pinewood flora: mainly heather, bilberry and cowberry, with scattered growths of creeping lady's tresses, a pinewood orchid. This is very much a speciality of north-east Scotland. It grows to about 8 inches (20 cm) and has pale yellow flowers.

The open pine wood on the left between the stream and the road should be checked for redstarts, spotted flycatchers, crested and coal tits; the introduced western hemlocks on the right are favoured by the ubiquitous goldcrest.

Several of the species mentioned will be seen on the walk back along the road to the car park; in addition, there are usually a few meadow pipits in the open, damp area opposite the forestry houses, and also the occasional skylark, sometimes seen trying to defend the nest against cuckoos. Swallows and swifts breed around the houses.

If the walk is done in late evening, the odd woodcock could be encountered on roding flights. There may be the hooting or 'kewicking' of tawny owls, and if long-eared owls are in residence, their long, moaning hoots may be heard in early spring. The wing-clapping display flights also help locate the bird, which is more often heard than seen.

1 Shetland – Yell & Unst
2 Shetland – Whalsay
3 Shetland – North Mainland
4 Shetland – South Mainland
5 Orkney – Northern Isles
6 Orkney – Mainland
7 Pentland Firth
8 Stornoway & North Lewis
9 Cape Wrath
10 Strathnaver
11 Thurso & Dunbeath
12 Thurso & Wick
13 West Lewis & North Harris
14 Tarbert & Loch Seaforth
15 Loch Assynt
16 Lairg & Loch Shin
17 Helmsdale & Strath of
    Kildonan
18 Sound of Harris
19 Gairloch & Ullapool
20 Beinn Dearg
21 Dornoch Firth
22 Benbecula
23 North Skye
24 Raasay & Loch Torridon
25 Glen Carron
26 Inverness
27 Nairn
28 Elgin
29 Banff
30 Fraserburgh & Peterhead
31 Barra
32 South Skye
33 Loch Alsh & Glen Shiel
34 Fort Augustus
35 Kingussie
36 Grantown & Cairngorm
37 Strathdon
38 Aberdeen
39 Rhum & Eigg
40 Loch Shiel
41 Ben Nevis
42 Loch Rannoch
43 Braemar
44 Ballater
45 Stonehaven
46 Coll & Tiree
47 Tobermory
48 Iona & Ben More
49 Oban & East Mull
50 Glen Orchy
51 Loch Tay
52 Pitlochry & Aberfeldy
53 Blairgowrie
54 Dundee
55 Lochgilphead
56 Loch Lomond
57 Stirling & The Trossachs
58 Perth & Kinross
59 St Andrews & Kirkcaldy
60 Islay
61 Jura & Colonsay
62 North Kintyre
63 Firth of Clyde
64 Glasgow
65 Falkirk & West Lothian
66 Edinburgh
67 Duns & Dunbar
68 South Kintyre
69 Island of Arran
70 Ayr & Kilmarnock

71 Lanark & Upper Nithsdale
72 Upper Clyde Valley
73 Peebles & Galashiels
74 Kelso
75 Berwick-upon-Tweed
76 Girvan
77 New Galloway & Glen Trool
78 Nithsdale & Lowther Hills
79 Hawick & Eskdale
80 The Cheviot Hills
81 Alnwick & Rothbury
82 Stranraer & Glen Luce
83 Kirkcudbright
84 Dumfries
85 Carlisle & Solway Firth
86 Haltwhistle & Bewcastle
87 Hexham & Haltwhistle
88 Tyneside
89 West Cumbria
90 Penrith & Keswick
91 Appleby
92 Barnard Castle & Richmond
93 Cleveland & Darlington
94 Whitby
95 Isle of Man
96 South Lakeland
97 Kendal & Morecambe
98 Wensleydale & Wharfedale
99 Northallerton & Ripon
100 Malton & Pickering
101 Scarborough
102 Preston & Blackpool
103 Blackburn & Burnley
104 Leeds & Bradford
105 York
106 Market Weighton
107 Kingston upon Hull
108 Liverpool
109 Manchester
110 Sheffield & Huddersfield
111 Sheffield & Doncaster
112 Scunthorpe
113 Grimsby & Cleethorpes
114 Anglesey
115 Snowdon
116 Denbigh & Colwyn Bay
117 Chester
118 The Potteries
119 Buxton, Matlock &
    Dove Dale
120 Mansfield & The Dukeries
121 Lincoln
122 Skegness
123 Lleyn Peninsula
124 Dolgellau
125 Bala & Lake Vyrnwy
126 Shrewsbury
127 Stratford & Telford
128 Derby & Burton upon Trent
129 Nottingham &
    Loughborough
130 Grantham
131 Boston & Spalding
132 North West Norfolk
133 North East Norfolk
134 Norwich & The Broads
135 Aberystwyth
136 Newtown & Llanidloes
137 Ludlow & Wenlock Edge
138 Kidderminster & Wyre Forest
139 Birmingham

140 Leicester & Coventry
141 Kettering & Corby
142 Peterborough
143 Ely & Wisbech
144 Thetford & Breckland
145 Cardigan
146 Lampeter & Llandovery
147 Elan Valley & Builth Wells
148 Presteigne & Hay-on-Wye
149 Hereford & Leominster
150 Worcester & The Malverns
151 Stratford-upon-Avon
152 Northampton & Milton Keynes
153 Bedford & Huntingdon
154 Cambridge & Newmarket
155 Bury St Edmunds & Sudbury
156 Saxmundham & Aldeburgh
157 St David's & Haverfordwest
158 Tenby
159 Swansea & Gower
160 Brecon Beacons
161 Abergavenny &
    The Black Mountains
162 Gloucester & Forest of Dean
163 Cheltenham & Cirencester
164 Oxford
165 Aylesbury & Leighton Buzzard
166 Luton & Hertford
167 Chelmsford & Harlow
168 Colchester & The Blackwater
169 Ipswich & The Naze
170 Vale of Glamorgan &
    Rhondda
171 Cardiff & Newport
172 Bristol & Bath
173 Swindon & Devizes
174 Newbury & Wantage
175 Reading & Windsor
176 West London
177 East London
178 The Thames Estuary
179 Canterbury & East Kent
180 Barnstaple & Ilfracombe
181 Minehead & Brendon Hills
182 Weston-super-Mare &
    Bridgwater
183 Yeovil & Frome
184 Salisbury & The Plain
185 Winchester & Basingstoke
186 Aldershot & Guildford
187 Dorking, Reigate & Crawley
188 Maidstone &
    The Weald of Kent
189 Ashford & Romney Marsh
190 Bude & Clovelly
191 Okehampton &
    North Dartmoor
192 Exeter & Sidmouth
193 Taunton & Lyme Regis
194 Dorchester & Weymouth
195 Bournemouth & Purbeck
196 Solent & the Isle of Wight
197 Chichester & The Downs
198 Brighton & The Downs
199 Eastbourne & Hastings
200 Newquay & Bodmin
201 Plymouth & Launceston
202 Torbay & South Dartmoor
203 Land's End, The Lizard
    & the Isles of Scilly
204 Truro & Falmouth

The RSPB

The Royal Society for the Protection of Birds, Europe's largest voluntary wildlife conservation body, is a charity with a membership of over 350,000.

Its headquarters are The Lodge, Sandy, Bedfordshire SG19 2DL.

The work of the Society is organized into three main fields: conservation of wild birds and habitats; information and education and sales and funding.

There are nine regional offices:

Scottish Office:
17 Regent Terrace, Edinburgh EH7 5BN
(Tel: 031-556 5624)

Wales Office:
18 Frolic Street, Newtown, Powys
SY16 1AP
(Tel: 0686 26678)

Northern Ireland Office:
Belvoir Park Forest, Belfast BT8 4QT
(Tel: 0232 692547)

English Regions:

North England Office:
'E' Floor, Milburn House, Dean Street, Newcastle upon Tyne NE1 1LE
(Tel: 0632 24148)

North-West England Office:
Imperial House, Imperial Arcade, Huddersfield, W. Yorkshire HD1 2BR
(Tel: 0484 36331)

Midlands Office:
44 Friar Street, Droitwich, Worcs
WR9 8ED (Tel: 0905 770581)

East Anglia Office:
Aldwych House, Bethel Street, Norwich
NR2 1NR (Tel: 0603 615920)

South-East England Office:
Scan House, 4 Church Street,
Shoreham-by-Sea, West Sussex
BN4 5DQ
(Tel: 07917 63642)

South-West England Office:
10 Richmond Road, Exeter, Devon,
EX4 4JA (Tel: 0392 32691)

The Young Ornithologists' Club is the RSPB's youth group, formed in 1965 to encourage birdwatching amongst young people up to the age of about 18 years. Most of the members are between 9 and 14 years of age.

The principal activities are local field outings organized by adult members of the RSPB and holiday courses.

Further information from the RSPB at the headquarters address.

The RSNC and local Nature Conservation Trusts

The Royal Society for Nature Conservation is the other organization that will be of considerable interest and importance to users of this book. Several of the walks are on reserves owned by the 44 trusts associated with the RSNC; membership of just one of them, or of the parent body, entitles birdwatchers to visit many trust reserves – excellent value.

The local trusts have a total membership of over 143,000 and between them manage 1,300 nature reserves in the UK. The RSNC advises and gives assistance to them and represents their interests at a national level. Together the RSNC and the Trusts give information and advice to local authorities and other official bodies, landowners and farmers about the management of wildlife habitats in the country.

A local trust is one of the most important voluntary organizations concerned with wildlife conservation in any county. Besides access to many of the reserves, membership is an excellent way of contributing actively to conservation on a local level. There are newsletters and a national magazine, *Natural World*.

Membership details for all trusts are available from the RSNC, The Green,

Nettleham, Lincoln LN2 2NR. Alternatively, contact your local trust:

Avon Wildlife Trust, 209, Redland Road, Bristol, BS6 6YU.

Beds. & Hunts. Naturalists' Trust, 38, Mill Street, Bedford, MK40 3HD.

Berks., Bucks. & Oxon. Naturalists' Trust, 3, Church Cowley Road, Rose Hill, Oxford, OX4 3JR.

Brecknock Naturalists' Trust, Chapel House, Llechfaen, Brecon.

Cambs./Isle of Ely Naturalists' Trust, 1, Brookside, Cambridge, CB2 1JF.

Cheshire Conservation Trust, c/o Marbury Country Park, Northwich, Cheshire, CW9 6AT.

Cleveland Nature Conservation Trust, 38, Victoria Road, Hartlepool, Cleveland, TS26 8DL.

Cornwall Naturalists' Trust, Trendrine, Zennor, St Ives, Cornwall, TR26 3BW.

Cumbria Trust for Nature Conservation, Church St, Ambleside, LA22 0BU.

Derbyshire Naturalists' Trust, Estate Office, Twyford, Barrow-on-Trent, Derby, DE7 1HJ.

Devon Trust for Nature Conservation, 35, New Bridge Street, Exeter, Devon, EX3 4AH.

Dorset Naturalists' Trust, 39, Christchurch Road, Bournemouth, Dorset, BH1 3NS.

Durham County Conservation Trust, 52, Old Elvet, Durham, DN1 3HN.

Essex Naturalists' Trust, Fingringhoe Wick Nature Reserve, Fingringhoe, Colchester, CO5 7DN.

Glamorgan Naturalists' Trust, The Paddock, Walterston, Barry, South Glamorgan, CF6 9AS.

Gloucestershire Trust for Nature Conservation, Church House, Standish, Stonehouse, Glos., GL10 3EU.

Gwent Trust for Nature Conservation, The Shire Hall, Monmouth, Gwent, NP5 3DY.

Hants & Isle of Wight Naturalists' Trust, 8, Market Place, Romsey, Hants, SO5 8NB.

Herefordshire & Radnorshire Nature Trust, Community House, 25, Castle Street, Hereford, HR1 2NW.

Herts. & Middlesex Trust for Nature Conservation, Grebe House, St Michael's Street, St Albans, Herts., AL3 4SN.

Kent Trust for Nature Conservation, 125, High Street, Rainham, Kent, ME8 8AN.

Lancs. Trust for Nature Conservation, Dale House, Dale Head, Slaidburn, Lancs., BB7 4TS.

Leics./Rutland Trust for Nature Conservation, 1, West Street, Leicester.

Lincs. & S Humberside Trust for Nature Conservation, The Manor House, Alford, Lincs., LN13 9DL.

Manx Nature Conservation Trust, Ballacross, Andreas, Isle of Man.

Montgomery Trust for Nature Conservation, 18, High Street, Newtown, Powys, SY16 2NP.

Norfolk Naturalists' Trust, 72, Cathedral Close, Norwich, NR1 4DF.

Northants Trust for Nature Conservation, Lings House, Billing Lings, Northampton, NN3 4BE.

Northumberland Wildlife Trust, Hancock Museum, Barras Bridge, Newcastle upon Tyne, NE2 4PT.

North Wales Naturalists' Trust, 154, High St, Bangor, Gwynedd, LL57 1NU.

Notts Trust for Nature Conservation, 33, Main Street, Osgathorpe, Loughborough, Leics., LE12 9TA.

Scottish Wildlife Trust, 25 Johnston Terrace, Edinburgh, EH1 2NH.

Shropshire Conservation Trust, Bear Steps, Shrewsbury, SY1 1UH.

Somerset Trust for Nature Conservation, Fyne Court, Broomfield, Bridgwater, Somerset, TA5 2EQ.

Staffordshire Nature Conservation Trust, 3A Newport Road, Stafford, ST16 2HH.

Suffolk Trust for Nature Conservation, St Edmund House, Ropewalk, Ipswich, Suffolk, 1P4 1LZ.

Surrey Trust for Nature Conservation, 'Hatchlands', East Clandon, Guildford, Surrey, GU4 7RT.

Sussex Trust for Nature Conservation, Woods Mill, Shoreham Road, Henfield, West Sussex, 5 9SD.

Ulster Trust for Nature Conservation, 11A, Stranmillis Road, Belfast, BT9 5AF.

Warwicks Conservation Trust, 1, Northgate St, Warwick, CV34 4SP.

West Wales Naturalists' Trust, 7, Market St, Haverfordwest, Dyfed.

Wilts. Trust for Nature Conservation, 19, High Street, Devizes, Wiltshire.

Worcs. Nature Conservation Trust, The Lodge, Beacon Lane, Rednal, Birmingham, B45 9XN.

Yorkshire Naturalists' Trust, 20, Castlegate, York, YO1 1RP.

Other organizations

British Trust for Ornithology, Beech Grove, Tring, Hertfordshire HP23 5NR. Works primarily to collect data from observers throughout the country to be analysed by scientists.

British Ornithologists' Union, c/o Zoological Society of London, Regent's Park, London NW1 4RY. For the advancement of the science of ornithology. Research work supported and initiated.

Wildfowl Trust, Slimbridge, Gloucester GL2 7BT. To conserve wildfowl and their wetland habitat and to help the public to a greater appreciation of wildfowl as part of our national heritage. Manages seven centres with collections of pinioned waterfowl.

International Council for Bird Preservation, 219c Huntingdon Road, Cambridge CB3 0DL. Seeks to protect birds throughout the world and has national sections in many countries, including Britain.

CHECKLIST OF BIRDS

This list of birds occurring in England, Scotland and Wales is adapted from the British Trust for Ornithology's *A Species List of British and Irish Birds*, reprinted with the editor's permission. The taxonomy is Voous, 1973–7.

ORDER GAVIIFORMES
Family Gaviidae

Gavia stellata	Red-throated Diver
,, *arctica*	Black-throated Diver
,, *immer*	Great Northern Diver
,, *adamsii*	White-billed Diver

ORDER PODICIPEDIFORMES
Family Podicipedidae

Podilymbus podiceps	Pied-billed Grebe
Tachybaptus ruficollis	Little Grebe
Podiceps cristatus	Great Crested Grebe
,, *grisegena*	Red-necked Grebe
,, *auritus*	Slavonian Grebe
,, *nigricollis*	Black-necked Grebe

ORDER PROCELLARIIFORMES
Family Diomedeidae

Diomedea melanophris	Black-browed Albatross

Family Procellariidae

Fulmarus glacialis	Fulmar
Pterodroma hasitata	Capped Petrel
Bulweria bulwerii	Bulwer's Petrel
Calonectris diomedea	Cory's Shearwater
Puffinus gravis	Great Shearwater
,, *griseus*	Sooty Shearwater
,, *puffinus*	Manx Shearwater
,, *assimilis*	Little Shearwater

Family Hydrobatidae

Oceanites oceanicus	Wilson's Petrel
Pelagodroma marina	White-faced Petrel
Hydrobates pelagicus	Storm Petrel
Oceanodroma leucorhoa	Leach's Petrel
,, *castro*	Madeiran Petrel

ORDER PELECANIFORMES
Family Sulidae

Sula bassana	Gannet

Family Phalacrocoracidae

Phalacrocorax carbo	Cormorant
,, *aristotelis*	Shag

Family Fregatidae

Fregata magnificens	Magnificent Frigatebird

ORDER CICONIIFORMES
Family Ardeidae

Botaurus stellaris	Bittern
,, *lentiginosus*	American Bittern
Ixobrychus minutus	Little Bittern
Nycticorax nycticorax	Night Heron
Butorides striatus	Green Heron
Ardeola ralloides	Squacco Heron
Bubulcus ibis	Cattle Egret
Egretta garzetta	Little Egret
,, *alba*	Great White Egret
Ardea cinerea	Grey Heron
,, *purpurea*	Purple Heron

Family Ciconiidae

Ciconia nigra	Black Stork
,, *ciconia*	White Stork

Family Threskiornithidae

Plegadis falcinellus	Glossy Ibis
Platalea leucorodia	Spoonbill

ORDER ANSERIFORMES
Family Anatidae

Cygnus olor	Mute Swan
,, *columbianus*	Bewick's Swan
,, *cygnus*	Whooper Swan
Anser fabalis	Bean Goose
,, *brachyrhynchus*	Pink-footed Goose
,, *albifrons*	White-fronted Goose
,, *erythropus*	Lesser White-fronted Goose
,, *anser*	Greylag Goose
,, *caerulescens*	Snow Goose
Branta canadensis	Canada Goose
,, *leucopsis*	Barnacle Goose
,, *bernicla*	Brent Goose
,, *ruficollis*	Red-breasted Goose
Alopochen aegyptiacus	Egyptian Goose
Tadorna ferruginea	Ruddy Shelduck
,, *tadorna*	Shelduck

CHECKLIST OF BIRDS

Aix galericulata	Mandarin
Anas penelope	Wigeon
,, *americana*	American Wigeon
,, *strepera*	Gadwall
,, *crecca*	Teal
,, *platyrhynchos*	Mallard
,, *rubripes*	Black Duck
,, *acuta*	Pintail
,, *querquedula*	Garganey
,, *discors*	Blue-winged Teal
,, *clypeata*	Shoveler
Netta rufina	Red-crested Pochard
Aythya ferina	Pochard
,, *collaris*	Ring-necked Duck
,, *nyroca*	Ferruginous Duck
,, *fuligula*	Tufted Duck
,, *marila*	Scaup
Somateria mollissima	Eider
,, *spectabilis*	King Eider
Polysticta stelleri	Steller's Eider
Histrionicus histrionicus	Harlequin Duck
Clangula hyemalis	Long-tailed Duck
Melanitta nigra	Common Scoter
,, *perspicillata*	Surf Scoter
,, *fusca*	Velvet Scoter
Bucephala albeola	Bufflehead
,, *clangula*	Goldeneye
Mergus cucullatus	Hooded Merganser
,, *albellus*	Smew
,, *serrator*	Red-breasted Merganser
,, *merganser*	Goosander
Oxyura jamaicensis	Ruddy Duck

ORDER ACCIPITRIFORMES
Family Accipitridae

Pernis apivorus	Honey Buzzard
Milvus migrans	Black Kite
,, *milvus*	Red Kite
Haliaeetus albicilla	White-tailed Eagle
Neophron percnopterus	Egyptian Vulture
Gyps fulvus	Griffon Vulture
Circus aeruginosus	Marsh Harrier
,, *cyaneus*	Hen Harrier
,, *macrourus*	Pallid Harrier
,, *pygargus*	Montagu's Harrier
Accipiter gentilis	Goshawk
,, *nisus*	Sparrowhawk
Buteo buteo	Buzzard
,, *lagopus*	Rough-legged Buzzard
Aquila clanga	Spotted Eagle
,, *chrysaetos*	Golden Eagle

Family Pandionidae

Pandion haliaetus	Osprey

ORDER FALCONIFORMES
Family Falconidae

Falco naumanni	Lesser Kestrel
,, *tinnunculus*	Kestrel
,, *sparverius*	American Kestrel
,, *vespertinus*	Red-footed Falcon
,, *columbarius*	Merlin
,, *subbuteo*	Hobby
,, *rusticolus*	Gyrfalcon
,, *peregrinus*	Peregrine

ORDER GALLIFORMES
Family Tetraonidae

Lagopus lagopus	Red (or Willow) Grouse
,, *mutus*	Ptarmigan
Tetrao tetrix	Black Grouse
,, *urogallus*	Capercaillie

Family Phasianidae

Alectoris rufa	Red-legged Partridge
Perdix perdix	Grey Partridge
Coturnix coturnix	Quail
Phasianus colchicus	Pheasant
Chrysolophus pictus	Golden Pheasant
,, *amherstiae*	Lady Amherst's Pheasant

ORDER GRUIFORMES
Family Rallidae

Rallus aquaticus	Water Rail
Porzana porzana	Spotted Crake
,, *carolina*	Sora Rail
,, *parva*	Little Crake
,, *pusilla*	Baillon's Crake
Crex crex	Corncrake
Gallinula chloropus	Moorhen
Porphyrula alleni	Allen's Gallinule
,, *martinica*	American P. Gallinule
Fulica atra	Coot

Family Gruidae

Grus grus	Crane
,, *canadensis*	Sandhill Crane

Family Otididae

Tetrax tetrax	Little Bustard
Chlamydotis undulata	Houbara
Otis tarda	Great Bustard

ORDER CHARADRIIFORMES

Family Haematopodidae

Haematopus ostralegus	Oystercatcher

Family Recurvirostridae

Himantopus himantopus	Black-winged Stilt
Recurvirostra avosetta	Avocet

Family Burhinidae

Burhinus oedicnemus	Stone-curlew

Family Glareolidae

Cursorius cursor	Cream-coloured Courser
Glareola pratincola	Collared Pratincole
,, *nordmanni*	Black-winged Pratincole

Family Charadriidae

Charadrius dubius	Little Ringed Plover
,, *hiaticula*	Ringed Plover
,, *vociferus*	Killdeer
,, *alexandrinus*	Kentish Plover
,, *asiaticus*	Caspian Plover
,, *morinellus*	Dotterel
Pluvialis dominica	Lesser Golden Plover
,, *apricaria*	Golden Plover
,, *squatarola*	Grey Plover
Chettusia gregaria	Sociable Plover
,, *leucura*	White-tailed Plover
Vanellus vanellus	Lapwing

Family Scolopacidae

Calidris canutus	Knot
,, *alba*	Sanderling
,, *pusilla*	Semipalmated Sandpiper
,, *mauri*	Western Sandpiper
,, *minuta*	Little Stint
,, *temminckii*	Temminck's Stint
,, *minutilla*	Least Sandpiper
,, *fuscicollis*	White-rumped Sandpiper
,, *bairdii*	Baird's Sandpiper
,, *melanotos*	Pectoral Sandpiper
,, *acuminata*	Sharp-tailed Sandpiper
,, *ferruginea*	Curlew Sandpiper
,, *maritima*	Purple Sandpiper
,, *alpina*	Dunlin
Limicola falcinellus	Broad-billed Sandpiper
Micropalama himantopus	Stilt Sandpiper
Tryngites subruficollis	Buff-breasted Sandpiper
Philomachus pugnax	Ruff
Lymnocryptes minimus	Jack Snipe
Gallinago gallinago	Snipe
,, *media*	Great Snipe
Limnodromus griseus	Short-billed Dowitcher
,, *scolopaceus*	Long-billed Dowitcher
Scolopax rusticola	Woodcock
Limosa limosa	Black-tailed Godwit
,, *lapponica*	Bar-tailed Godwit
Numenius borealis	Eskimo Curlew
,, *phaeopus*	Whimbrel
,, *arquata*	Curlew
Bartramia longicauda	Upland Sandpiper
Tringa erythropus	Spotted Redshank
,, *totanus*	Redshank
,, *stagnatilis*	Marsh Sandpiper
,, *nebularia*	Greenshank
,, *melanoleuca*	Greater Yellowlegs
,, *flavipes*	Lesser Yellowlegs
,, *solitaria*	Solitary Sandpiper
,, *ochropus*	Green Sandpiper
,, *glareola*	Wood Sandpiper
Xenus cinereus	Terek Sandpiper
Actitis hypoleucos	Common Sandpiper
,, *macularia*	Spotted Sandpiper
Arenaria interpres	Turnstone
Phalaropus tricolor	Wilson's Phalarope
,, *lobatus*	Red-necked Phalarope
,, *fulicarius*	Grey Phalarope

Family Stercorariidae

Stercorarius pomarinus	Pomarine Skua
,, *parasiticus*	Arctic Skua
,, *longicaudus*	Long-tailed Skua
,, *skua*	Great Skua

Family Laridae

Larus ichthyaetus	Great Black-headed Gull
,, *melanocephalus*	Mediterranean Gull
,, *atricilla*	Laughing Gull
,, *pipixcan*	Franklin's Gull
,, *minutus*	Little Gull
,, *sabini*	Sabine's Gull
,, *philadelphia*	Bonaparte's Gull
,, *ridibundus*	Black-headed Gull
,, *genei*	Slender-billed Gull
,, *delawarensis*	Ring-billed Gull
,, *canus*	Common Gull
,, *fuscus*	Lesser Black-backed Gull
,, *argentatus*	Herring Gull
,, *glaucoides*	Iceland Gull
,, *hyperboreus*	Glaucous Gull

CHECKLIST OF BIRDS

Larus marinus	Great Black-backed Gull
Rhodostethia rosea	Ross's Gull
Rissa tridactyla	Kittiwake
Pagophila eburnea	Ivory Gull

Family Sternidae

Gelochelidon nilotica	Gull-billed Tern
Sterna caspia	Caspian Tern
,, *maxima*	Royal Tern
,, *sandvicensis*	Sandwich Tern
,, *dougallii*	Roseate Tern
,, *hirundo*	Common Tern
,, *paradisaea*	Arctic Tern
,, *anaethetus*	Bridled Tern
,, *fuscata*	Sooty Tern
,, *albifrons*	Little Tern
Chlidonias hybridus	Whiskered Tern
,, *niger*	Black Tern
,, *leucopterus*	White-winged Black Tern

Family Alcidae

Uria aalge	Guillemot
,, *lomvia*	Brünnich's Guillemot
Alca torda	Razorbill
Pinguinus impennis	Great Auk (extinct)
Cepphus grylle	Black Guillemot
Alle alle	Little Auk
Fratercula arctica	Puffin

ORDER PTEROCLIDIFORMES
Family Pteroclididae

Syrrhaptes paradoxus	Pallas's Sandgrouse

ORDER COLUMBIFORMES
Family Columbidae

Columba livia	Rock Dove
,, *oenas*	Stock Dove
,, *palumbus*	Woodpigeon
Streptopelia decaocto	Collared Dove
,, *turtur*	Turtle Dove
,, *orientalis*	Rufous Turtle Dove

ORDER CUCULIFORMES
Family Cuculidae

Clamator glandarius	Great Spotted Cuckoo
Cuculus canorus	Cuckoo
Coccyzus erythrophthalmus	Black-billed Cuckoo
Coccyzus americanus	Yellow-billed Cuckoo

ORDER STRIGIFORMES
Family Tytonidae

Tyto alba	Barn Owl

Family Strigidae

Otus scops	Scops Owl
Bubo bubo	Eagle Owl
Nyctea scandiaca	Snowy Owl
Surnia ulula	Hawk Owl
Athene noctua	Little Owl
Strix aluco	Tawny Owl
Asio otus	Long-eared Owl
,, *flammeus*	Short-eared Owl
Aegolius funereus	Tengmalm's Owl

ORDER CAPRIMULGIFORMES
Family Caprimulgidae

Caprimulgus europaeus	Nightjar
,, *ruficollis*	Red-necked Nightjar
,, *aegyptius*	Egyptian Nightjar
Chordeiles minor	Common Nighthawk

ORDER APODIFORMES
Family Apodidae

Hirundapus caudacutus	Needle-tailed Swift
Apus apus	Swift
,, *melba*	Alpine Swift
,, *affinis*	Little Swift

ORDER CORACIIFORMES
Family Alcedinidae

Alcedo atthis	Kingfisher

Family Meropidae

Merops superciliosus	Blue-cheeked Bee-eater
,, *apiaster*	Bee-eater

Family Coraciidae

Coracias garrulus	Roller

Family Upupidae

Upupa epops	Hoopoe

ORDER PICIFORMES
Family Picidae

Jynx torquilla	Wryneck
Picus viridis	Green Woodpecker
Sphyrapicus varius	Yellow-bellied Sapsucker
Dendrocopos major	Great Spotted Woodpecker
" *minor*	Lesser Spotted Woodpecker

ORDER PASSERIFORMES
Family Alaudidae

Melanocorypha calandra	Calandra Lark
Melanocorypha bimaculata	Bimaculated Lark
Melanocorypha leucoptera	White-winged Lark
Calandrella brachydactyla	Short-toed Lark
Galerida cristata	Crested Lark
Lullula arborea	Woodlark
Alauda arvensis	Skylark
Eremophila alpestris	Shore Lark

Family Hirundinidae

Riparia riparia	Sand Martin
Hirundo rustica	Swallow
" *daurica*	Red-rumped Swallow
Delichon urbica	House Martin

Family Motacillidae

Anthus novaeseelandiae	Richard's Pipit
" *godlewskii*	Blyth's Pipit
" *campestris*	Tawny Pipit
" *hodgsoni*	Olive-backed Pipit
" *trivialis*	Tree Pipit
" *gustavi*	Pechora Pipit
" *pratensis*	Meadow Pipit
" *cervinus*	Red-throated Pipit
" *spinoletta*	Rock Pipit
Motacilla flava	Yellow Wagtail
" *citreola*	Citrine Wagtail
" *cinerea*	Grey Wagtail
" *alba*	Pied Wagtail

Family Bombycillidae

Bombycilla garrulus	Waxwing

Family Cinclidae

Cinclus cinclus	Dipper

Family Troglodytidae

Troglodytes troglodytes	Wren

Family Mimidae

Toxostoma rufum	Brown Thrasher

Family Prunellidae

Prunella modularis	Dunnock
" *collaris*	Alpine Accentor

Family Turdidae

Cercotrichas galactotes	Rufous Bush Robin
Erithacus rubecula	Robin
Luscinia luscinia	Thrush Nightingale
" *megarhynchos*	Nightingale
" *calliope*	Siberian Rubythroat
" *svecica*	Bluethroat
Tarsiger cyanurus	Red-flanked Bluetail
Phoenicurus ochruros	Black Redstart
" *phoenicurus*	Redstart
Saxicola rubetra	Whinchat
" *torquata*	Stonechat
Oenanthe isabellina	Isabelline Wheatear
" *oenanthe*	Wheatear
" *pleschanka*	Pied Wheatear
" *hispanica*	Black-eared Wheatear
" *deserti*	Desert Wheatear
" *leucura*	Black Wheatear
Monticola saxatilis	Rock Thrush
Zoothera dauma	White's Thrush
" *sibirica*	Siberian Thrush
Catharus guttatus	Hermit Thrush
" *ustulatus*	Olive-backed (or Swainson's) Thrush
" *minimus*	Grey-cheeked Thrush
" *fuscescens*	Veery
Turdus torquatus	Ring Ousel
" *merula*	Blackbird
" *obscurus*	Eye-browed Thrush
" *naumanni*	Dusky Thrush
" *ruficollis*	Black-throated Thrush
" *pilaris*	Fieldfare

CHECKLIST OF BIRDS

,, *philomelos* — Song Thrush
,, *iliacus* — Redwing
,, *viscivorus* — Mistle Thrush
,, *migratorius* — American Robin

Family Sylviidae

Cettia cetti — Cetti's Warbler
Cisticola juncidis — Fan-tailed Warbler
Locustella certhiola — Pallas's Grasshopper Warbler
,, *lanceolata* — Lanceolated Warbler
,, *naevia* — Grasshopper Warbler
,, *fluviatilis* — River Warbler
,, *luscinioides* — Savi's Warbler
Acrocephalus melanopogon — Moustached Warbler
Acrocephalus paludicola — Aquatic Warbler
Acrocephalus schoenobaenus — Sedge Warbler
Acrocephalus agricola — Paddyfield Warbler
,, *dumetorum* — Blyth's Reed Warbler
,, *palustris* — Marsh Warbler
,, *scirpaceus* — Reed Warbler
Acrocephalus arundinaceus — Great Reed Warbler
,, *aedon* — Thick-billed Warbler
Hippolais pallida — Olivaceous Warbler
,, *caligata* — Booted Warbler
,, *icterina* — Icterine Warbler
,, *polyglotta* — Melodious Warbler
Sylvia undata — Dartford Warbler
,, *conspicillata* — Spectacled Warbler
,, *cantillans* — Subalpine Warbler
,, *melanocephala* — Sardinian Warbler
,, *rueppelli* — Rüppell's Warbler
,, *nana* — Desert Warbler
,, *hortensis* — Orphean Warbler
,, *nisoria* — Barred Warbler
,, *curruca* — Lesser Whitethroat
,, *communis* — Whitethroat
,, *borin* — Garden Warbler
,, *atricapilla* — Blackcap
Phylloscopus trochiloides — Greenish Warbler
,, *borealis* — Arctic Warbler
,, *proregulus* — Pallas's Warbler
,, *inornatus* — Yellow-browed Warbler
,, *schwarzi* — Radde's Warbler
,, *fuscatus* — Dusky Warbler
,, *bonelli* — Bonelli's Warbler
,, *sibilatrix* — Wood Warbler
,, *collybita* — Chiffchaff
,, *trochilus* — Willow Warbler
Regulus regulus — Goldcrest
,, *ignicapillus* — Firecrest

Family Muscicapidae

Muscicapa striata — Spotted Flycatcher
Ficedula parva — Red-breasted Flycatcher
,, *albicollis* — Collared Flycatcher
,, *hypoleuca* — Pied Flycatcher

Family Timaliidae

Panurus biarmicus — Bearded Tit

Family Aegithalidae

Aegithalos caudatus — Long-tailed Tit

Family Paridae

Parus palustris — Marsh Tit
,, *montanus* — Willow Tit
,, *cristatus* — Crested Tit
,, *ater* — Coal Tit
,, *caeruleus* — Blue Tit
,, *major* — Great Tit

Family Sittidae

Sitta europaea — Nuthatch

Family Tichodromadidae

Tichodroma muraria — Wallcreeper

Family Certhiidae

Certhia familiaris — Treecreeper
,, *brachydactyla* — Short-toed Treecreeper

Family Remizidae

Remiz pendulinus — Penduline tit

Family Oriolidae

Oriolus oriolus — Golden Oriole

Family Laniidae

Lanius isabellinus — Isabelline Shrike
,, *collurio* — Red-backed Shrike
,, *minor* — Lesser Grey Shrike
,, *excubitor* — Great Grey Shrike
,, *senator* — Woodchat Shrike

Family Corvidae

Garrulus glandarius	Jay
Pica pica	Magpie
Nucifraga caryocatactes	Nutcracker
Pyrrhocorax pyrrhocorax	Chough
Corvus monedula	Jackdaw
,, *frugilegus*	Rook
,, *corone*	Carrion (or Hooded) Crow
,, *corax*	Raven

Family Sturnidae

Sturnus vulgaris	Starling
,, *roseus*	Rose-coloured Starling

Family Vireonidae

Vireo olivaceus	Red-eyed Vireo

Family Passeridae

Passer domesticus	House Sparrow
,, *hispaniolensis*	Spanish Sparrow
,, *montanus*	Tree Sparrow

Family Fringillidae

Fringilla coelebs	Chaffinch
,, *montrifringilla*	Brambling
Serinus serinus	Serin
,, *citrinella*	Citril Finch
Carduelis chloris	Greenfinch
,, *carduelis*	Goldfinch
,, *spinus*	Siskin
,, *cannabina*	Linnet
,, *flavirostris*	Twite
,, *flammea*	Redpoll
,, *hornemanni*	Arctic Redpoll
Loxia leucoptera	Two-barred Crossbill
,, *curvirostra*	Common Crossbill
,, *scotica*	Scottish Crossbill
,, *pytyopsittacus*	Parrot Crossbill
Bucanetes githagineus	Trumpeter Finch
Carpodacus erythrinus	Scarlet Rosefinch
Pinicola enucleator	Pine Grosbeak
Pyrrhula pyrrhula	Bullfinch
Coccothraustes coccothraustes	Hawfinch
Hesperiphona vespertina	Evening Grosbeak

Family Parulidae

Mniotilta varia	Black-and-white Warbler
Vermivora peregrina	Tennessee Warbler
Parula americana	Northern Parula
Dendroica petechia	Yellow Warbler
,, *tigrina*	Cape May Warbler
,, *coronata*	Yellow-rumped (or Myrtle) Warbler
,, *striata*	Blackpoll Warbler
Setophaga ruticilla	American Redstart
Seiurus aurocapillus	Ovenbird
,, *noveboracensis*	Northern Waterthrush
Geothlypis trichas	Common Yellowthroat
Wilsonia citrina	Hooded Warbler

Family Thraupidae

Piranga rubra	Summer Tanager
,, *olivacea*	Scarlet Tanager

Family Emberizidae

Pipilo erythrophthalmus	Rufous-sided Towhee
Zonotrichia melodia	Song Sparrow
,, *leucophrys*	White-crowned Sparrow
,, *albicollis*	White-throated Sparrow
Junco hyemalis	Dark-eyed (or Slate-coloured) Junco
Calcarius lapponicus	Lapland Bunting
Plectrophenax nivalis	Snow Bunting
Emberiza leucocephalos	Pine Bunting
,, *citrinella*	Yellowhammer
,, *cirlus*	Cirl Bunting
,, *cia*	Rock Bunting
,, *hortulana*	Ortolan Bunting
,, *caesia*	Cretzschmar's Bunting
,, *rustica*	Rustic Bunting
,, *pusilla*	Little Bunting
,, *aureola*	Yellow-breasted Bunting
,, *schoeniclus*	Reed Bunting
,, *melanocephala*	Black-headed Bunting
Miliaria calandra	Corn Bunting
Pheucticus ludovicianus	Rose-breasted Grosbeak

Family Icteridae

Dolichonyx oryzivorus	Bobolink
Icterus galbula	Northern (or Baltimore) Oriole

INDEX OF PLACE NAMES

Place names at or near starting points of walks or bird locations.

INDEX OF PLACE NAMES

ORNITHOLOGICAL INDEX

Bold type denotes an illustration of the species on that page.

ACKNOWLEDGEMENTS

Front cover photographs: Oystercatchers: R. Thompson (Frank W. Lane); Puffins, Dennis Green (Survival Anglia); Kestrel, Brian Hawkes (The Robert Harding Picture Library); Linnet feeding young, Brian Hawkes (The Robert Harding Picture Library).

Peter Hayman drew the symbol silhouettes.

All other illustrations are the work of Ken Wood, with the exception of: 2–3 David and Katie Urry/Ardea; 18–19, 20–21 Jim Robbins; 22–23, 26 Andrew Popowitz; 27 Ian Wallace; 24–25 Peter Hayman; 34–35, 62–63 David and Katie Urry/Ardea; 80 Tony Graham; 180–81 Richard Vaughan/Ardea; 122–23 Don Smith/Nature Photographers; 94–95 Bill Paton/Nature Photographers; 159, 162–63, 165, 169 Trevor Boyer/Linden Artists; 156–57 David and Katie Urry/Ardea 210–11 Uno Berggren/Ardea.

Stanley Davies RSPB Regional Officer, South-west England; **Tony Prater** RSPB Regional Officer, South-east England; **Roger Lovegrove** RSPB Regional Officer, Wales; **Dr Stephanie Tyler** Conservation Officer, Gwent Trust for NC; **Graham Williams** RSPB Deputy Regional Officer, Wales; **Philip Burton** Scientific Officer, the British Museum (Natural History), Tring; **Linda Williams** RSPB Midlands Office; **P. W. Richardson** Conservation Trust Warden, Pitsford Reservoir; **Michael F. Wallace** excursion secretary, the Shropshire Ornithological Society; **Frank Gribble** BTO Regional Representative, Staffordshire, and Organiser of the national Nightjar Survey; **Barrie Robertson** contributor to the *Atlas of Breeding Birds*; **David Cohen** RSPB local representative, West Midlands; **John O'Sullivan** RSPB Regional Officer, East Anglia; **Peter Rumsey** RSPB Local Representative and Group Leader, Epping Forest; **John S. Armitage** RSPB Regional Officer, North-west England; **Ian Armstrong** RSPB Regional Officer, North England; **Ray Hawley** Ken/Dee Marshes Warden; **Peter Bowyer** Nature Centre Warden, Lochwinnoch Nature Centre; **Stephen Warman** Ranger, St Abb's Head Wildlife Reserve; **Alister Clunas** Ranger, John Muir Country Park; **Stewart Taylor** Warden, Loch Garten Reserve; **Ken Smith** RSPB South-east England Office; **John Hunt** RSPB Scottish Office.

Our thanks also to Carl Nicholson, RSPB Midlands Office; Frank Hamilton, RSPB Scottish Office; the British Trust for Ornithology; the RSNC and the local Conservation Trusts; Trevor Dolby for researching the original concept; Malcolm Rush and Martin Tither of the WCC; Robin Wright of the National Trust; Douglas Bremner of the National Trust for Scotland; The Forestry Commission, particularly staff at its regional conservancy offices; Dorothy Bashford; Camilla Baring.

John Parslow is author of *Breeding Birds of Britain and Ireland* (Poyser) and co-author of the *The Birds of Britain and Europe* (Collins) and *The Birdlife of Britain* (Mitchell Beazley) to which he contributed the maps. He is a leading authority on the distribution of British and European birds.